49-00

WITHDRAWN

COACHING AND MENTORING

Coaching and Mentoring

Nigel
MacLennan

Gower

© Nigel MacLenann 1995

Published by
Gower Publishing Limited
Gower House
Croft Road
Aldershot
Hampshire GU11 3HR
England

Gower
Old Post Road
Brookfield
Vermont 05036
USA

Nigel MacLennan has asserted his right under the Copyright, Designs and Patents Act 1988 to be identified as the author of this work.

British Library Cataloguing in Publication Data
MacLennan, Nigel
  Coaching and Mentoring
  I. Title
  658.3124

Reprinted 1996, 1999

ISBN 0-566-07562-8

Library of Congress Cataloging-in-Publication Data
MacLennan, Nigel, 1961–
  Coaching and mentoring / Nigel MacLennan.
    p. cm.
  Includes bibliographical references and index.
  ISBN 0-566-07562-8
  1. Mentors in business. 2. Employees – Training of. 3. Employees –
  Counselling of. I. Title.
HF5385M232 1995
658.4´07124–dc20   94–24811
                                                         CIP

Printed in Ehrhardt by Poole Typesetting (Wessex) Ltd, Bournemouth and printed in Great Britain by Biddles Ltd, Guildford

CONTENTS

ILLUSTRATIONS

PREFACE

What this book can do for you

It will show you:

- How to gain maximum performance from your staff, on both an individual and team basis.
- How to coach and mentor your staff and empower them with a sense of ownership and commitment.
- The skills, techniques, methods and logistics of effective coaching/mentoring.
- How to coach and mentor in and through difficult situations.
- How to coach and provide mentoring in the key commercial skills.

What can it do for you?

- The coach/mentor: It is a comprehensive manual of coaching and mentoring for general business skills.
- The manager: It will show you how to obtain staff and department performance levels way beyond anything conventional management methods can offer.
- The Chief Executive Officer (CEO): It will show you what your directors and senior managers could be doing to increase company performance overall. It will show you how to implement a company wide coaching/mentoring programme.

People, people, people

Every company is as good as the people in that company. For any grouping of individuals to succeed in a world of people, they must provide what people want, in the way people want it, and they must be skilled in their handling of people.

Every chief executive wants his or her company to succeed. The best CEOs do so by encouraging their people to succeed through people. This book is a manual of the best methods known today of getting people to succeed, namely, a manual of coaching and mentoring.

Anyone wishing to contact the author may do so at:

1733 Coventry Road,
South Yardley,
Birmingham,
B26 1DT,
United Kingdom

Nigel MacLennan

ACKNOWLEDGEMENTS

Without the help of a huge number of people you would not be holding this book. My thanks to all the wonderful staff at Gower, particularly Malcolm Stern for having so much faith in me, and to Solveig Servian and Dorothy Stewart for editing and copy editing so effectively. My thanks to David Newton for yet again taking my simplistic child-like cartoon designs and professionally illustrating them. To Sarah Allen for editing one of my early manuscripts. To all my previous staff for helping me develop my coaching skills, often at their expense. To my great friends who have provided unwitting mentoring over many years, namely my mother and brother, Patricia and Gordon MacLennan (how do you put up with me?). To a friend and high achiever, Andrew Nicholson: thanks for letting me bounce my ideas off you. My thanks also to the many people whose ideas have helped me develop and enhance my thinking.

NM

Part I

Foundations

1

INTRODUCING COACHING AND MENTORING

Needs for and benefits of coaching and mentoring

Directing people to 'Do' has always produced inferior results compared to inspiring people to want to do. Increasingly we are finding out why. But *why* makes no profit; *how to* does. Coaching and mentoring are the 'how to'.

Being told versus being asked

Coaching and mentoring, if provided skilfully, inspire people 'to want to'. They can provide enormous benefits by satisfying an organization's needs for:

- Enthusiasm and commitment.
- Productivity and loyalty.
- Flexibility and persistence.
- Responsive crisis management and conscientious crisis prevention.
- Team work and mutual support.
- Creativity and co-operation.
- Managed risk taking and perpetual self-regeneration.

- Staff ownership of problems and responsibility for solutions.
- Adaptability and responsiveness to change.
- Vision and purpose.
- Purposeful, specific and appropriate staff development.
- and so on ...

As you go through the material, you will see exactly how coaching and mentoring provide these benefits. But for now, let's start as we intend to go on by providing a developmental exercise: What benefits do you most need to obtain for your company? What benefits have been missed in the above list?

Definitions and parameters: coaching, self-coaching, mentoring

What is coaching?

Well, it is NOT teaching, instruction or training. The coach does not have to be a relative expert in the field being coached (more on this later). It is not managing. The coach has no responsibility for the performer's behaviour.

Coaching helps performers unlock their ability

So what is it? A coach is someone available for the performer to learn WITH. Coaching is the process whereby one individual helps another: to unlock their natural ability; to perform, learn and achieve; to increase awareness of the factors which determine performance; to increase their sense of self-responsibility and ownership of their performance; to self-coach; to identify and remove internal barriers to achievement.

EXERCISE

Definitions in every field are dependent on the user, the context and other factors. What is your definition of coaching? Don't worry that you have not enough knowledge to provide an accurate definition; your definition will evolve with your knowledge base. In fact, making what you recognize to be a naïve definition at this stage will help your motivation to learn more, and give you an indication of how much you need to learn.

The self-coach

Ultra-high performers are typically self-coaches who do all of the above for themselves in any way they can (more on this later). The best performers seem able to self-coach through the most unbelievable adversity. Some analysts even suggest that a history of serious adversity is a prerequisite of outstanding achievement.

Self-coaching

What is mentoring?

A mentor is someone available for the performer to learn FROM. At least that is the theory. In practice a mentor will be the assigned 'teacher' of an individual. There is enormous variation of expectation in the function and behaviour of people bearing the same title – mentor. Some of the roles lead to the following definitions: Mentoring is the process whereby one senior individual is available to a junior –

- To form a non-specified developmental relationship.
- To seek information from.
- To regard as a role model for the purposes of emulation.
- To pick up what the organization/department/company expects.
- To show the performer how the organization works; to ensure cultural compliance.
- To guide the performer through a phase of operational, professional or vocational qualification.
- To provide feedback and appraisal.
- To teach all the relevant facts that will enable the junior individual to perform effectively in an organization.

EXERCISE

What is your definition of mentoring?

The coach–mentor distinction

The two roles are worlds apart and overlapping, depending on which dimension they are compared. In terms of volition, a mentor can be unwitting or even unwilling, but still a successful mentor. How? By a performer choosing a role model at a distance. A coach could never be unwitting, and is unlikely to engage in the process if unwilling.

The roles overlap when a person performs successfully as a coach. He or she is likely to be adopted as a mentor of coaching skills. The reverse is not true. A mentor can never be a coach unless they deliberately adopt the skills involved in successful coaching. Time for honesty. Who were/are your unwitting mentor(s)? Who are/were your 'witting' and willing mentors? Who were your favourite coaches? Who were your most effective coaches?

Focus distinction

The coach concentrates on helping the performer learn how to achieve more. The mentor's aim is to be available for the performer to use as a resource. You will find the answers to the following questions as you go through the book, but generating your own ideas at this stage will give you a clear picture of the process as it unfolds. With what aspects of performance do you think the coach will help? What is the performer most likely to want to learn from the mentor?

Skills distinction

A mentor can fulfil the role quite adequately with basic management, people and training or teaching skills. An effective coach must have the knowledge, technique and skill to help the performer achieve, without directing. As always with definitions, the difference between coaches and mentors is not defined in theory, but in practice. Whatever an organization defines for each role creates the parameters of that role.

Ownership distinction

We will come back to the word 'ownership' with irritating frequency. The level of ownership assumed and encouraged in the performer is one of the dimensions on which it is easiest to define the coach–mentor distinction. Coaching assumes more self-responsibility on the part of the performer. Mentoring assumes more performer responsibility than a conventional training course, but not quite as much as a participant-led course.

The coaching continuum diagram below expresses the relationship between level of ownership and the various performance enhancement methods.

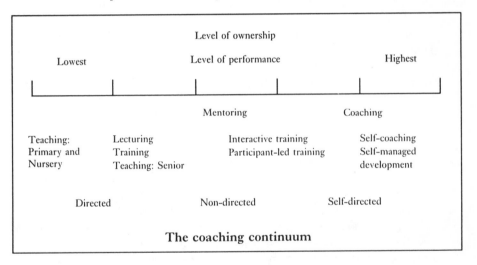

The coaching continuum

Ownership and performance: the connection

The diagram also conveys the level of direction expressed at each level of ownership. Note there is an assumed direct correlation between level of performance, ownership and self-direction in the achiever. How accurate do you think the assumed correlation is? Is it absolute?

On occasion, mentoring can be more performer-centred than coaching but, in general, coaching will be more performer-led and therefore better at facilitating performance enhancement.

Preview and overview of the material

Several assumptions inform this book. Genuine adoption of these assumptions is central to the success of any coaching effort undertaken. The principles of high-level achievement are timeless. But they will only work if practised as actions, as skills, as behaviours. They will not work if merely presented as convincing platitudes. For a company to bring out the best in its staff, it must assume and act on the assumption that its people – its intellectual resources – are its most valuable asset by far. The most powerful force in history is people power. Coaching and mentoring are mechanisms to switch on that power. But if high performance were as easy as flicking a switch we would all be super-achievers. As performers, each of us has to discover that electricity, learn to generate and control it, from first principles, before we can flick the metaphorical switch to achievement. We must develop our own model and mechanisms of achievement. Watching a super-achiever at work may provide some useful ideas, but we still have to learn and practise the skills ourselves. Our learning process can be assisted if there is a super-achiever on hand who also has a conceptual understanding of how to get to that level of performance, and who has the attitude and skills to help others get there too. That is the role of the coach and, to a lesser extent, the mentor.

This book uses coaching methods (as far as possible within the confines of the printed page) to help you develop your coaching skills. The exercises interspersed throughout the text will give you an opportunity to acquire the knowledge, adopt the attitudes, rehearse the behaviours, and practise the skills necessary to become an effective coach. Since the core skills of coaching are both few and straightforward, you will be in a position to start coaching before you are a quarter of the way through the book. The more advanced skills, which make up the bulk of the coach's tool-bag, are practised only a fraction of the time. Amongst the most useful of the advanced skills is the ability to help performers identify and overcome the barriers to their achievement – and most useful within that skill cluster is the ability to help the performer identify and remedy the beliefs they hold which block their achievement.

Coaching and mentoring can be used to help both teams and individuals enhance their performance. The skills required and used are very similar. Additional knowledge of group formation and operation processes is required, as are some tools with which to analyse what is happening.

Perhaps the most challenging and exciting role for those involved in coaching at a senior level is the design, introduction and implementation of a suitable coaching system for the company. The factors which ought to be considered to complete that task successfully are covered in detail.

The last Part of the book, Part V, provides summaries of the factors performers and coaches will consider during the development of the most common business or organization skills.

Now let's get down to business.

2

THE NATURE OF ACHIEVEMENT

Why an understanding of achievement is essential

Would a product designer stand any chance of success if she or he did not understand the operational principles of the proposed product? Would a finance director be able to prepare a company finance report with no knowledge of accounting (non-finance directors are asked to restrain themselves at this point!)? Would you search for gold if you didn't know what it looked like? Of course not, and for obvious reasons. For the same reasons, coaches and mentors need an understanding of achievement and the principles of performance.

Understanding achievement

Such knowledge will also equip coaches and mentors with confidence in their abilities to carry out the role successfully, credibility in the eyes of the performer, the confidence to have confidence in the performer (an aid to decision making), and a healthy bullshit detector (human potential is second only to the availability of excuses as the world's most abundant resource).

EXERCISE

Give five reasons why an understanding of achievement is essential to successful coaching and mentoring.

The principles of performance and achievement

The simplest view

The simplest explanation of the mental life of successful performers is: they choose an objective; focus on it exclusively; and take complete personal responsibility for directing their thoughts, feelings, behaviours and skills towards achieving their goal, and persist until they see results.

In general terms that description is probably close to reality, although most of us have other commitments which prevent concentrating on one goal exclusively. When we are able to focus on our objective, we can do so exclusively, if we choose. Whatever our situation, we can always choose to take total responsibility for what we think, what we feel, how we behave, and what skills we choose to acquire in the pursuit of our goal. What excuses do under- or non-achievers most frequently use for not taking control of their thoughts, feelings and behaviours? Which have you heard recently?

No absolute prescription

The way you choose to achieve or perform is entirely up to you. Yes, the market you are aiming to satisfy may place some constraints or boundaries on the range of your behaviours. But within those boundaries you have total control.

There is no absolute prescription for successful performance. Of course, the ingredients are influenced by what kind of success you want to create. You probably wouldn't spend your time practising your writing skills if you wanted to be the world's best salesperson. The ingredients of success are tied to the objective; the recipe is your choice. To be a successful performer you have to acquire the ingredient skills and put them together in your own unique way. Look at the recipes others have used; make some notes, but don't make a copy.

EXERCISE

What are the success ingredients in your particular industry and role? What are the skill ingredients in the roles you aspire to?

Variety of strategies

Any number of strategies can be used by the aspiring business success. There seems to be a core of effective methods available to those who seek them. The main ingredients are: direction; desire and motivation; self-image; belief structure; persistence; a willingness to learn; and support systems.

Direction

Direction is essential for successful performance. A noble purpose with no achiever and a noble achiever with no purpose are equally ineffectual. A determined achiever with a worthwhile goal is an extremely powerful force. Ultra-high achievers in all disciplines exhibit this intense sense of purpose and direction. Many report that they actively create and enhance their sense of direction. Others report that it seemed to be innate, but they focus and develop it on an ongoing basis. Still others report that their sense of direction was determined by chance, but once 'selected', it was, and continues to be, nurtured. All report an ongoing evolution of their life purpose and of the methods used to enhance and draw on it as a source of motivation. Their life purpose is continually evolving, being updated and fine tuned. They have a vision or a mission. It pervades their souls with the passion of a religious missionary. For the high achiever 'mission' is much more than a paragraph to be trotted out when the boss asks what the company strategy is!

EXERCISE

What is your direction? What is your life's purpose? What direction have you chosen? If you have not consciously chosen or at least articulated your life purpose, compile a list of the goals or objectives you have pursued over the period of your life and try to distil the common purpose behind them.

Another way to determine the purpose you have chosen is to consider the goals you have in the four main areas of your life – personal, family, organization/career and departmental/functional – and find the common ground between them. If you can't find it or there is no common ground, something must give.

Desire and motivation

The degree to which direction is converted into results, as measured by the level and speed of achievement, seems to be directly related to the level of focus, intensity and constancy of desire in the performer. As hinted at above, successful people tend to do what they enjoy and enjoy what they do. They maximize their motivation by controlling what they do, or at least how they do it, and by finding ways of increasing their desire and motivation towards what they do. What can you do to increase your desire and motivation? Name five things.

Self-image

Successful performers have a healthy self-image, and a high level of self-esteem. Non-successful performers argue they too would have those characteristics had

Self-image

they won, achieved or performed. It is consistently evident that performers use self-image, self-esteem and the expectancy of achievement to help them to succeed. They consistently strive to improve their self-image, to increase their self-esteem, to intensify their expectancy of success. Performers use mental affirmations regularly, mental imagery and rehearsal frequently. They do things for themselves and others that will boost their self-image/self-esteem and give them a sense of 'deserving' to achieve, of expecting to achieve. What do you plan to do to enhance your self-image?

Achievers create success in the mind as the cause, and find success in reality as the consequence.

Belief structure

Everyone has the choice of what they want to believe in. As children, our beliefs are affected by factors beyond our control, but as adults we can choose exactly what we wish to believe. Successful people have beliefs that empower them; unsuccessful people have beliefs that hinder and disempower them. Believers are achievers.

Many high performers believe that it is easier to succeed than it is to fail. Failure requires considerable skill and dedication. To illustrate: the thinking and energy required to fail is probably greater than that necessary for success. It must be extremely difficult to fail every time an attempt is made; to become blind to every opportunity that appears or could be created; to dismiss every useful idea; to avoid meeting people who could be helped, or who could offer help; and to turn each of the above into an efficient habit and expend the necessary energy to maintain the habit. Looking at failure from that perspective, it would be logical to assume that the average failure is more successful at what they do than the average success.

Head games are normally associated with less than well-balanced individuals. Successful people play head games with a difference: head games that enhance achievement, head games that empower them. For instance, it is smart to forget one's failures, it is smart to use all sorts of denial strategies to protect ourselves from pain. We know that successful people tend to have an unrealistic optimism about the future; have exaggerated perceptions of personal control, and have unrealistically positive views of themselves. The strange thing is that although these beliefs never turn into reality, they come closer to doing so in high performers than in non-achievers who don't believe! Playing head games is clearly beneficial. What head games are you going to start playing? Which do you already use?

Persistence

High achievers have more failures than low achievers do! Why? Because they try more often. Failures don't try and therefore don't fail; they don't succeed either. Successful performance requires persistence through failure. Persistence requires a healthy attitude to failure. What is that attitude? Failure is:

- A necessary item in the tool-box of success.
- The dimension that makes success three-dimensional.
- The opponent who forces you to learn and improve.
- A barrier which is nice enough to offer you directions for a diversion.

Failure is a necessary learning tool. Given that failure is inevitable, what views can you adopt other than those just expressed? What beliefs will empower you in the face of defeat?

High-level achievers carry out a skilled balancing act. They tread the best

Persistence is a balancing act

line between too much persistence (pigheadedness) and too little (quitting too soon). They make sound judgements about when to force their way through some barriers, when to alter course to navigate round others, when to accept that a barrier is insurmountable, when the cost of surmounting a barrier is greater than the potential rewards, and when to change course entirely. They are persistent in their efforts to achieve their goal, but flexible about the methods used to achieve it. How can you decide where the line between pigheadedness and persistence lies? What can you do to improve your level of persistence?

A willingness to learn

A willingness to learn, to become expert, and a commitment to keep on learning, to engage in continual self-development, seems central to successful performance. Particularly, willingness to learn from the basics up, one step at a time; by sticking to one level until it is mastered before proceeding to the next level; by observation of others; by actively seeking feedback from constructive others; by transferring skills acquired in one context to another; by trial and error; by making mistakes; by focusing on what works and ignoring the rest; by choosing functionality rather than perfection; by using mental rehearsal and thought experiments; by controlling stress and tension levels; by concentrating on the objective and ignoring the performance until complete; by thinking about the performance when not performing; and by practising skills until they become automatic.

From numerous studies of ultra-high performers in many fields we know that the acquisition of expertise happens as follows:

1   They learn the components of the skills required.
2   And gradually acquire some understanding of the context.
3   They form a mental hierarchy of the contexts in which the skills are used.
4   They perform by using a repertoire of recognizable mental patterns of the skill area, in conjunction with some analytical thought.
5   Through practice, they eventually acquire a comprehensive and extensive repertoire of patterns, to which recognition and responses are automatic.

EXERCISE

At which stage in this sequence should each of the learning strategies listed under 'Willingness to learn' be placed?

Support systems

Everything in life seems to function as an ally to the successful. Sleep, family, exercise, friends, peers, bosses, regulators, failure ... you name it and the ultra-high achiever seems to have it set up in such a way that it supports their success. Anything that detracts from their success is worked on until it is either neutralized or is actively supportive of their efforts. At least that's the way it appears from the outside. In reality, performers control their minds to view problems as allies. If they have to do something that could detract from their success, they will do it in such a way that it supports them.

The conventional understanding of 'support systems' is family, work friends, social friends and so on. While kindly support from our nearest and dearest is clearly necessary for most of us, it is not nearly sufficient to achieve success. High performers have their own internal support system developed to an extremely high level.

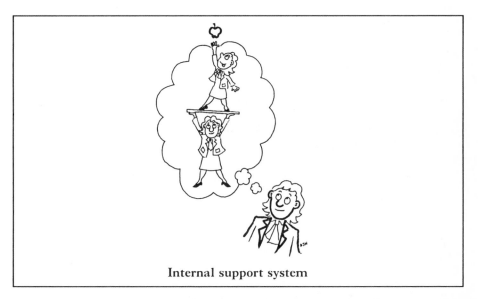

Internal support system

Internal support is achieved by telling yourself good things about you. It is achieved by choosing to have an empowering inner dialogue. It involves choosing to believe those things that will help you achieve your goal, having empowering thoughts, making empowering attributions. Internal support is concerned with maintaining your most valuable achievement tool – your mind – or, more specifically, your state of mind. How can you enhance your internal and external support systems and encourage your performers to do the same?

Some other common factors in successful people

The above points have already started a listing of what successful performers share. Following is a list of the bare minimum required for success:

1 Maintain physical and mental health within genetically and environmentally imposed limits.
2 Have a sense of usefulness, satisfaction and purpose: high fliers have a sense of purpose way beyond themselves, reaching levels religious devotees would be proud of.
3 Rest and recreation should be adequate to achieve point 1: for the achiever

who sees work as play, the prospect of a 'day off' is horrifying. Why should they be deprived of the thing they love?

4   Have a sense of being involved.

5   Have a confidant: In business it is often difficult to find a confidant with no axe to grind.

6   Take responsibility for your life and all its problems

7   Be objective about and have insight into yourself, although, not so objective that you lose your optimism.

8   Don't take yourself too seriously. (Extreme performers often take their goal too seriously, causing an occasional spill-over on to their view of themselves.)

9   Live in the here and now, while enjoying the journey into the there and then.

EXERCISE

Which of the items do you practise, in reality, not in a wish list? When will you start practising those you currently do not? Make a plan, decide on some regular action, set a date to start implementing, set a date for ongoing evaluation. If you already practise the above regularly, have you set up a mental structure to run through this checklist when things are not looking too wonderful?

Motivation

Motivation as a field of human study has generated enormous output. Why? Because an understanding of it still eludes us. Elusive maybe, yet it is central to performance achievement, and to coaching/mentoring people to that end. We will present what is known about the most effective motivational methods under the following headings:

- Objectives of this section.
- Introductory issues.
- The factors which affect motivation.
- Physical motivations.
- Environmental motivators.
- Self-motivation

  - Level 3 'The achiever'
  - Level 2 'The potential achiever'
  - Level 1 The 'achieving elsewhere'.

- Motivation and control – An operational model.
- Motivational dispositions – POP RIOT.
- Motivation and choice of rewards.
- Motivation factors checklist.

Objectives

This section seeks to equip the coach/mentor with a realistic and operational – as opposed to a theoretical and academic – understanding of motivation as it affects performance at work.

Introductory issues

Each individual's motivators are unique. If it could be reliably documented, each of us would have our own motivation profile as distinct as our fingerprints. With one main difference, our motivation profile changes and evolves with experience. More on motivational dispositions later.

The ways in which we become motivated are as different as the means by which we achieve satisfaction of our needs. To help your performers maximize their motivation you must help them to understand the unique way in which their natural motivations are aroused. Then help them find the optimum way(s) they can be enhanced and harnessed. Note the assumption: the performer finds ways of increasing their own motivation with the coach/mentor's help. This assumption is critical to effective performer assistance. Those who cannot accept it have no business and no future in workplace coaching. Why do you think this assumption is so important to the likely outcome of a coaching and mentoring session, and of the achiever's performance?

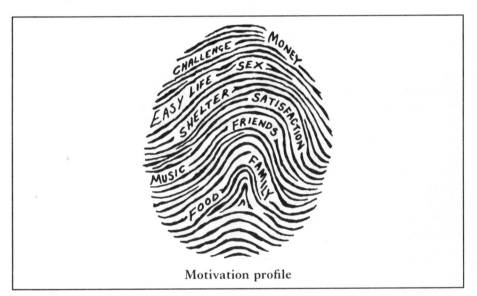

Motivation profile

The factors which affect motivation

What ingredients make up our unique motivation profile? Described very broadly, motivations can be voluntary, involuntary, external or environmental, internal or physical, and self-determined.

Physical motivations

The involuntary, life-preserving motivations are of little concern to us here since they are satisfied for everyone (or should be) in a civilized society. They consist of the drive towards satisfying the need for air, food, water, shelter, warmth and survival. Involuntary motivation as a non-survival issue is of concern to us. An individual who can make a voluntary motivation so habitual and so powerful that it attains the irresistibility of the involuntary motivation can achieve unbelievable results. Super-achievers persuade themselves they absolutely need a result.

EXERCISE

List the physical motivations in order of priority or in terms of the necessary frequency of satisfaction. Which on this list can be used to enhance voluntary motivations and how?

Environmental motivators

External motivators are those factors (heat, light, fair pay and so on) in the performer's working environment which, if not satisfied, can cause substantial demotivation. A lesser manifestation is often the diversion of the performer's energies from the main purpose of their job to rectify or remove the de-motivator. The most frequent manifestation is a suppression of overall motivation with no attempt being made at rectification. The environmental motivators seem to affect motivation in an on or off way. The thinking goes something like: 'I can either get what I want or want what I've got. Since I've tried but can't obtain the small thing I desire, I'll just content myself with what I have.' That conclusion then spreads, or generalizes, to other aspects of the person's work performance, as more and more ideals are not met. Before long you have a workplace automaton.

Internal motivators are those factors which, if present or provided in the working environment, create internal motivation. The satisfaction of external motivations coupled with the non-satisfaction of internal motivators will produce barely adequate performance. Where both are present, above-average performance can be expected in direct proportion to the level at which internal motivators are present.

EXERCISE

Which members of staff can you think of who resign themselves to putting up with things that seem unbearable? What is their level of motivation? When was your motivation last detrimentally affected by your superior's failure to look after your interests? Which was greater, the cost of the non-provided element or the value of lost productivity from you?

Self-motivation

Superior performance starts here. Throughout history the individuals who made the greatest impact, those producing the most outstanding achievements, have always been self-motivated. The most successful entrepreneurs and business leaders are always those who have acquired superior self-motivation skills. In every company, the highest actual achievers (as opposed to those most skilled at gaining credit for the work of others) are certainly the most highly self-motivated. An important part of the coaching/mentoring process is to help performers find, harness and enhance their self-motivation.

Self-motivation

EXERCISE

What do you think or do to enhance your own self-motivations? Do you think those methods would work for everybody? How did you find your self-motivation methods? When did you first start using them? How long did it take to make your self-motivation patterns automatic? Has it been so long since you acquired self-motivation methods that you have forgotten why you had once needed to do so?

So what are the internal and external environmental motivation factors? What are the techniques of self-motivation and self-motivation enhancement? In the first instance, a three-level listing of what is involved in each will help:

Level 3: 'The achiever' (using self-motivation factors):

- Is focused on a purpose larger than themselves.
- Has an intense sense of direction.

- Has opportunity and preferably a requirement to learn new skills on an ongoing basis.
- Has the willingness to experiment with ideas.
- Forms their own detailed/comprehensive belief structure and view of the world.
- Has a feeling of total ownership, commitment and self-responsibility.
- Has a willingness to do whatever is required to achieve results or make results attainable.
- Develops a willingness to persist in the face of adversity.

Level 2: 'The potential achiever' (using internal environmental motivation factors) needs:

- Challenges and interest.
- Interesting projects chosen or assigned.
- Developmental experiences made available.
- Increasing responsibility offered.
- Worthwhile and attainable objectives set or agreed.
- Overcoming barriers encouraged and rewarded.

They also need:

- To be involved and accepted.
- To be valued and informed.
- To be consulted in regard to all decision making to the maximum extent possible within the remit of the department or company.

Level 1: 'The achieving elsewhere' (using external evironmental motivation factors) needs:

- Rewards:

  - Basic needs met.
  - Fair wage/salary.
  - Appreciation/recognition and acceptance.
  - Holiday entitlement.

- Security of rewards:

  - Sickness provision.
  - Employment security.
  - Relative income protected.

- Physical needs:

  - Food.
  - Water.
  - Air.
  - Shelter.
  - Warmth.
  - Safety.
  - Space.

– Peacefulness when required.
– Hygiene.

EXERCISE

Several theories of motivation could be worthy of further study e.g. Herzberg's 'two factors' theory, Maslow's 'hierarchy of needs'. Seek out information on those and other theories of motivation.

Readers who are familiar with established theories on motivation will recognize that the three-levels notion presented reorganizes known motivators (as described by Maslow, Herzberg and others) into categories that list the concerns likely to be present at different levels of achievement. The direct implication of structuring motivation factors in this way is that the level of performance required can be seen in terms of what must be present to achieve it. A company should satisfy all the motivations of the level at which they require their staff to perform. A company wishing for superior performance should provide the possibility for its staff to satisfy the motivations listed in Level 3, and ensure that the two previous levels are satisfied. A Level 2 performance requires Levels 1 and 2 to be satisfied. A Level 1 performance will be provided if Level 1 motivations are satisfied.

Motivation and control

From the point of view of the performer, the more possibility of control there is over the known motivators, the higher their potential achievement. Note that we are saying the 'more control', not the 'more satisfaction' of the motivators. Ultra-high achievers in most fields are able to suppress their lower motivations to focus more on the upper levels. Fledgling entrepreneurs often have to risk everything to get started, and do so willingly – because they have control. Reports of entrepreneurs living in their business premises, with zero social life, extremely long hours, over a prolonged period and several other severe deprivations by any standards are not just common, but almost standard. By comparison, there is little chance of a conventional employee ('The achieving elsewhere') sacrificing anything other than their time to do the job in hand in exchange for a fixed salary.

Such contrasts in behaviour suggest there is some high-level process going on that not only influences motivation, but probably creates it too. That sounds like a cue for a model. For several years I have used the mental conception of motivation shown in the figure overleaf. It helps me analyse my own and others' motivations, but more importantly it helps to identify, predict and enhance motivations. It facilitates focus on the issues that make a difference, namely rectifying under-motivation and enhancing high motivations. It is not meant to be an academically accurate model; it is meant to be useful!

At the top of the model is the conscious mind; it functions as the master controller making all the 'director level' decisions about our needs and motives.

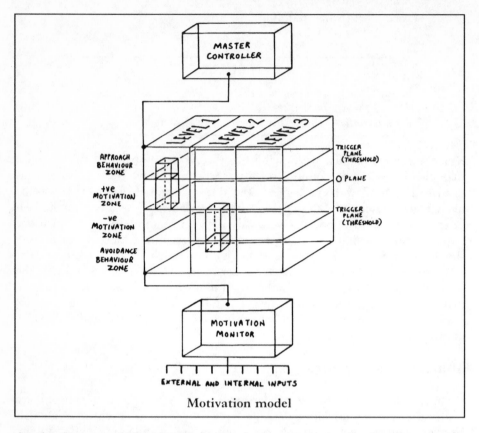

Motivation model

At the bottom of the model is the junior manager who carries out the instructions from above. The needs or motivation monitor conducts semi-conscious monitoring of our state on an ongoing basis; it evaluates and adjusts the level of motivation appropriate to each motivator. It receives signals from the environment and alters the intensity of each motivation as directed by the standing orders of the master controller. The needs/motivation monitor has staff build a tower of motivation as signals are received from the body and environment that a deficit of whatever kind is appearing. For instance, as hunger starts to appear the motivation monitor tops up the eating motivation tower. As hunger gradually turns into hunger pain, the tower/motivation is progressively topped up. At some point, determined by the master controller, the needs monitor is required to alert the master controller that the level of deficit has reached the trigger plane. The motivation has then entered the behaviour zone. The master controller then makes a decision about whether or not to act on the information. If the decision is to act, the person concerned seeks food intensely – it becomes the primary concern. After eating, the individual has satisfied the motivator and the column/tower is drained. If they have over-eaten there will be a surplus situation and the motivation column/tower will be drained below the zero plane. In this state, the thought of eating will feel uncomfortable, the smell of food may even be repulsive. There is a strong motivation not to eat. That particular motivation has moved into the avoidance zone. The master controller has already issued standing orders to move away from the source of the food smell.

The master controller can override any motivation, even the desire to survive (resulting in suicide); it can also determine the rate at which a motivation column fills or is emptied, in either positive or negative directions. The conscious mind or master controller can decide the trigger point at which motivation turns into actual behaviour. It can decide to fill or empty a column contrary to the other signals gathered by the needs monitor. It can decide which of several motivations that have reached or exceeded their trigger plane should be attended to first. The more a motivator protrudes through the trigger plane into the behaviour zone, the more intense will be the behaviour aimed at satisfying the motivator.

Higher-level motivators will, as a general rule (see entrepreneur exception above), only be attended to when the lower levels have been satisfied. When higher-level motivations are being expressed as behaviours, the emergence of a lower-level need will, generally, take greater priority. High-level behaviours will then be temporarily suspended until the louder demands of the lower levels have been silenced.

The master controller is also capable of setting up multi-tasking behaviours; it can react to different needs at different levels simultaneously. For instance a hungry writer formulating a new theory can make a trip to the kitchen or supermarket while continuing to think; Level 3 and Level 1 needs are being satisfied simultaneously.

The master controller is influenced by upbringing, education, experience and so on. But it is not bound by any of these factors. In fact it can override all of them. It can choose to re-interpret any experience. It can choose what it believes. It can choose what it will regard as a motivator. It can choose to change the motivations available. It (your conscious mind) can choose to alter the trigger point of any motivation.

How can we enhance motivation using the concepts of this model? Which are the elements open to influence?

Areas of influence

There are two main ways to influence motivation: change either the internal or the external motivations. Since the master controller or conscious thought has control over the whole process, motivation can be influenced by:

- Deciding what environmental cues are attended to.
- How they are attended to.
- Generating internal motivation cues.
- The rate at which motivation builds up.
- The point at which motivation becomes behaviour.
- The behaviour used to address the motivation.
- The rate at which the behaviour satisfies the motivation.
- The point at which the behaviour satisfies the motivation.

Re-programming

Each of the above can be altered by 're-programming' the master controller and reinforcing the new programme to the level of an automatic response. As will be shown later there is only one realistic option to change or re-programme motivations, and that is to alter the beliefs of the master controller. The method to achieve re-programming can be found in the section on Belief change method (page 200). There are less drastic ways of improving motivation which can be found under Peak motivation methods (page 136).

Alter the external or environmental factors (input signals)

If your employer is not satisfying your motivations, you can attempt to persuade them that it is in their best interests to do so. If they continue to provide an environment less than conducive to the performance you want to offer, you have three options:

1   Put up with it and try to perform in spite of the demotivation effect.
2   Carry on and accept you will perform at a level less than that which you would like.
3   Seek an environment where you can perform at the level you and every-one else except your previous employer will benefit from.

Motivational dispositions

There are seven main areas in which individuals can direct their motivations. Collectively the seven form a 'POP RIOT'. Power, Order, Production, Relationships, Imagination, Operations, Tao. Most of us have a little motivation in most of the seven and strong motivations in two or three, with one being our primary motivation. They involve motivation towards:

POP RIOT

- *Power*: recognition, status and authority. The power-oriented achiever gets results by influencing others. Such achievers are extremely results-oriented, highly passionate and emotional, and thrive on challenge and competition.
- *Order*: planning, prediction control and assessment. Order-oriented performers achieve by exercising responsibility to make sure things run smoothly and in accordance with the rules. They have enormous capacity for accuracy, detail and thoroughness.
- *Production*: the creation or generation of something physical. It can be physical or intellectual production. Production-oriented performers are pragmatic, physical, and good at solving problems.
- *Relationships*: people and getting on with them. Relationship-oriented performers achieve by virtue of their ability to obtain and maintain good-will from others. They are sociable and optimistic about others.
- *Imagination*: vision, purpose, mission, inspiration and enthusiasm. Imagination-oriented performers achieve by devising and developing a vision and pursuing it with relentless enthusiasm and dedication, their purpose is bigger than themselves. They are willing to make enormous sacrifices to achieve their goals and can inspire extraordinary loyalty and dedication in their peers and staff.
- *Operations*: processing information and understanding systems. Operations-oriented performers achieve by gaining understanding that is ahead of its time, or at least ahead of their peers. They are highly change-oriented, innovative and prefer to work on the intellectual coal-faces of their chosen disciplines.
- *Tao*: harmony, balance, intuition, feeling, and meaning. The Tao-oriented performer achieves by seeing imbalance, disharmony and meaning, by

observing trends, by interpreting the world in ways that others fail to see until pointed out. They are highly alert to market changes, staff morale, and opportunity. They make first-rate facilitators and change agents.

EXERCISE

Which of the POP RIOT motivators do you most associate with? Which least? Go the rest of the way and put them in order one to seven.

Motivation and choice of rewards

As mentioned earlier, the greater the control a person has over their motivators the more likely they are to be motivated. It makes sense therefore to let performers choose the rewards they wish. A knee-jerk reaction to that suggestion may be that staff will set ridiculously high rewards for ludicrously low effort or results. But surprisingly the reality does not work out that way. In several companies, workers are choosing their targets and what rewards they should expect for attainment of them. At one company, to be described later, employees set fair and reasonable targets. In fact in conditions of employee democracy staff usually produce more per capita than they did when they had no choice of their rewards.

What reward choices can be offered? The question misses the point! The employees should decide what reward options should be offered. A coach can encourage his or her performer to take more control over their rewards, to tell management what they want, and how they are prepared to link that to achievement on some sort of reward scale. How can you most persuasively explain to those holding the purse strings what the benefits of letting performers choose their own rewards will be?

Motivation: choice of rewards

Motivation factors checklist

Here is a list of some of the factors a team leader or manager can use to maximize motivation and in turn performance.

- Targets agreed, set and understood.
- Take time to get to know each individual.
- Recognition of individuals by team members and team leader.
- Always recognize and respond to achievement with praise and rewards.
- Keep staff informed.
- Criteria against which they will be judged are open and fair.
- Co-operation is encouraged and rewarded.
- Destructive competition is dealt with.
- Give responsibility and delegate.
- Have team make decisions and mutually support each other.
- Demonstrate trust.
- Provide opportunities for training and personal development.
- Encourage advancement – even if it means the performer has to leave the team, department or company to achieve it – and even if it means promotion above your own level.

EXERCISE

Take the list, combine it with the factors mentioned in the three-levels theory, and make your own motivational checklist. What are the factors that motivate you? When and under what conditions are you really motivated at work? When outside work? What really turns on your motivation? The dimensions along which your motivation varies are contained in the differences between your last two answers. What are the dimensions?

EXERCISE

On a scale of 1 to 10 how would you rate the importance of each motivation dimension? Which motivators would you like to have most control over? Which would you most like to increase? How could you influence those dimensions to further enhance your motivation in the situations when it matters most? How do you control your self-motivation levels, not in theory, but in practice? List five ways in which you could improve your self-motivation. What new strategies could you adopt? Which could you apply more rigorously? If you are a manager and coach/mentor, who is the person who knows what motivates each individual? Have you asked each of your staff what motivates them? Use this chain of questions to help your performers identify their motivators.

Success styles

The preceding section gave a broad indication of many of the known motivators and motivations. Each of the motivations described in our 'POP RIOT' (Power, Order, Production, Relationships, Imagination, Operations, Tao) can form a particular success style. Within each of the seven styles – and the list is by no means exhaustive – there is a potential for variation in style between extremes of the relevant motivation dimensions. The individuals' unique experience of life will vary the expression of each dimension in each style. Complicate that further with such factors as age, life stage, industry type, work environment, social environment, available motivators and so on, and it soon becomes clear that every individual must have their own unique achievement style.

Success styles

There are innumerable styles of success and achievement. Each performer will achieve in their own individual way. The coach's/mentor's role is to help the performer achieve using their own style. In the past some coaches have tried to make people a success by teaching the performer the coach's style. Which of us cannot remember being told at school that there was 'a way' of doing something, and that we'd be a success if only we adopted that way and dropped our own 'silly ideas'? How many left-handed people were inhibited by parents and others insisting that they do it the 'correct way', the right-handed way? Trying to teach someone 'a way' to be successful is just as illogical. Each of us has to find and develop our own ways. The coach is there to help us on that journey, NOT to give us directions. The coach is there to help us match our style to the environment in which we operate. The coach is there to help us build on our style, NOT choose it.

We can identify our style of success by asking questions about what motivates us most. When in the past have we achieved the greatest results? What ways did we operate to achieve those results? We can ask our friends, peers, bosses, teachers, subordinates. Our coach can help us enhance our style, discover when it works best, and just as usefully identify in which situations our style is rendered ineffective.

EXERCISE

By distilling the last three paragraphs, what are the key responsibilities of the coach in terms of helping the performer with his or her success style?

An introduction to acquiring new skills

Another of the central issues in coaching and mentoring is the acquisition of skills. To help anyone learn new skills, the coach should have an understanding of the process. More particularly he or she will help best if they know what is required to learn rapidly and thoroughly. The material will be covered under the following headings:

- Awareness of ignorance.
- The components of learning skill.
- The learning cycle.
- The learning cycle enhanced.
- The world's most effective trainer.

Acquiring new skills

Awareness of ignorance

Before any worthwhile learning takes place, the learner must become aware of his or her ignorance or inadequacy. The learner must know enough to know they are lacking in knowledge or skill, and need to learn, or acquire, new skills. How do performers acquire an awareness of their ignorance? By comparing their objective against their current knowledge and skill base. Sounds elusive, eh? Perhaps this six-stage thinking/question structure will help:

1   Is the objective set?
2   Are the sub-goals set?
3   Requirement of sub-goals analysed in terms of 'what is required to achieve this?' What tasks must be performed?
4   What skills/knowledge are required to complete these tasks?
5   Do I have this knowledge/skill? If so, do I have them to the required degree?
6   If not, do I acquire them or hire them?

Of course this circuit can be bypassed by someone spelling out exactly what the potential performer needs to know or acquire to be successful. Or at least it appears to be bypassed. In reality it has not been. Only the performer can establish what they need for their style. What works for Bloggs will probably not work for the performer. The route to success is in the hands of the individual. Only they can make the journey.

For example, someone aspiring to CEO level on the basis of their strong analytical, problem-solving and strategic analysis style doesn't need to spend years developing the skills of a charismatic leader if he or she has decided to employ a figure-head to satisfy that requirement. The same is true for those wishing to become charismatic leaders but who don't wish to spend years acquiring commercial analysis skills.

EXERCISE

How can you encourage your performers to engage in the above six-stage process? Better still (from the point of view of the performer retaining ownership), what can you ask that will help the performer to see the need for and benefit of such a process, and ideally to generate it themselves?

The components of learning skill

There are four components to the learning of any skill. They are best expressed in diagrammatic form (see the skill triangle opposite). Mental skills are usually acquired by developing understanding of the process, identifying and adopting the necessary attitudes and mental rehearsal of the required behaviours prior to trying out in the real world. Physical skills are usually acquired by observing, copying and practising in the real world, without much analytical thinking.

Interpersonal skills are usually acquired by trial and error through social exposure as a child. They can best be enhanced by using the existing skills as a baseline and encouraging the performers to analyse the skill in terms of knowledge, attitude and behaviour and then practise it. Perhaps you should do that for your own benefit first, as in the next exercise. I use the term 'intra-personal' to demonstrate the obvious but rarely appreciated similarity between the skill of handling others and the skill involved in managing one's self.

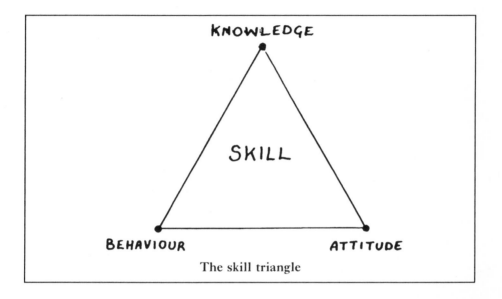

The skill triangle

EXERCISE

What is your most prized skill? Break it down into its component elements: knowledge/beliefs, attitudes and behaviours. You should have three short lists. Now take a skill you do not possess and do the same.

The learning cycle

The actual process is the same for all kinds of skill learning. First the theory is acquired, then it is practised, the outcome is observed, then evaluated, the theory or understanding is then modified and the whole cycle starts over again, as illustrated overleaf. What should be the coaching input at each stage of the cycle? There is more information available on the learning process later, under 'learning styles'.

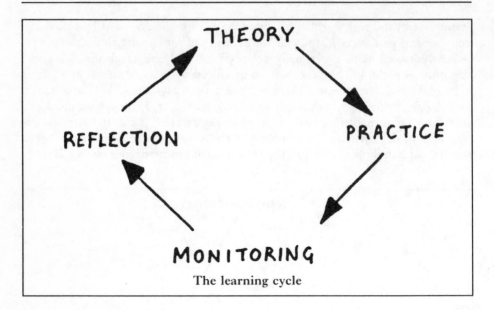

The learning cycle

The learning cycle enhanced

Each component of a skill is subject to the learning cycle. Knowledge, attitude and behaviour are processed in terms of theory or modelling before completing the rest of the cycle. The skill as a whole is also subject to the learning cycle. The individual components of a skill are processed at the detailed or micro level whereas the skill as a whole is processed at the macro level. More on this later.

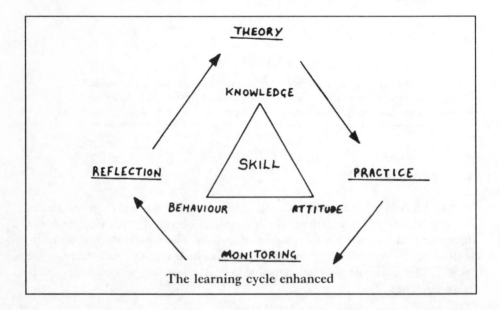

The learning cycle enhanced

The world's most effective trainer

Who is it? You. The performer is always his or her own best teacher. Time and time again in all sorts of different fields the most outstanding performers are self-taught. Einstein was. Steven Spielberg was: despite being denied entry to film school his career has been head, shoulders and body above his film school educated contemporaries. Thomas Edison was considered a dunce at school. He left before he was 16 and went on to train himself. The list of high achievers who never attended or completed a formal education in their field could fill several books. Virtually none of the world's top entrepreneurs went to business school. The very few that did either quit early or had professors dampen their ideas and enthusiasm, but later recovered.

YOU NEED YOU
THE WORLD'S MOST
EFFECTIVE TRAINER

There seems to be a negative connection between an individual's likelihood of serious achievement and having a high-level education. Yes, well educated people earn more than poorly educated people, on average. But poorly educated people have more 'chance' of being seriously successful. Why? Probably, because they are not constrained by knowledge of 'the rules of the system', or an awareness of what is considered possible and what is not. It could equally be because, having missed out on education, they choose to educate themselves (with a convert's zeal) in the things that matter, ignoring what they see as academic drivel.

Certainly no one would claim that these people were not experts in their field. Quite the contrary, many are so expert as to be virtually peerless. In short, superior performance almost certainly comes from self-taught performers. The performer is their own best teacher. The coach is there to reinforce that notion, to help the performer write his or her own achievement course.

EXERCISE

The performers you coach/mentor will probably be so used to being guided and taught that they may be shocked at the respect you wish to show them, and the trust you wish to assume in their abilities to achieve. How will you explain to them that you will not be directing them? How can you try to ensure that they don't see your non-directive approach as weakness and indecision?

Concluding comments and summary

To provide coaching successfully in the workplace, a first-hand understanding of business achievement is essential, as is a conceptual understanding of the processes involved. Both are required; one without the other is useless. High achievers – although vastly different as individual people – have much in common. They share a strong sense of direction, motivation and self-image. They have a strong belief structure which supports and creates their direction and enthusiasm. They are flexible in their persistence and have developed support systems from within and without. They engage in continual self-development. All those wishing to perform at a high level should adopt the behaviours of successful performers.

The role of the coach or mentor is to help their performers to acquire the mental and other behaviours of achievement. The acquisition of any new skill follows a predictable cycle. All skills and each component of each skill (knowledge, attitude, and behaviour) are individually and collectively acquired and improved by the application of the basic learning cycle. Only the performer can develop their skills of achievement. They are their own best trainers. They can, however, benefit enormously from having an assistant – the coach or mentor. Successful coaches and mentors use their knowledge, experience and understanding of commercial achievement to help the performer learn how to be commercially successful.

Motivational levels in performers will to a large extent be determined by the degree and nature to which each of the three motivation levels are satisfied. Low levels of motivation should be expected when only survival needs are met or will be met. Intermediate levels of motivation can be expected when higher-order needs such as recognition and acceptance are satisfied or will be satisfied. High-level motivation will be found in performers whose lower-level needs are satisfied and they are in pursuit of a purpose greater than themselves. The factors which create optimum levels of motivation will vary between individuals. In the world of work there seem to be seven motivational preferences. Together the coach and performer will work to find the best ways of using and enhancing the performer's motivational preference.

There is one factor which can override all other motivations, namely conscious control. The mind can negate the demotivating effects of the most motivationally hostile environments. Conscious will can turn what others may perceive to be overwhelming demotivations into optimum inspiration. The coach/mentor works with the performer to enhance motivation and to find ways of harnessing or converting demotivations.

Part II

The essentials

3

OBJECTIVES AND PROCESSES

The main objective of coaching and mentoring is to improve staff performance. That generates several subsidiary aims:

- To increase enthusiasm and commitment.
- To improve productivity and loyalty.
- To encourage flexibility and persistence.
- To create responsive crisis management and conscientious crisis prevention.
- To facilitate team work and mutual support.
- To engender creativity, open communication and co-operation.
- To achieve managed risk taking and perpetual self-regeneration.
- To have staff ownership of problems and responsibility for solutions.
- To allow adaptability and responsiveness to change.
- To inspire vision and purpose.
- To increase confidence, happiness and self-esteem in staff.
- To help performers overcome internal and external barriers to performance.
- To facilitate staff self-motivation.

And so on.

EXERCISE

The above list has been left deliberately incomplete. Complete the list. Write a list of coaching/mentoring objectives for your company.

The coaching and mentoring processes – an overview

The purpose of presenting an overview at this stage is to enable you to see the context in which all the relevant skills fit. The coaching and mentoring processes follow the same general sequence of stages, which are

1 Creation of a rapport.
2 Vaguely formulate the objective(s).

   – Agree the process, methods and goals of coaching and mentoring.

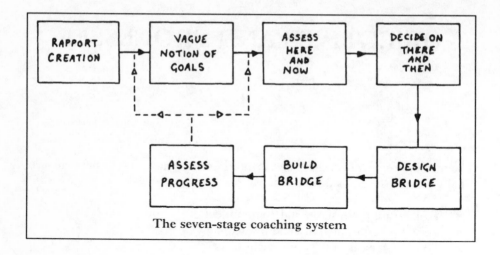

The seven-stage coaching system

3   Assess the 'here and now'.
4   Decide on the 'there and then':

  − Objective setting
  − Aligning missions

5   Choose a bridge between 'here and now' and 'there and then':

  − Ingredients analysis/situational analysis.
  − Barrier analysis.
  − Paradigm analysis.
  − Learning/success style analysis.
  − Choosing between bridge design options.
  − Drawing up the achievement plan.

6   Building the bridge.
7   Assessing progress to the other side:

  − Monitoring and performance observation.
  − System feedback and looping.

EXERCISE

Picture yourself doing what you think is implied by each of the stage headings (ignore the sub-headings at this stage). How would you choose to structure and order the coaching/mentoring process? How could you turn it into a three-stage process, a four-, a five-stage process?

The process in more detail

Rapport creation

As must be obvious, if the coach/mentor and performer have a poor relationship not very much is going to be achieved. On the other hand if they have mutual trust, respect and a genuine interest in each other's lives, the outcome will be highly positive. The specific skills involved in creating good rapport will be covered in the key skills section.

Vague formulation of goals

At the start of the process there will probably be a vague sense of objectives by both parties, and that is how it should be. The objective setting can only become precise when both parties have a clear picture of the point of departure. At this stage they should agree how to structure the coaching/mentoring sessions. They might decide to adopt this seven-point plan. Or they might take more charge of their lives and devise their own structure.

Assessing the here and now

The performer's current achievement level – the departure point – must be objectively assessed and agreed against whatever are the appropriate dimensions for that role.

Deciding on the there and then

Both parties discuss and agree an arrival point, in terms of both actual performance and the time at which that level will be reached.When I say 'discuss', I mean the coach/mentor helps the performer to decide. Some mentoring programmes are designed to help the performer achieve a particular qualification, in which case the 'there and then' is already set. Despite that, the performer should take as much responsibility as possible for deciding how to get to the there and then.

Choosing a bridge

The performer will examine the gap between the current and the desired situation and decide what options are available for crossing it. The most appropriate options are then chosen and turned into an agreed formal achievement plan.

Building the bridge

The performer sets about implementing the achievement plan. Coaching or mentoring input at this stage is, and should be, minimal. If the performer requests input the most effective assistance is usually to ask questions aimed at enhancing focus on, and observation of, the relevant factors.

Coaching and mentoring: start to finish

Assessing progress to the other side

The coach is there:

- To help the performer confront and overcome the inevitable obstacles to success.
- To help decide whether the goals should be fine-tuned or whether the method of achieving them should be improved or altered.
- To enhance ownership and focus.
- To encourage perseverance and resilience.

EXERCISE

Now that you've gone through the process in more detail, sit back and imagine what you would do in each of the stages based on your current level of knowledge. The purpose of this exercise is to encourage your imagery to aid your memory and raise issues that will motivate further development of your understanding.

4

THE REQUIREMENTS

A coach needs to know, to be, to do...

What does a coach need to know? Do they need to be expert in the field of the performance? NO. They do need to be practical (not academic) experts in the principles of performance. An academic or a psychologist is the last thing a coach should be. What is required is a person who has performed some business skill or discipline at a high level. They need to know and to feel at first hand what is involved in achievement. They need to have been through the pain and pleasure, the elation and frustration, the battles, the defeats, and workplace victories on their way to success. The actual business discipline is not as important as an experiential understanding of achievement.

Sitting on top of that experientially acquired knowledge, the coach can be maximally effective by having a good theoretical understanding of the principles of achievement. Perhaps theoretical is the wrong word. The right word is structural. The coach should have a structural understanding or framework with which she or he can process and organize their vast experience, a structure through which they can communicate their knowledge by asking the right question, not by providing the right answer. This book aims to help the coach develop that structure.

The non-expert as coach

Is knowledge a handicap? Can ignorance be an asset? There is some evidence to suggest that high achievers in one field who are also skilled coaches can be even more effective coaches in disciplines about which they know nothing. The explanation seems to be that if the 'ignorant' coach has no technical knowledge, he or she is forced to concentrate more on the performer than on the technical performance. The performer then has total ownership, and all the coach can do is help the performer to focus, plan and self-teach by asking appropriate questions. Whereas those with technical expertise are tempted to use it by offering advice on the technical aspects of the performance, despite their better judgement – thereby depriving performers of ownership.

The non-expert as coach

What the coach needs to be: the attitudes

In addition to having superior communication skills, the coach should exhibit attitudes that facilitate the performance of others. Attitudes that facilitate an increase in the purpose and ownership of the performer are desired. Specifically coaches should be:

- Supportive, but not to the point of depriving the performer of his or her responsibility for themselves.
- Nurturing – a positive attitude towards the performer's progress and their desire to achieve results.
- Interested and judgemental in the sense that she or he seeks to see the best in performers.
- Other-focused.
- Other-empowering.
- Empathetic (but not soppy).
- Open.
- Responsive.
- Trusting and trustworthy.

The practice of the necessary skills (to be covered later) will express these attitudes automatically.

EXERCISE

What does your ideal coach or mentor need to be? What attitudes do they need to possess? What attitudes does your performer most want to see in their coach?

Coaching credibility

Which of us likes being taught or coached by someone who last learned something new the day they left college? The best teachers are those who never cease being students. Well actually, they are the second best teachers, as we've already mentioned. The best coaches are those striving to improve their own performance, preferably with the help of their own coach.

What the coach needs to do: the behaviour

The behaviours of the coach are direct manifestations of the knowledge and attitudes just covered. A good coach will:

- Listen.
- Ask questions designed to increase performers' focus and enhance their self-responsibility.
- Provide a sense of hope and an expectation of success.
- Provide opportunities to experience success.
- Provide a structure/format/context/intellectual environment for performer development.
- Provide the kind of coaching the performer will respond to.
- Provide opportunities for emotional release.
- Provide objective and honest feedback.
- When asked, provide rationales for action and aetiologies of failure.

A mentor needs to know, to be, to do...

The requirement for knowledge on the part of the mentor is greater than on that of the coach. Since the mentor is someone available for the performer to learn FROM (as opposed to 'with') she or he must have technical expertise in all the areas the performer seeks to develop. They should have great experience of life generally, and specifically have good knowledge of the organization or structure within which she or he is working with the performer. They should have a good knowledge of the performer's background and capabilities, and an awareness that the knowledge may be misused to impose limiting expectations on the performer, or – potentially just as bad – unrealistically high expectations which set the performer up for failure. Mentors should possess an awareness of the emotional difficulties a relatively young person may have in dealing with someone whose skills and abilities are likely to be at a higher level than anyone they've ever been close to before: the 'awe factor'.

Mentors should be: secure in their own position; not feel threatened by their rising star; inclined to seek ways of motivating people; supportive; reassuring; credible; authoritative but not authoritarian; and approachable.

What the mentor should do will depend very much on the purpose of the mentoring role. The purpose may be to provide induction, general development mentoring, or indeed any of the other purposes mentioned earlier. Speaking broadly the mentor should:

- Establish human rapport quickly.
- Establish the level of confidentiality being provided and stick to it.
- Provide good instruction, training, explanations, guidance and advice, and counselling.
- Provide representation and liaison on the performer's behalf.
- Provide long-term developmental support.
- Provide career overview and options advice.
- Provide information on the company's interest in the performer to complement that provided by the departmental manager.
- Provide analysis of the skills required to succeed in the role, and critical feedback.

The differences

Mentors need to form relationships very quickly. The mentor is less performer-centred than the coach and as such is required to have even better rapport development skills than the coach. The mentor is most needed in the early stages and least needed as the performer finds his or her feet. By comparison, the coaching process lends itself to an easy rapport development: it is totally performer-focused; the performer is the centre of attention. Coaching is mainly a 'pulling out' activity. Mentoring is mainly a 'putting in' activity.

EXERCISE

Compile a list of the differences between the coach and mentor roles – for the most performer-focused coach and the most performer-directive mentor.

Coaching styles

There are as many coaching styles as there are coaches. Coaching styles vary from the outright 'Machiavellian' to the 'protective parent' – with all the possible 'in betweens', such as the 'detached rationalist', the 'taskmaster' and the 'evangelist'. Each of these styles has its benefits and drawbacks:

- *The Machiavellian coach* will tell the performer whatever needs to be said to produce a performance. If that means lying, coercing or provoking, so be it. The style can be effective, but usually only in the very short term.

It will rapidly produce resentment, anger and distrust.

- *The protective parent coach* operates on the basis of 'softly, softly catchee monkey'. They are gentle and reassuring. It works wonders when recovering from failure, but soon becomes associated with failure.
- *The detached rationalist coach* works miracles at getting performers to think for themselves. But rapport formation is poor: who wants a trusting relationship with a computer?
- *The taskmaster coach* pushes, confronts and criticizes. Wonderfully useful at maintaining staying power when the going gets tough, but is likely to eventually generate resentment and loss of self-control in the performer.
- *The evangelist coach* inspires by painting wonderfully optimistic pictures of the world and future achievements. The level of energy displayed by them is positively contagious, at least until the performer sits down and thinks it through, when it becomes naïve idealism. However, if the performer generates their own evangelical passion towards their own achievements they are more likely to achieve results than those not possessing that level of passion.

Technically there is only one true coaching style, and that is where the coach is totally performer-focused – where the performer views the coach as an assistant to their attempts to increase focus and self-responsibility. The coach is required to be flexible and do what is most desired by the performer, NOT what is thought by the coach to be most needed. You cannot 'know' what the performer needs at any one time. You cannot know what coaching style will be best for each scenario the performer presents you with. If you don't or can't know something the obvious strategy is to ask the person who can and does know – the performer. The performer will tell you what they want or need. They will also tell you, if you ask, whether they want you to provide what they need (for instance, support), or help to figure out for themselves what to do next.

The range of workable coaching is very broad. At any point, in any role, on the continuum appearing on page 7, coaching could be effectively employed. For instance using predominantly formal teaching methods does not rule out the use of pure coaching as and when required.

EXERCISE

How would you use coaching methods? In formal teaching environments like senior schools, universities and conventional training courses?

The range of expression of the one true coaching style: options, formats, tools and questions

Variations of the style can be identified partly or at least distinguished by the tools used. There is an enormous number of self-training methods available with which the coach can help the performer: role play, behaviour rehearsal, humour-based problem presentation, puzzle provision, illustrations, exercises, debate and argumentation, self-debate, list formation, structured thinking, brainstorming, detached analysis, teach me, give it to me from another perspective, tell it like a story and so on. (More on this later.)

Variation in coaching style is also inevitable because of the variety of thinking styles possessed by individual coaches. People tend to think in particular styles. Logically/analytically, intuitively/emotionally, pictorially/mechanically... there are as many thinking styles as there are people who think.

There is also room for variation in the habitual questioning pattern of the coach, and the extent to which questions, and not statements, are the main communication output by the coach. (We will come back to the asking of questions soon.)

Try to identify the way your performers think and tune into it. If possible, phrase your questions in that way. You can identify their style from the key descriptive words they use and the way they present information. For instance, do they present information on the basis of cause and effect, chronologically, in terms of relationships, in terms of the overall picture, in terms of the skills involved, in terms of the emotional content of the events, in terms of who said what, in terms of ...? Identifying a performer's thinking style need not be done at the level of articulation. Much of our effective understanding is at the pre-articulation level. For instance, when was the last time you articulated the mathematics and physics behind the decisions you make to hit a moving tennis ball? Never? Point taken?

But note: no one thinks in all one style. Some people vary their style depending on the context, or the people they are dealing with. Some highly sophisticated performers adopt the thinking style they have found is most effective for the task at hand. When managing people, they think intuitively/emotionally. When financial-planning they think logically/numerically. When managing production they think pictorially, and so on.

People's thinking style seems to be strongly connected to their motivational preference. The ingredients of POP RIOT can help you here. Predict what the thinking style of each POP RIOT motivator is most likely to be.

Mentoring styles

The range of acceptable mentoring practices is even more broad. It can be prescriptive, informative, supportive, catalytic (the main coaching requirement), confrontational or even cathartic. Everything that was said about coaching styles applies to mentoring styles, especially where the mentor is operating using coaching principles.

Mentors can operate effectively while being either passive, neutral or active in their interaction with the performer. Directive and non-directive mentoring variations are also widely practised. Passive, non-directive mentors can operate effectively by being like a human library. The performer asks questions and the mentor gives answers to those and only those questions. Directive mentors tell the performer what they should be learning, what they should be asking.

EXERCISE

Which thinking styles do you think are most suitable for mentoring? Which do you think would be least suitable or even counter-productive for mentoring? Rank the 'POP RIOT' motivation dispositions in the order you think would give the best performance in a mentoring role. Note: if your personal style is one of the least productive, that does not mean you should avoid mentoring. It means you should be aware of the weaknesses in the style and seek ways to maximize the strengths.

EXERCISE

Conduct the same exercise for coaching styles.

Combining roles

Very few work roles are pure roles. Most of the levels from junior management up have an element of several different functions involved. The purchasing manager, for instance, has to organize and maintain his or her staff, and the purchasing activities, and the problems and opportunities generated by that interface.

Increasingly she or he also has responsibility for organizing and providing (or at least liaising with others to organize) the training, development and coaching or mentoring of staff. In some companies cross-coaching is common, where a performer is coached by someone other than their direct manager, and that manager coaches other departments' staff.

Combining roles – the ethics

As with all combining of roles, there are numerous situations with potential conflicts of interest. Research shows that people under even a small amount of stress (most executives) will resolve conflicts in THEIR best interests, and either justify that action in terms of 'the greater good', 'I had no choice' or attribute motivations that their audience will best believe. Needless to say, coming to that conclusion didn't need any research; it's common knowledge now and it was several hundred years ago. Remember old Nick, alias Machiavelli?

Most intelligent people recognize that a person with two roles has considerable leeway to decide how best to resolve such conflicts. The performer will probably think about the motivations of the coach/mentor and make his or her personal decision about what level of trust is to be expected in respect of which subject areas. Although from the performer's view such self-protection is necessary, it is likely to inhibit the effectiveness of any subsequent coaching, unless addressed and clarified.

A tip for performers. Ask your coach/mentor to sign a confidentiality agreement with you, perhaps based on the above, with each party keeping a copy. If they refuse, regardless of the ingenious and creative reasons offered, you have a good indication as to their likely trustworthiness, or at very least that their interests are not primarily with your development. The old adage, 'Who pays the piper calls the tune' applies.

Whom do you deal with who has two roles, each of which can affect you? If it was safe to tell that person something while they were wearing one hat, but unwise if they were wearing the other hat, would you:

a) Not tell them?
b) Not tell them and tell them you were not telling them?
c) Tell them?
d) Ask for a confidentiality agreement, before telling them?
e) Ask for a confidentiality agreement, but still not tell them?
f) Pretend to have absolute trust in their integrity in carrying out the twin roles, and tell them nothing that may compromise you, ever?
g) Do what was best for the company regardless of your interests?
h) Do as you would expect your aspiring performers or any other upwardly mobile person to do?
i) Lie and tell them what they want to hear?

Decide on your response. Now look at the answer at the end of the chapter and compare your answer to mine. Point taken?

Combining roles successfully – ethical guidelines

It would be sensible to have a set of guidelines for combining roles in such a way that the coach protects themselves from accusations of less than ethical behaviour, and the performer knows exactly how any conflicts will be identified and resolved. The following list provides some guidelines.

1 Clearly define the requirements and responsibilities of each adopted role.
2 Clearly identify the potential conflicts of interest.
3 Decide on the general principles that will guide the resolution of actual conflicts.
4 Compile a set of rules based on 3 above. Most professional associations have very similar codes of ethics: perhaps you could adopt and upgrade such a code to apply specifically to the combined roles.
5 Publicize 1, 2, 3, and 4 above to all to whom you are providing coaching/ mentoring.
6 Agree some kind of confidentiality pact based on your guidelines.

7 Completing stages 1–4 with your performers is likely to establish good rapport and high trust levels quickly.

8 If you ever break the rules you have laid down yourself, your trust is finished.

9 Note: even if you have completed the above, the astute performer will not offer absolute trust. You will not be given information in one role which you may be able to use in your other role against the performer's interest. You are, after all, human. We all look after our own best interests first, and we all know that.

Combining specific roles with coaching or mentoring

Having raised the issues involved in combining roles, it's time for me to take a break. It's your turn to do the work – only because I am in no position to cover all the possible combinations that exist in the organizational world: trainer/coach, personnel/mentor, counsellor/coach, director/mentor...

EXERCISE

How will you combine your main role with your mentoring/ coaching responsibilities? Establish a set of guidelines. If you completed the last exercise with your combination in mind ignore this one.

Summary

The coach's primary responsibility is to do everything possible to enable the performer to take responsibility for their own achievements. The mentor by comparison should be sufficiently equipped for the performer to learn from. There are a number of possible coaching and mentoring styles, but in reality there is only one effective coaching style – namely, performer focused coaching. There is room for considerable, and probably inevitable, variation in the delivery of coaching and mentoring.

In the situations which require coaches and mentors to combine their roles with say that of manager or director, there is considerable scope for the emergence of conflicts of interest. Both coach and mentor have a responsibility to set up an ethical system which is geared towards handling the inevitable ethical dilemmas.

The effective coach does not need to be an expert in the particular field of business being coached; in fact it may be preferable for their expertise to lie elsewhere. But they must be commercially skilled, they must be credible, and they must be continuing to develop themselves. An academic or theorist is the last thing a coach or mentor in the business world should be.

ANSWER TO EXERCISE

Answer: Well done. I thought you'd choose that one. What would I choose? The same as you, of course! Anyone of any merit always prefers that option.

5

THE KEY SKILLS

It is possible to coach effectively with limited knowledge, as long as what knowledge there is, is made up of the core ingredients, the key skills. Those skills will be considered under four headings:

- Rapport creation.
- Listening and listening skills.
- Ownership, focus, questions and objectives.
- Questions: the master tool – a user's manual.

Rapport creation

What do people who create good rapport with others do? What do they think? What attitudes do they take to the meetings? What exactly is involved in creating a good rapport?

Meeting – first impressions

Whether we like it or not the most important factors in the early stages of rapport development are physical. We do judge others by appearance and by first impressions. We should expect to be so judged ourselves. Appearance means physical characteristics, dress, behaviour, voice, and attitude. Most of these characteristics can be controlled and refined. Physical characteristics too have room to be made an ally in the impression-formation stakes. People who keep themselves in good physical shape are generally better regarded than those over- or underweight.

The introduction

For good rapport development, eye contact should be prolonged but not aggressively so. Both parties normally make a detailed scan of the other's face. The smile is best if warm and genuine, not forced or short. The handshake should be firm, not crushing. And the verbal greeting should convey pleasure in the experience appropriate to the level of knowledge you have of the other party.

First impressions

Immediately begin the habit of addressing the other party by their name. If you wish to appear totally false, then follow the advice given by some communication specialist to repeat the other party's name several times in the first few minutes. Otherwise, use the name when it is natural and appropriate to do so, don't force it. The first exchanges should be superficial open questions.

Getting to know you

With the appropriate attitudes, rapport-building behaviour seems to flow naturally. The most important attitude is a genuine desire to get to know, understand, and find interest in the other party, to establish what she or he likes, dislikes and finds interest in. The unstated assumption is that every individual has the right to be the way they choose and it is up to us, the other party, to find what we like in them.

The people who are most skilled at developing rapport – the world's super-salespeople – report a sense of 'unconscious communication' when good rapport has been established. The conversation flows spontaneously and both people feel that the other is genuine, and all barriers to open communication have been removed. This is the point where sterile academic debate could start, so let's return to the 'how to'.

The attitudes adopted by the coach/mentor or performer wishing to form a good rapport are quite specific and are characterized by the following behaviours:

- Asking open questions.
- Active and reflective listening.
- Asking questions which pick up on the point made by the other speaker.
- Self-disclosures with question add-ons.
- Self-deprecation, admission of fears and weaknesses, and humour.

- Clear, brief and coherent communication.
- Matching and pacing – language, breathing, intensity, non-verbal communication.
- Building trust.

Open questions

We'll go into more detail on questions shortly. For now, an open question is one which cannot be logically answered with a yes or no. It is a question which requires to be answered in the form of information provision. Asking open questions says to the listener, 'I am interested in you and in what you have to say'.

Active and reflective listening

So important that this will have its own section.

Pick up and carry questions

A powerful way of demonstrating that you are both listening and have understood your speaker is to pick up on a point just made and ask for the speaker to carry on, to elaborate, or carry it on yourself, and/or make a self-disclosure about the issue raised. Or make reference in some other way to the speaker's key point.

Self-disclosure with question add-ons

Providing information about yourself is essential for good rapport. You can do this as a follow-on from a self-disclosure by the other party. Or you can make a self-disclosure and invite the other to express their views on the particular issue.

Self-deprecation, admission of fears and weaknesses, and humour

Making fun of yourself is a great way of showing that you don't take yourself too seriously. Those able to do this seem better adjusted than those unable to do so. We all make mistakes and all have a healthily unhealthy collection of fears and weaknesses. Showing them rather than hiding them demonstrates our humanity. As for humour, which of us is not happiest when having a good laugh with friends? Humour lubricates learning and oils the wheels of business. When the going gets tough, if you find the funny, the bizarre, the unusual and the ridiculous, and the relationships between, the tough will really get going.

Make clear, brief, relevant and coherent communications

Alternatively, you could hog the conversation and talk about things the listener has absolutely no interest in for hours and hours, while doing your best to be utterly incoherent. Have you ever noticed how our enemies know instinctively to use that style as a weapon against us?

Matching and pacing

A method used by highly skilled rapport developers. Aristotle Onassis was a master. The technique is to match every aspect of the other party's behaviour, to adopt their style of language, breathing, intensity and non-verbal communication, and to do so at the same speed or pace. Outsiders looking in feel the process is insincere, unethical and patronizing, but have great difficulty deciding who is matching who, particularly if they have no knowledge of the previous behaviour of either party. Further, people who have known each other a long time adopt each other's mannerisms, especially when they are with the person concerned. The skilled user of pacing and matching would argue that she or he is only doing what will end up happening in the long term anyway, and that in fact by doing so early they will develop the relationship faster than might otherwise have been the case. That, of course, is exactly the reason why one should use matching: to develop rapport.

Matching and pacing

One final benefit occurs: while trying to match and pace someone you have no choice but to focus on the individual, and while doing so, you inevitably come to understand and appreciate them. It's difficult not to appreciate someone whose behaviour you have been exhibiting for some time! You will identify with your communication partner and they will sense you trying to do so, and appreciate it.

Will other people detect and perceive pacing as mimicry and take offence? Not if your motives are pure. The acid test must be: how many times have you detected and taken offence at someone matching and pacing you? Probably never. Not because you have never been matched. On the contrary. With so many skilled communicators in the business world you most certainly have been matched and paced, regularly.

Building trust

The most powerful action for building trust is to demonstrate trust, to be honest about one's fears, weaknesses, mistakes, hopes, aspirations, ambitions, to show one's real self, warts, bunions, carbuncles and all.

EXERCISE

Devise an exercise that you and your performers can use to enhance each of the skills mentioned under the above headings. That should be a total of eight exercises. You will have to read some of the next section to complete some of the exercises.

Listening and listening skills

Listening is often misperceived as a passive process. It is most certainly an active process as will be demonstrated under the following headings:

- What to listen for.
- Reflective listening.
- What makes people listen.
- What is it about the message that interests people in listening?
- What puts people off listening?

What to listen for

Words spoken account for around 20 per cent of the information we communicate. The other 80 per cent of the information comes from our interpretations of non-verbal communication sources: hand, eye, mouth, body movements; voice tone, pace, pitch, intensity, timbre; language style, structure and accent. The 'science' of interpreting these signals is extremely primitive. Our brains can process the information instinctively and almost instantaneously, but we have yet to successfully analyse how we do it. Trying to analyse your listening while you are listening will destroy your listening. Are you listening? Don't do it. So what do you listen for? Understanding. Simply concentrate on understanding what is being said.

Reflective listening

Reflective listening demonstrates and encourages listening by requiring the listener to bounce what has just been heard back to the speaker for confirmation. Re-phrasing, paraphrasing and summarizing the perceived message also allows the speaker to check that they have communicated what they intended. Concentrate on the total meaning conveyed, not just the words. And if you pick up a conflict or contradiction in communication, reflect that too.

What makes people listen?

The four most important factors are self-interest, source credibility, the presentation method of the message – and the fourth factor is an absence of communication turn-offs.

Listening switch

What is it about the message that interests people in listening?

Much of this question has already been answered in the rapport development section. A collection of descriptive words can serve as a summary: warmth, friendliness, sincerity, openness, honesty, confidence, organized thinking, enthusiasm, inspiration, creativity, knowledge, listener 'centricity' and excitement.

What puts people off listening?

The barriers include deceit, pomposity, monotony, irrelevance, lethargy, stuffiness, hypersensitivity, patronizing behaviour, formality, complexity, statistics, vagueness, insecurity, nervousness, distractibility, inconsistency, mixed messages. The most effective listening skill is to remove all the barriers to listening.

EXERCISE

Time for a bit of honesty. When was the last time you realized that someone had stopped listening because of your communication turn-offs? What particularly did you do to turn them off? Think back to other communication failures. What seems to be your most consistent blocker?

Some people cause the above problems by trying too hard to be good listeners. For instance, listening well does not mean trying to decide what to say next while the other party is speaking. In fact that's a pretty good definition of listening badly, and a good example of the distractibility turn-off.

EXERCISE

Devise an action plan for improvement based on the above, that will enable you to practise and develop the known effective listening behaviours.

Objectives, ownership, focus and questions

The third key coaching and mentoring skill is actually a mixture of operating principles, interpersonal skills and intrapersonal skills.

Objectives: the unifying thread

In coaching or mentoring 'Objectives are achieved by using questions to enhance the ownership and focus of the individual performer'. Every aspect of coaching and mentoring should be directed towards increasing the ownership and awareness of the performer. Or more precisely, towards having the performer increase his or her focus and ownership.

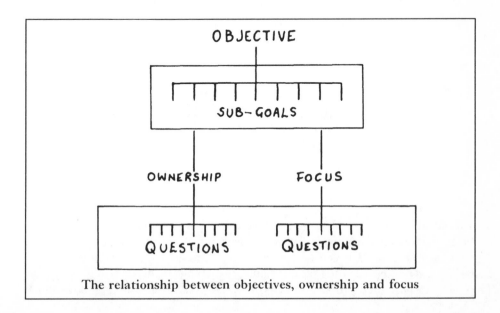

The relationship between objectives, ownership and focus

Ownership

How can the world's top-level business performers work 14 to 18 hours a day every day for years and still enjoy it? Simply because they have ownership. Not necessarily ownership of the company (although that often becomes the case over the years – because of their capacity for work) but ownership of their efforts. They take total and unconditional responsibility for their beliefs, thoughts, feelings, skills, behaviours, and results. If they need to learn a new skill to complete some task, they don't run off to the training department and request 'a course', and whine when the request is denied. They acquire the skill any way they can. If they have a problem that the best brains in the world could not solve, they don't throw up their hands and give up. They can't do that: it's their problem, so they create a workable or operating solution and fine-tune it as they continue to perform. The Wright brothers were out there fine-tuning their flying machine while the world's academics were arguing over why mechanical flight was impossible. The Wrights owned the problem of flight. They were totally committed to solving the problem. Edison owned the problem of creating the electric light bulb ('lamp', for the technical boffins). The NASA team responsible for putting the first human on the moon owned the problems standing in the way of their dream.

Ownership

A sense of ownership is central to commitment and persistence. If you own a problem – if that problem is inside you, if it has become part of your soul – finding the energy, commitment and persistence to solve it is easy. So how is ownership acquired? It can be sought or it can be given. If it is given it must be willingly accepted to be of any value. Ownership is increased by asking the performer how they propose to...? how they will...? what they might do to...?

EXERCISE

When was your performance level at the highest you can remember? What did that sense of ownership feel like to you? What sparked it off? What maintained it?

Focus

What is meant by 'focus'? Focus is what we do when we concentrate on something we are trying to achieve. It is the single-minded application to one goal. Focus is enhanced by asking questions that require the performer to pay even more attention to the task to be able to answer sensibly. If a performer were trying to improve their cash flow projection or management skills, you would ask questions like, 'How regularly does ABC Plc pay us? When do accounts write payment cheques?' Note that the questions, while being open, require only a short or one-word answer. The idea is to increase observation/ awareness, but not to engage in analysis – unless of course the skill being performed is analysis. Let's assume our performer is now seeking ways to make the cash flow more positive, or at least less negative. 'Which areas could you examine to find cash flow savings? Which creditors could we negotiate extensions with? Which suppliers may be willing to accept a delayed payment? Which debtors could pay us earlier? From which customers could we insist on cash in advance, or at least cash with order?'

Can you see the pattern? Each question is designed to help the performer focus, to increase their awareness of the critical factors in the skill. Note that we don't say things like 'Pay attention to the details'. These kinds of statement are to be avoided because they offer nothing more than harassment. They don't encourage awareness for any particular purpose whereas the specific requests above create awareness for a particular purpose. Focus can become a habitual part of a performer's repertoire if she or he finds benefit in it. 'Pay attention to the details' and its unhelpful relatives do not offer the promise of anything other than more of the same after one's concentration has lapsed through boredom. What questions can you ask yourself to enhance your focus on the performer?

Here is a little word structure to help you remember the importance of focusing:

- *Focus* increases awareness.
- *Awareness* increases understanding.
- *Understanding* increases control.
- *Control* increases performance.
- *Performance* increases results.

Focus: observation v. analysis

The relationship between observation and analysis is a stormy one. Analysis during observation reduces performance; it serves as a very effective distraction.

They are like a couple who cannot live together and cannot live apart. Observation during analysis is distorted by the analytical process. Scientists have known this for at least a century. The two processes are linked but should be separate for best use. To illustrate: observations spark scientists' curiosity. They analyse the information gathered, then go back to observing again to see whether their analysis was accurate. Then they return to thinking and explaining (analysing), to devising experiments. Then they conduct the experiments (observing) and analyse the results. Each process provides information which helps the other. The two processes are always kept separate; they interfere with each other. The brain functions better at both when they are conducted separately. When has your performance been impaired by analysing when you should have been observing?

In a workplace coaching setting, the performer should be encouraged to keep the two thinking processes apart. When performing/developing an interpersonal or business skill, there should be intense concentration on the other party; the analysis comes after. When acquiring negotiations skills, for instance, the performer should set their game plan, concentrate on carrying it out, focus on the process, and afterwards analyse what happened. Some performers will suggest that they can undertake both processes at the same time, or at least that they can switch between them very rapidly during a performance. If they can, and can do so effectively, say hello to the next international business mega-star!

It is possible to observe and analyse at the same time, but only with different kinds of abilities and with skills so highly developed that they can be carried out automatically – driving and talking simultaneously, for instance (visual-spatial and verbal abilities), or conducting a telephone conversation while preparing a spreadsheet (numerical and verbal). The higher the level of processing power required, the less performing two skills at once is likely to be a success. Keep thinking and doing separate; they're both happier and more effective that way.

General and specific, overview and detail, macro and micro levels

One thing the two processes – analysis and observation – do have in common is that they are naturally conducted by starting with the general and moving towards the specific. As explained by the learning cycle, we hold models or theories in our heads. The precise nature of the model pertaining to any specified skill varies from individual to individual, but all have a general overview of the skill and specific or micro details. Both observation and analysis can be conducted at the overview or detail levels.

The successful acquisition and performance of any skill requires an understanding at both general and detail levels. The two levels have an effect on each other. Indeed successful performers integrate the micro with the macro, the detail and the overview. The overview of the skill area being practised determines what micro level skills are required, and practice at the micro level is used to modify and improve the performer's macro-level model.

Analysis at this stage needs a partner: synthesis. Analysis is used to break down the elements of an observation in an attempt to isolate the 'active ingredient' or 'inactive ingredient' as the case may be. Synthesis pulls together the conclusion from the analysis to create a modified and hopefully improved model.

Analysis is usually conducted when thinking from the general to the specific. Synthesis is usually conducted when thinking from the specific to the general. Like analysis, synthesis should be kept separate from observation, as illustrated below.

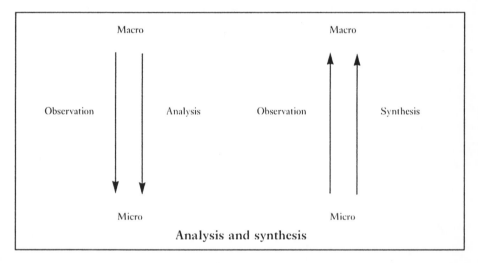

Analysis and synthesis

The process of acquiring or improving understanding is a continuing journey from the overview to the detail level of the skill being developed. Eventually performance becomes so skilled and practised that it can be carried out without reference to the detail level; the responses are made automatically on the basis of recognizing patterns.

In practical terms the coach should encourage the performer to develop their skill by asking for observations at both macro and micro level as appropriate, then seek analysis of the observations, followed by a synthesis of the new conclusions. The modified model is then tested by the performer, after which the coach should ask for observations. And on the process goes.

Questions: the master tool – a user's manual

Questions are immensely powerful. They serve a multitude of different purposes. Coaching at its ideal best is a never-ending chain of performer-centred questions. The perpetual use of questions is probably the most striking difference between coaching and teaching. Let's examine them in more detail. Questions can be:

Questions: the master tool

- Thought directors.
- Empowering mechanisms.
- Belief forming.
- Catalysts for change.

Thought directors

If I asked you to tell me the time, what would come into your head? If you were asked what you did for a living, what would you be thinking about? If you asked yourself how you would write a business plan, what would come into your mind? If you asked whether or not questions asked by yourself or others dictated what you thought, what would come into your mind? Questions are the steering system of our thinking ship. Questions set you off in a particular direction, and like a supertanker, the more power and speed you acquire in that direction, the harder it is to stop or change direction. Questions are intellectual rudders. With astute questioning you can steer your performer into wonderful waters, or leave them in pieces on the rocks.

EXERCISE

What questions could you ask that would enable performers to see the value in asking questions of themselves?

Empowering mechanisms

Questions empower the high performers. They use questions to find ways of achieving, when low performers use questions to justify leaving. Successful people habitually ask themselves empowering questions.

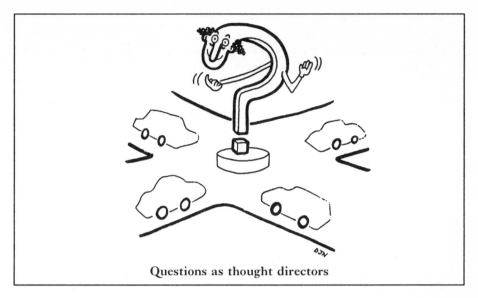
Questions as thought directors

'OK, so conventional sources of finance won't respond to this project. What are the unconventional sources? Where can I find them? How do I go about persuading them? How can I make the case irresistible?' Who do you think is more likely to find finance, our hero/ine just mentioned or the habitual disempowering questioner: 'Why won't they lend me the money? What's wrong with these people? Why can't they recognize a good idea when it jumps up and bites them? Why are these bankers strangling our economy? Why are they collectively giving away billions to developing countries and they won't LEND for profit in their own backyard? Why do they always lend at the top of the property cycle, when it's bound to go down, and refuse to lend at the bottom

Empowering mechanisms

of the cycle when it's bound to go up?'

The list of disempowering questions could go on for ever, and for some people they do. There are always more disempowering questions that can be asked. There are far fewer possible empowering questions to ask of any situation. Their fewer number actually makes empowering questions much easier to find. The empowered thinker asks a few helpful questions, finds the appropriate direction to apply their efforts to get results, and gets on with it.

EXERCISE

Provide five reasons why it is wise to concentrate on empowering thoughts and asking empowering questions.

Belief forming

The questions asked by yourself or others can form new beliefs or reform old ones. Why do people in some cultures celebrate the death of a loved one? Why is commercial failure virtually certain to end a business career in the UK, but taken as statement of an opportunity to acquire new expertise and experience in the USA?

Exploring the first question might lead you to think about whether grieving was a phenomenon dictated by culture or an in-built physical reaction. The information you would obtain if you researched this area in more detail would lead you to certain conclusions. Your conclusions would certainly change your belief, if only by a tiny degree. Exploring the second question might lead to the conclusion that persistence and merit were differently valued in the US, or that preventing proven failures from risking others' money was more important than encouraging enterprise and economic growth in the UK. Again, having asked the question your belief is bound to be changed, however imperceptibly. But imperceptibly is not enough to make a serious performance difference. What is required is an intense effort to identify the beliefs that will most empower yourself as the performer.

Set about asking yourself a range of questions that will help you really believe. Questions like: Can I give five reasons why empowering questions can positively affect my performance? When in my past have I noticed that the answer to a problem came to me after I phrased the question in a way that assumed an answer was available to me? When have I missed solutions, opportunities and other benefits because I didn't see them, only to witness someone else ask the right empowering question and come up with the obvious solution? How can I make sure I generate empowering questions for myself on an ongoing basis?

Catalysts for change

Questions can act as the factor that changes your behaviour. Salespeople have known this for centuries. The persuasion method of the top salespeople world-wide is asking catalytic questions. 'You can get a better widget cheaper with

Bloggs and Co. Why pay more for less?' Of course, if you are in the market for a widget, why should you pay more for less? No reason! Off to Bloggs we go.

Every coaching question aims to be a catalyst for change. When people want a particular benefit, they actively want to hear from or about the person who can genuinely offer it. In the coaching situation the performer is both the customer and the supplier. The coach is the sales representative who persuades the customer to buy from themselves. What do you most want to hear right now to change your behaviour into that of a wonderful coach or mentor?

Pulling out – putting in

Questions are used by the coach/mentor for pulling achievement out of the performer. Questions are used by the coach to inspire the performer into putting in whatever is necessary to help their performance, to encourage the performer to decide what they have to add to their performance to improve it.

Questions – what to ask

All questions are aimed at increasing either awareness or ownership. Questions aimed at enhancing ownership can do so by provoking thinking about a relevant issue, stimulating the performer to learn about a particular aspect of the field or by seeking ways to overcome internal or external blockages to ownership and awareness. Questions aimed at increasing awareness seek to help the performer develop their mental model. Awareness can be enhanced with observation, analysis or synthesis at either the micro or the macro level of the performer's mental model.

Question types

Let's turn our attention to the different types of question. There are basically two types: open and closed questions. While that distinction is accurate it is not nearly informative enough. There needs to be a much greater understanding of questions than black or white, open or closed. There are numerous types of useful questions between the two extremes, as you will see.

Open questions

As we saw earlier on, an open question is one you cannot logically answer yes or no. 'Open question' should also be taken to mean a question which encourages an answer of more than one word.

As you may have noticed, when dealing with an unwilling communicator who is reluctant to assert that they do not wish to speak, any and every question you ask can be answerable with a single word or phrase, no matter how open, skilled or interesting the question.

Open questions are the most effective tool for increasing focus and awareness. Asking the performer to make an observation that requires an enhancement of awareness should be done in an open way. For example you might ask 'who contributes most in your staff meetings?' to increase the performer's awareness of staff behaviour, perhaps as part of a leadership development programme.

Very open questions

There are degrees of openness in open questions. 'What time is it?' is an open question which requires a single short phrase answer, the format of which requires no thought; the response to which is almost automatic. 'What methods did you use to re-organize the company?' is a very open question. It requires an elaborate, well thought-out and almost certainly unique answer.

Very open questions are best used when trying to increase ownership. 'How do you propose to arrive at your sales plan? How can you identify the source of your quality problems? Which processes will you use to find ways of reducing your stock?'

Closed questions

Those which require a yes or no answer: in conversation they are the poor relative of open questions. Many communications experts frown on the closed question in the formation of interpersonal relationships, and rightly so. However, that advice is then widely misunderstood to mean that closed questions are a bad thing generally. Poor relatives they may be, but they have their place, a very effective place. Can you imagine a conversation where there are no yes or no responses? Hmm, neither can I, at least not in a conversation between two sane people who were not playing party games.

Closed questions are best used when confirming agreements and commitments, when confirming information or facts, confirming that you understand what the other party is saying, while making a subtle statement that you are ready and waiting for them to continue. 'You mean the engineering director hasn't given you the material and components order, so you can't plan the purchasing programme?' 'Yes. ... and ...'

Closed questions are an essential part of the listening behaviours' repertoire. Use them to show your performers that you are listening, that you understand, that you want them to continue their line of thought.

Socratic questions

More properly known as the Socratic method, this is a teaching method devised, or at least made famous by Socrates a great many years ago. The principle is that the teacher asks a series of questions that enable the learner to come to the desired understanding by themselves. It is extremely effective, mainly because conclusions we come to by our own thinking are much more memorable than something that has been provided. In coaching, the Socratic question is used when the coach knows the conclusion the performer ought to be coming to and asks a question that will require partial or total formation of that conclusion. I say partial, because the leap required between two positions can often be better made in a series of small leaps.

This kind of questioning, if done badly, can appear pointless, wasteful and excessively controlling. It is done badly when the steps are too small, the questions too vague or all-encompassing, too simple to be worth answering, or the teacher offers no interaction with the answers, or is not flexible in asking the next question based on the response to the last. Done badly this method will be less effective than a soporific lecture, and more alienating than outright verbal abuse. It is done properly by providing an overview of where the questioning/reasoning is leading, and in the coaching context that should be the performer's decision, at best, and by agreement at least.

A variant of this method is used by those whose learning is self-managed. They decide on what they want to learn at an overview level, then they ask progressively more detailed questions of one or more individuals until they have the whole picture. That is the ideal mentoring arrangement. The mentor is available for the performer to question Socratically.

Stage jump questions

Occasionally, when using the Socratic method, or helping a performer be a user of the Socratic method, you will hear a hint that the person has understood related to a point several stages ahead of your/their current position. If you do, you can speed things up by asking a question that could only be answered if they have made the stage jump you suspect.

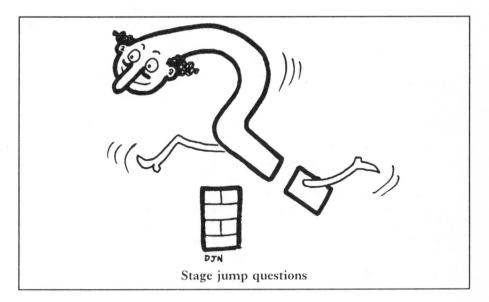

DJN

Stage jump questions

Assertion questions

Those used to assert the speaker's opinion/view or knowledge while at the same time seeking a response or feedback from the listener are assertion questions. They show the speaker values him/herself and the other parties. 'Instead of

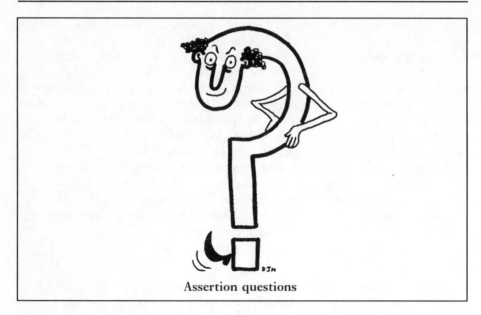

Assertion questions

paying a fortune for an outside consultant, I think we should conduct a skills audit to determine whether or not we have someone in the company with those skills. What do you think?'

Assertion questions should be infrequently used while coaching, they necessitate an equality of input by both parties and that is not desirable. Coaching should be performer focused. The conventional mentor can use these questions with great effect. 'You need more marketing experience. How about we try to arrange a spell in the marketing department with Christine? What do you think?'

Leading questions

These are the little devils whom you love when you agree with their assumptions, and resent when you don't. Their assumptions and intent are invisible if you share them, but luminous and glowing larger than life otherwise. 'Why did you download the entire database on to tapes that were due to be destroyed?' Seems innocuous enough as a question if, and only if, you share the assumption that the computer operator knew the tapes were due to be scrapped. If they didn't know that, and had no logical reason to think about it, or if discovering it would have required enormous forethought, the assumption behind the leading question is flawed.

Since leading questions are undetectable when you share the assumptions with the listener, they can be used to great effect in coaching and mentoring. They can be used to reinforce shared but unstated assumptions. 'How can you solve this marketing problem?' assumes, first, that it is solvable, second that the performer owns the problem and third, that she or he is going to try to solve it. If you are an enthusiastic achievement-oriented member of staff, all these assumptions will be invisible.

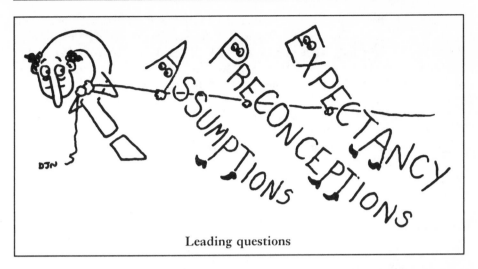

Leading questions

The technique is often used by salespeople. If you have ever bought a house you will recognize this: 'What do you think is nicest about that lovely view from the lounge window? Let's have a look at your master bedroom now. Where would you put the bed?'

Why do you believe leading questions can increase ownership and focus all in one? Buy yours today!

Probing questions

These are questions designed to check the finer points of the speaker's or performer's assumptions, opinions, facts or plans. Probing questions are used in coaching to help the performer identify or clarify some pre-articulate notion.

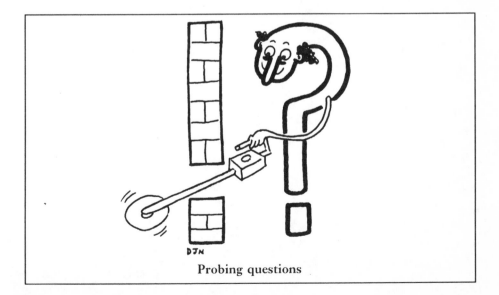

Probing questions

It may help give form to a vague barrier. Probing questions can bring out influential factors that the performer had missed. As a guide, the probing question can be used when you detect lack of clarity in the thinking of the performer, or when you think there is something behind the scenes influencing the performer's thinking which has not been made explicit.

'All I have to do is get the finance director to see my way of thinking.'
'How do you propose to do that?'
'I'll just tell her what the best action is for the company.'
'What will you tell her?'
' ... and naturally I'll try to be as persuasive as possible.'
'What will be your persuasion strategy?'

Hypothetical questions

These questions are designed to get the performer to think about the way they would respond to some potential situation. Their greatest power is in focusing attention on contingency planning. 'What do you think the finance director's reaction will be to your presentation?' 'If the best interests of the company come first, my ideas will be accepted.' 'What will you do if your plan is rejected?'

Note the choice of responses open to the coach after the last answer – the performer hinted that the finance director may not make a decision in the best interest of the company – that could have been probed further before exploring the 'hypotheticals'. The performer also made the assumption that their plan was the only one in the best interests of the company. Since we know that in business there is very rarely only one acceptable solution, we may be witnessing the manifestation of an attitude barrier – that too could be explored. So how do we decide which option to focus our questions on? In the strictest coaching

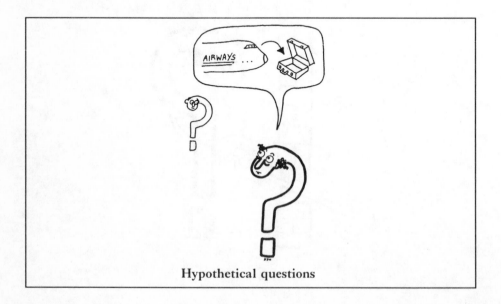

Hypothetical questions

practice we should go with the performer. If it is not clear where the performer is going with their last statement, we should ask a question like: 'What is the most important issue in what you've just said?' or 'Where does that lead you to?' or 'What's next?'

Justifying questions

Justifying questions are relatives of probing questions. Justifying questions are aimed at exploring the rationales behind the performer's assumptions. They invite the performer to justify their position, but without threat or challenge. If the basis of their assumptions turns out to be unreasonable, the performer will notice that when you reflect what is said back to them. Unreasonable positions invariably require extreme, unsustainable or downright irrational assumptions and rationales as support. The normally rational performer will recognize and change their error when you (a normally rational person, of course) reflect in your own words the basis of their beliefs/position. (Here we are not talking of the authoritarian, racist, misogynist, 'anything that isn't like me should be shot' bigot but of the relatively well adjusted human being.)

Justifying questions

If the basis of the position taken by the performer seems to be factual and empowering, then your request for justification will have served to enhance their conviction.

Open self-persuasive questions

Coaching in the strict sense would not use this technique; it is too directive. However, pragmatism must prevail, so here it is. An open self-persuasion question is one that requires the performer to provide justifications for taking a certain action or adopting a certain belief, and in the process she or he is

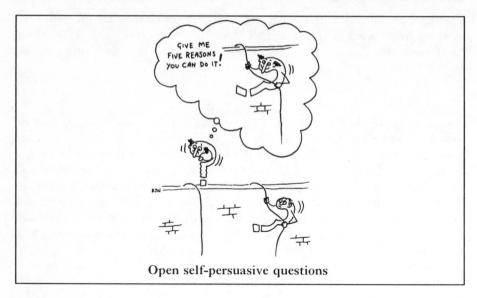

Open self-persuasive questions

actually self-persuading. 'Can you give me five reasons why you should sit this exam?' 'What in your background are the reasons that you are likely to be a successful coach?' This is an extremely effective technique; it is used by professional brainwashers of all kinds – cult leaders, prisoner of war interrogators, psychiatrists, advertisers and so on. For those with a social sciences background, the technique is based on 'counter-attitudinal advocacy' (where the subject is required to argue for a point of view which they would normally argue against. The result is usually a marked shift in attitude away from the previously held position toward the view for which they argued).

A mentor could use this method if she or he were trying to persuade the performer to adopt a particular view, or to comply with a company rule or norm.

Prefix/suffix questions

These are questions formed from statements simply by adding a prefix or suffix. For instance 'You perform best when working on your own' could become: 'What makes you perform best ...?' or 'You perform... on your own. Why is that?'

This method is best used when you've nearly made a mistake by making a statement instead of asking a question and want to save yourself at the last moment. Resist the temptation to use this method to make a disguised statement: you will be detected, you will take responsibility away from the performer and, worst of all, you will probably weaken the level of trust the performer has in you. If you must make a statement or provide information, ask the performer if you can do so. If you're mentoring, just go ahead and make the statement.

Prefix/suffix questions

Empathetic questions

Since good feeling is so central to success, there needs to be a tool in the questioner's box that will help the performer target the emotional aspect of the goal, particularly one that encourages the focus on others' feelings. The occasional empathetic question can help the performer get the best results through people. It can also prevent the emergence of self-centredness and egocentricity, a serious risk in those whose lives are the focus of those helping them. 'How do you feel about that?'

Discrepancy questions/puzzle presentation questions

A serious coaching dilemma is whether the coach should draw the performer's attention to some harmful opinion, a disempowering belief, a piece of incorrect information, an outright prejudice, a... well, anything the performer believes, thinks, says or does that is harmful to their likelihood of success. Purists argue that it is for the performer to discover for themselves; we know that self-learned lessons are better retained. Pragmatists argue that the company is not a Buddhist monastery or a self-exploration charity, that there is no room for sterile debate; there is a job to do which must be done or there will be no company in which to debate the issue. Guess which side of the debate I fall on?

The company, the coach and the performer want results. When the coach needs to take issue with the performer, it should be done. The performer won't thank the coach for giving him or her six months to self-discover something that could be taught in five minutes flat. Yes, the coach should encourage the performer to take responsibility for learning the new information, but it should not be withheld to satisfy ideological or educational dogma that harms everyone. So ask a question that seeks a resolution of the discrepancy.

Often the best way to present information that the performer needs to know is to give them a puzzle which requires the desired (but non-possessed) information to reach a solution. For example, the performer needs to learn how to manage his or her divisional finances, but they don't know about cash flow projections or the formats used to compute them. Set a puzzle: how much money will be in the bank on the 5th of 'Mayober' this year. Most performers will try to work it out (and may succeed by working out a method from first principles), some will ask for the appropriate format, others will simply ask how they should do it. All will become aware of the need for a system. They will become aware of their ignorance and take steps to rectify it.

Negative feeling questions

We've already covered this indirectly in the section on reflective listening. If the coach detects some negative feelings coming from the performer, a request should be made for elaboration. The temptation is to ignore the feelings component of communication, especially if it is unpleasant or hostile. Ignore it at your peril. Any feeling so intense that it comes through in the voice or attitude is more than powerful enough to have a detrimental effect on the level of performance. Ask about it, get it out in the open where the cause can be addressed.

The reverse may happen. You, the coach/mentor, may feel some hostility to the performer for some reason. Assess the state of your relationship before deciding what to do about it. In an ideal world we should be able to say 'I feel some resentment towards you. I don't want to. Help me figure out what's causing it. What do you think it might be?' Alternatively you may know why you feel hostile. What do you do? Sit on your hands, or open your mouth? If it looks as though you'll not be detected, carry on regardless? If you think it will interfere with your coaching then get it out and get it resolved.

On a personal note, I prefer to be honest mainly because of my own reaction to people who I can see have problems with something about me but who visibly suppress themselves or give some diplomatic response: I just don't trust them.

Consequence analysis questions

Frequently the meaning, implications or consequences of something a performer says or proposes will not be clear, either to you or to them. Or perhaps the implications are clear to you and you want to ensure they are to the performer. Encourage the performer to think about consequences or implications by asking appropriate questions. Consequence thinking allows empowering judgements to be made about any proposed action or belief. What will be the consequences of believing that 'all accountants are boring, semi-articulate and lacking in initiative'? What level of co-operation do you think holding that belief will provoke?

Consequences can be analysed on several dimensions: desirability, undesirability, manifest benefits or costs, potentially latent benefits or costs, the implications for other tasks and people... and so on. Ask consequence questions about whatever dimension seems most important or most prominent in the performer's mind.

EXERCISE

Devise one coaching-relevant example question from each of the above categories. In what other ways could you improve your understanding and memory of the different question types and their usage?

EXERCISE

How could it be beneficial for your performers to know and use the different question types?

EXERCISE

On page 154, you will find a list of team behaviours under the heading 'Some role-determined team behaviours'. Scan the list and convert some of the more empowering behaviours into appropriate types of question you can ask your performers.

Silence

Often the most powerful question you can ask is no question at all. Respond by showing the performer you are still listening, but say nothing. The silence will be filled by whatever is most prominent on the performer's mind. Silence also ensures that you don't impose on the performer that which you think is most important. While being a genuine non-verbal question, silence can also help you out if you don't know what to ask next!

Questions are the ideal

There will be many occasions when a discussion about the relevant issues will be more productive, appropriate or simply easier than asking questions. If you must discuss rather than ask, choose issues that facilitate self-responsibility in the performer: issues such as their mental models of the task or objective they are addressing, or the processes/methods they plan to use, or any of the issues that you would normally ask questions about.

EXERCISE

Compile a list of those things you can discuss which will maximize the performer's self-responsibility.

Deciding what to ask – an operational model

The greatest worry in coaching for those who can see the value of empowering the performer is: What do I ask? How can I decide when to ask what? Having glanced at the model we're about to use, you are probably even more worried. With good cause. Many nights were spent making this model as complex as possible. Well, perhaps I exaggerate just a little. There are five main stages in generating the appropriate question, and I promise you, after a short while the whole process will be virtually automatic. The five stages are:

1   Purpose or objective: Checking the desired direction of the questions.
2   Sub-goal: Setting the purpose of the question.
3   Question type: Deciding what type of question to use.
4   Question formation: Structuring the sentence for the individual.
5   Assessing the answer: Assessing the new level of understanding/focus/ownership.
5a   Loop back to stage 1 to modify objective and repeat.

Sounds easy, eh? Now look at the model in more detail. Each of the five areas above has its own little process going on. Take a little time now to think about the processes. Have I included everything that should be in each stage? If not, write to tell me what I missed.

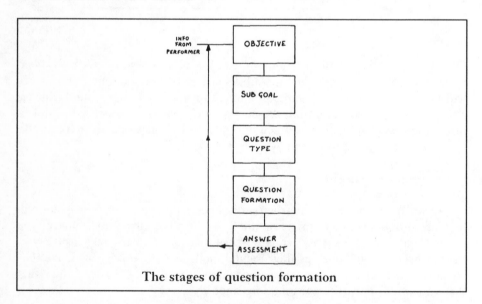

The stages of question formation

1   Purpose or objective: checking the desired direction of the questions

Stage one in the question formation model, the objective analysis stage, is largely dictated by whatever stage of the coaching process you are currently engaged in. Here is an abbreviated reminder:

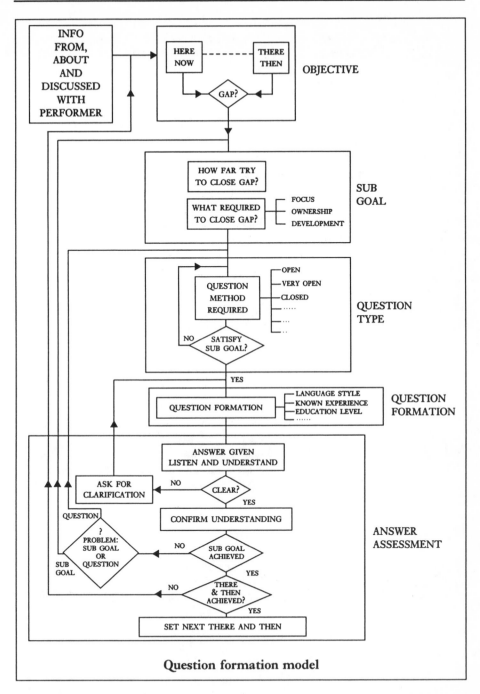

Question formation model

1 Rapport creation.
2 Vague formulation of objective(s).
3 Assessing the here and now.

4 Deciding on the there and then.
5 Designing a bridge between here and now, and there and then.
6 Building the bridge.
7 Assessing progress to the other side.

2 Sub-objective: setting the purpose of the question

The decision to be made at this stage is: is a question aimed at enhancing owner-ship or awareness/focus most appropriate? As with every apparently simple decision there are complicating factors. There must always be some play-off between focus and ownership, at least on a temporary basis. There can be no perfect resolution. Asking the performer to concentrate on some aspect of performance takes away some ownership. Enhancing ownership necessarily dulls focus for a short while. 'To make an omelette you have to break some eggs'. Make a commitment: is ownership or focus most important given the factors involved?

3 Method decision: deciding what type of question to use

Having set the objective and sub-objective, you now have to decide what questions are most likely to achieve the purpose. Here is a summary of what each type of question will achieve.

Open questions	All questions except confirmation reflections should be open-focus enhancement questions and should require short predictable answers.
Very open questions	Ownership-enhancement questions should require involved free-ranging answers.
Assertion questions	Used when you want to express an opinion or fact, an issue on which the performer's opinion is sought.
Leading questions	Naughty little beasties, used to reinforce shared assumptions and encourage ownership.
Probing questions	Ideal in helping performers clarify pre-articulate thinking.
Hypothetical questions	Best used to get achievers to contingency plan.
Justifying questions	Used to invite performer to justify a shaky position.
Open self-persuasion questions	Used to have the performer persuade themselves of a desired belief/action.
Prefix/suffix questions	Most often used when digging yourself out of the statement-making hole.
Socratic questions	Used when you have decided on a conclusion the performer should come to.
Stage jump questions	Used to establish whether performer has under-standing ahead of the current position.
Empathetic questions	Design them to encourage the achiever to think of the other party's feelings.

Discrepancy questions	Used to take issue with the performer.
Negative feelings questions	Used to air, seek explanation, and resolve negative feelings.
Consequence analysis questions	Used to have performer focus on the likely consequences of their thoughts or plans.

EXERCISE

Above are suggested uses for each question. Expand the list. What other coaching and mentoring uses can you think of for each question type? Devise some question formats for each question type in such a way that when you use the question you just have to fill in the blanks. By devising the formats you'll develop your understanding, skill and confidence in asking coaching questions.

---

4 Question formation: structuring the sentence for the individual

In this stage you plan how to communicate with the listener in the language of the listener. That involves considering their thinking/communication style, educational level, experience and a whole host of other factors. Don't worry too much about this stage; you already have a lifetime's experience of relating to others and most of us do this automatically. Highly skilled communicators do seem to consider these factors more.

As noted earlier, there are numerous different thinking and communication styles. After we have tuned in to someone's thinking and communication characteristics once, the mind seems to take over from then on. The way we then phrase subsequent communications is done with the listener in mind.

EXERCISE

On what can you concentrate to help increase your awareness of and harmony with the performer's style?

---

5 Assessing the answer: assessing the new level of understanding/focus/ownership

This process, like the last, is virtually automatic. Communication involves a continuous process of checking whether or not the respondent has picked up our message as we intended. We also check whether the question has been answered and, to a lesser extent (than we should), to see if we have understood the response. If our listener has not understood the question as indicated by the answer, our responsibility is to clarify our communication. If the question has not been answered, the performer may have deliberately chosen to do so by focusing on what they see as a more important issue – in which case the coach has to decide whether to rephrase the question, or adopt the newly identified successor to the sub-goal behind the question. Strictly speaking the performer should be asked if he or she has identified a more important point, and if that ought to become the new focus.

EXERCISE

The next time you communicate with someone, take a moment after they have answered one of your questions to examine how you decided whether or not they had answered your question.

5a   Loop back to stage 1 to modify the objective or sub-objective and repeat

When the question has been answered, or the performer has satisfied the purpose of the question in some other way, the coach/mentor will make a decision as to how far along the road to closing the gap, defined by the sub-goal, the answer has gone. That decision will then lead to the next decision which is, if the gap has been closed, what is the next sub-goal? If the gap has not yet been closed, what has still to be achieved?

Questions to avoid

Avoid any question that contains over-generalization: 'Why do you ALWAYS let me down?' Or questions that are used to shroud ultimatums or threats: 'Who do you think will be first to go if your project fails?' Or questions which are so vague as to be confusing: 'What is the economic basis of business?' And questions which contain accusations (the leading questions we don't like) 'When did you stop beating your spouse?' Those kinds of questions create instant resentment, and naturally are to be avoided in a coaching or mentoring environment.

Example of the model in use

To learn how to use the model, we need a performer case history. Jean is a 31-year-old production manager with a degree in mechanical engineering. She has some lofty ambitions: she wants to run the most efficient, cost-effective and productive factory in her industry. She is brimming with ideas on stock control methods, quality improvement, staff-motivation enhancement, employee-friendly induction methods; she even has some ideas on industrial democracy that make her bosses' hair stand on end. Where she has been allowed to implement ideas she's had great results.

You are her coach; you have been chosen and you accepted because you have substantial commercial experience and know little or nothing about manufacturing methods. The coaching sessions have started. You've had the first meeting in which you both worked hard and successfully at setting up a good rapport. She has told you her outline goal. You have just finished your greetings at the start of the second session.

To complete this development exercise to best effect, take a piece of paper and, as you go along, cover all but the next sentence: What would be a sensible starter question for this session? Try to answer this before looking at the answer.

Following the seven-stage plan, the 'right' question would be aimed at assessing the here and now. Of course, reality is a lot more flexible than that. There are two possible starting points; it doesn't really matter which you decide to take first. They are: 'How do you propose to define your target in measurable terms?' and 'What is your starting point?'

While you have a model to help your decision making, it may be tempting to allow that to dictate your coaching sessions. The performer is the purpose of the activity, and any model is the servant of the performer, to be used when required, or be told 'That will be all, Jeeves'. The performer should decide what comes first. So a third possible starting point in your coaching session with Jean could be 'What do you think would be best to look at first?' or 'Where would you like to start?'

This may prove difficult to those used regularly to taking control. Make it work by choosing to take control of giving control to your performer.

Now a little further into the session, Jean says 'The people who stand to benefit most from the new methods – my board of directors, most of whom are also shareholders – are the people who are most actively resistant.' What would be a good next question?

A   'If they stand to gain from the improvements, what could be their objections?'
B   'What do you think is behind their resistance?'
C   'Do you think the key issue is trying to understand the resistance of people you are trying to help?'

Which of these three questions seems to be most in line with our assumptions? I think it is the last question (although closed) because it asks the performer to confirm what they perceive as the important issue while offering a reflection of what it seemed to be. In other words, the performer keeps maximum control, but is invited to focus more intently. The other questions assumed that resistance was the central issue and immediately asked the performer for an analysis. While A and B increase focus, they take away an element of control; they remove a little ownership of the process from the performer.

Jean replies, 'And what's more they won't even allow me to make a formal presentation or submit any other kind of proposal; they just won't discuss my ideas!'

What is your next question? It should be based on your purpose, which at this stage is to assess the here and now.

'If you were to define the situation as it stands, what would you say?' is one option. Jean's reply might be: 'I'd say they were blocking me. I'd say they were cutting off their noses to spite their face. I'd say there was great potential for improvement, but they are frightened of change or, rather, the risks involved in changing.'

You have a reasonably clear definition of the here and now. What is your next question? Let's try 'So, what do you want to achieve? What is your target?'

'Quite simply to implement all these great ideas for the benefit of the company.' Jean has now broadly defined her 'there and then'. Following the seven-stage coaching sequence, what should be the purpose of your next questions?

To encourage Jean to start designing a bridge between here/now and there/then. One final point about deciding what the coach should ask the performer: if in doubt, ask the performer what they think the next stage should be!

EXERCISE

Practise using the model with examples or cases that you are familiar with. Get into the habit of deciding what to ask and how to ask it.

The coaching and mentoring process in practice

Let's turn our attention from the detail of deciding on questions to the issues involved in carrying out the seven-stage coaching sequence in practice. For the purposes of clarity we will look at practical issues from the view of the manager/coach combination (probably the most common) under the following headings:

- Overt and covert coaching and mentoring.
- Planned and unplanned coaching and mentoring.
- Rapport creation.
- Vague formation of goals.
- Assessing the 'here and now'.
- Deciding on the 'there and then':
  - Aligning missions.
  - Changing goals.
- Designing a bridge.
- Monitoring progress.

Overt and covert coaching and mentoring

Overt coaching is clear for all to see. It is organized, planned, and both parties know exactly what is going on. Covert coaching or mentoring takes place when one party does not realize what is really happening, or thinks that one thing is happening when in fact it's another. The non-aware party can be the performer or the coach. Performers can find themselves being coached during a 'manage ment chat', or briefing meeting for example. On the other side, someone may be coaching when they planned to pass on some basic information. The performer may discover that they do not have the context to process the new information, and discreetly asks questions which effectively put the provider in the position of coaching/mentoring the performer to a new level of contextual understanding.

EXERCISE

What will be your strategy when you realize than a covert coaching demand is being made? Will you arrange a formal coaching session? Will you 'switch on' your coaching skills and provide what is required there and then?

Planned and unplanned coaching/mentoring

The seven-stage coaching/mentoring process will probably occur naturally whether it was planned that way or not. Often the coaching or mentoring process will be conducted on an unplanned, unscheduled spontaneous basis. Opportunities and requirements for coaching occur regularly throughout the course of the executive's average day. Opportunities to help a member of staff improve their performance will arise spontaneously. If a formal session was then planned to discuss whatever the issue, the sense of immediacy and reality of the situation will have gone. This is particularly true of coaching performance where *in situ* observation is required. Analytical, detached reasoning in a quiet office three days later will not enhance a performer's observation of the events. Focusing and awareness enhancement should take place when they are most likely to be of benefit.

EXERCISE

If you find yourself in an unplanned but overt coaching situation what will be your mental strategy for confirming that coaching is appropriate and for switching into coaching skills mode?

Rapport creation

The practical implications have already been covered. It is worth restating that the success of this stage will affect the whole coaching programme. The foundations of the coaching/mentoring partnership must be well laid, and maintained on an ongoing basis.

Vague formulation of goals

It is difficult to set goals without an awareness of the current situation. The nature of the assessment of the current situation will largely be determined by the purpose for which it is undertaken. It is therefore wise at this stage to create only a vague sense of purpose. What can be achieved with clarity is an agreement between coach and performer on the processes, methods and procedures that will be followed. Since what is sought is agreement, you won't be expecting me to provide any prescriptions, will you?

Assessing the here and now

The performer's current achievement level, the departure point, must be objectively assessed against whichever are the appropriate dimensions for that role, by both parties. There are several ways in which the here and now can be assessed. It can also be assessed from different perspectives.

Here and now can be seen and assessed in terms of the current levels of performance, consistency of performance, the skill level of the performer, their beliefs, knowledge, standing in the organization, standing of the organization and so on.

Details of other criteria against which the here and now can be assessed can be found in the section on performance assessment. A collection of assessment methods is also presented in that section. They include: video and audio assessment, self-set criteria judgement, peer assessment, supervisor assessment, appraisal history assessment, customer assessment, supplier assessment, significant other assessment and so on.

One of the simplest ways of assessing a performer's current situation is to conduct a comparison against their job description. Job descriptions are usually written by a person other than the post holder and they are notoriously inaccurate and unrealistic. Re-write the JD with a greater level of realism, giving more detail to the skill and behavioural requirements. Do a Pareto guesstimate on the skills involved: which 20 per cent of skills account for 80 per cent of the

Assessing here and now

job performance? Having identified the key skills, rate the performer against them. Or rather, have the performer rate themselves, or at very least manage their assessment through others. Self-assessment is preferable, if not essential, in maximizing the self-responsibility and ownership in the performer.

Some of the other techniques provided later in the book can also be used during the here and now assessment stage, namely, performance observation, skills analysis and personal paradigm analysis.

Deciding on the there and then

It is worth noting that the 'there and then' need not be a definable objective; it could be a process. Many successful people take the view that if you look after the process well, the outcome will take care of itself. Others use the final objective to set up the processes and then ignore the target to concentrate on making the process as effective as possible. For example, you might set a goal of having the fastest growing and most innovative company in your industry. You set up all the systems and processes which will achieve that goal, then forget the goal, and focus on implementing the processes as well as you can.

There are several factors to be considered before a performer can set an objective. They include:

- Personal strengths and weaknesses.
- Organizational strengths and weaknesses.
- Aligning missions:
  - personal
  - family
  - departmental
  - organizational.

The most important of these is the last.

Aligning missions: personal, family, departmental and organizational

As we noted in the section on the principles of achievement, highly successful people tend to align the goals in the different aspects of their lives in such a way that they complement each other. Aligning goals is central to successful performance. Maximum motivation comes from many sources – one of the most powerful is unity of purpose. Most of us have personal, family, organizational and societal goals. Let's drop societal goals: this is a book on coaching and mentoring, not social change.

One would predict that maximum motivation and performance would occur when all three goals are perfectly aligned. Certainly that is the ideal situation for entrepreneurs and other self-controlled individuals. But it is not as simple as that for most people in employment. Few people are willing to tie their future, security, personal and family interests totally to one company or organization; employment security is not guaranteed or within their control. Most

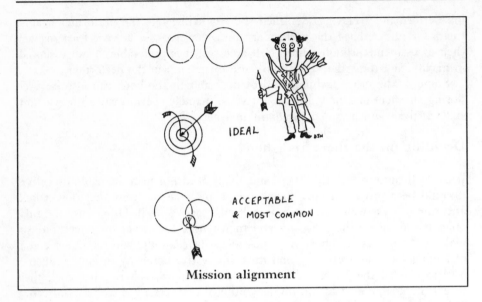

IDEAL

ACCEPTABLE
& MOST COMMON

Mission alignment

will experience an overlap. The point at which all three goals overlap is still the point of theoretical maximum motivation. As an informative aside let's ask what happens when it IS safe to tie personal and family goals to an organization.

In the UK the 'jobs for life' culture generally produces lower performance, and the more secure the position the lower the performance. For much of the time in the 1970s, work was a place where people went to conduct political activity and pick up a pay-cheque for 'face time' (face time is the process by which if a person's face is seen on the premises, it is assumed they are working, whether or not anything is actually produced). But in Japan, where employment (at least until the early 1990s) was virtually guaranteed for life, performance is extremely high.

It could be that when security is seen as a right (UK) performance is low, but when it is seen as a valuable privilege and an honour which must be repaid (Japan), performance and commitment are high. Whatever the explanation, it is clear that the result of perfect mission alignment with an organization is dependent on culture among other things.

The coach's role during the aligning missions phase of the process is to help the performer find the overlap point, or more accurately the overlap area, for there is usually considerable scope for overlap. To find the overlap area the goals of the organization must be understood and clearly defined, as must the family and personal goals. The greater the trust in the coach the more honesty will be forthcoming.

However, the performer will not reveal their genuine motives (goals) if they feel that will be to their detriment. If an employee is only in the company long enough to find out how it all works prior to setting up in competition, you can hardly expect to see their cards on the table can you? But, and this is a very big but, if the company concerned genuinely has the interests of its staff as a priority it would welcome such people, and offer to provide some of the venture capital (in exchange for equity) to get them started.

Why? Can you imagine the dedication you would get from someone of that calibre with that kind of ambition? Since you can't stop them, you might as well have shares in their company. In fact, the more you help them the more your company and their company will be likely to have a productive and symbiotic relationship. Instead of being threatened by this kind of person the smart organization should be actively recruiting them. Alas they don't. Why? You tell me.

Let's assume the performer is in an environment in which it is smart rather than stupid to be honest. How do the performer and coach/mentor find the overlap? In four stages:

1   Clearly identify the missions/goals for each of the four areas: personal, family, departmental, organizational.
2   Compile a list of ways in which the goals in each area could be satisfied.
3   Explore the ways in which the overlap between personal and family goals is currently being satisfied.
4   Explore the ways in which the organization's goals could be satisfied by satisfying the personal/family overlap goals.

In short the coach/mentor should help the performer find the common factors in the four mission areas. The common factors can then be used as a checklist against which to devise a strategy for achievement.

EXERCISE

Devise a list of questions that will enable you to help the performer find the overlap area between their four missions. Create a similar range of questions to have the performer create a guidelines list against which to assess and devise the achievement plan.

Changing goals

It should not be taken as a sign of weakness for someone to change their goals. In fact it should be regarded as a sign of strength. Most of us find that our life's purpose is continually evolving. As we grow and develop we often outgrow our goals. Changing goals is to be expected of a high performer. The purpose may stay pretty much the same, but the means of achieving it will improve over time like a good wine.

Designing a bridge between 'here and now' and 'there and then'

In this stage the performer decides how they are going to close the gap between the actual and the desired. The conclusion of this stage is a completed achievement plan. As with the other stages there are several factors to be considered to reach that end point. The process will be considered more fully in the section on situational analysis. The factors to consider include:

- What are the obstacles (barriers and overcoming them will be considered later)?
- What communication is involved, and with whom?
- What support is needed and available?
- How and when can access be gained to the support?
- If any performer development is involved, what is the performer's learning style (see learning styles)?
- What is the performer's certainty that she or he will carry out the plan?
- How can that level be increased?
- What other considerations are there?

The maximum number of alternative bridge designs should be generated. Quantity of options should be the first priority; the performer should not censor their ideas for achievement. The coach or mentor can take notes on the ideas generated. Judgements for quality can then be made and a final decision reached from the maximum number of available options.

Ideally the achievement plan should include an element of parallel planning. It should specify the sequence of objectives and include some parallel ways of achieving them.

EXERCISE

There is a simple achievement plan in the appendix. How could you improve the plan format?

Building the bridge

As was stated previously, the coach should be available for whatever kind of support the performer wishes. Issues likely to be raised by the performer include the 'How to ... Who ... Where ... When ... Why ...' of unforeseen barriers and problems. The coach should resist solving problems, overcoming barriers and so on for the performer. The performer should be encouraged to address and resolve any difficulties themselves with the assistance of the coach.

Assessing the other side – monitoring progress

Additional or superior solutions and possible bridges may only become obvious after the implementation and monitoring phase has started. A decision then has to be made about whether it is better to go for the improved design or stick with the predecessor.

In this stage, the performer and coach will decide how they are going to assess and evaluate progress. The simplest effective method is to decide on a set of criteria, the here and now starting point and so on, as shown in the figure below. Build assessment into the achievement plan.

Dimension/ Criteria	Here & Now Starting Point	There Arrival Point	Then When	Assessment Method
1				
2				
3				
4				
5				
...				

Assessing and evaluating progress

EXERCISE

What possible errors could interfere with the assessment process?

Concluding comments and summary

Of all the skills the expert coach should possess the most important are rapport creation, listening skills and questioning skills. The questions asked by the coach/mentor are aimed at increasing performers' ownership and awareness of the factors which affect their performance. Awareness can be enhanced by observation or analysis but not simultaneously. Questions are immensely powerful; they can empower, form or change beliefs in an instant. There is a huge variety of questions available to the coach or mentor, each with its own purpose and power – so many in fact that novice coaches often feel unable to decide what to ask. A practical model aimed at helping the new coach or mentor decide what to ask has been provided. The coaching process in practice was examined and revealed the importance of several tasks such as aligning missions, and being prepared for covert and unplanned coaching and mentoring.

6

ADVANCED DEVELOPMENT SKILLS

Coaching and the learning cycle

Learning takes place in a repetitive cycle as shown in the figure. The relative positions of the coaching and mentoring inputs are not fixed. They are meant as a guide. Ownership is best enhanced and analysis best conducted on the top left side of the cycle. Focus and observation are best conducted on the bottom right. As a guide, top left processes should be kept separate from bottom right processes. Analysis of performance should not be conducted during performance, as has been mentioned on numerous occasions.

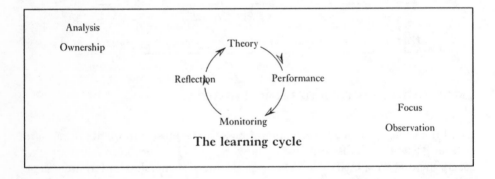

The learning cycle

Learning styles: making it memorable for the individual

The world's best trainers are students who engage in self-training. The most powerful form of learning is self-managed development. The learner knows how they learn best. That's probably the way they enjoy learning most. They usually don't have or need a label for it either. For those with the initiative and determination to use this method, the less interference from outsiders the better. The lesson for the coach is that the performer should not have his or her responsibility for learning weakened or removed. In fact the opposite applies:

the coach should engage in enhancing the learner's ownership.

The coach should have the learner decide:

- How they want to plan their learning (system).
- What they want to learn (objectives).
- The sub-components of what they wish to learn (aims).
- How they want to learn it and the style in which they will learn best (method).
- How to trade off maximum learning with minimum cost (logistics).

And so on. What series of questions will you ask to help the performer make those learning decisions?

The performer may decide that the coach should provide some input. The coach then has a responsibility to tell the performer of his or her preferred training style – especially if the training input requested by the performer specifies another style. Obviously if the coach is not prepared to undertake the training, or do so in the style requested, an alternative should be found. There is much virtue on both sides in realizing the performer's best interests are not served by the coach's style and having the good grace to do something about it. The level of trust in the relationship can only be improved with such honesty.

Self-managed development

In the section entitled 'A willingness to learn' (page 14) we talked about the stages a performer goes through to get to the point of high-level performance:

1 They learn the components of the skills required.
2 And gradually acquire some understanding of the overview or context.
3 They form a mental hierarchy of the contexts in which the skills are used.
4 They perform by using a repertoire of recognizable mental patterns of the skill area, in conjunction with some analytical thought.
5 Through practice, they eventually acquire a comprehensive and extensive repertoire of patterns, to which recognition and responses are automatic.

But we didn't fully explain how they managed to do so. The learning cycle on page 92 and the enhanced learning cycle mentioned earlier is a summation of a more detailed process. Self-managed developers use the following sequence of steps, or something close to it, to improve their skills:

1 Create a model/devise a personal theory of 'how to...'.
2 Mentally prepare/rehearse the performance/commit to action.
3 Carry out the behaviour or skill.
4 Focus on the relevant aspects of the performance while performing.

5 Observe self in action/maintain high awareness of the process.
6 Define the outcome and processes.
7 Decide if method/behaviour/skill needs improving or altering.
8 Decide if model or theory is to be altered or improved.
9 Loop back to stage two.

Stage nine reads 'Loop back to stage two'. It should also say 'perpetually'. Learning is an ongoing cycle and those who stop pedalling are left behind.

The world's second best trainers

There is an enormous amount of information available on what are the most effective learning methods as used by the world's second best trainers. A brief summary of the learning enhancement factors follows.

Relaxation and interest

If you are going to teach, your learners should be relaxed and interested in the subject. It is the trainer's responsibility to provide as conducive and peaceful an environment as possible, to make the material as interesting as possible.

Playful and entertaining

As above. For best results, bake performers in an oven of entertaining playfulness for the duration of the session(s). Make jokes, have fun and take the mickey.

Primacy effects and recency effects

Material conveyed at the beginning of a training session (primacy) and at the end (recency) is better remembered than that in the middle of a session. The effect can be maximized by organizing training with lots of little breaks. No section should be more than 20 minutes long without some form of natural break, and no more than 40 minutes without a total stop. Note that this book is divided into many sections and sub-sections.

Distinctiveness

Distinctive material is more memorable than (yawn) dull material. The more distinctive, outrageous, bizarre or even controversial the better it is for the memory. This is the principle which informs many of the cartoons provided in this book.

Multi-sensory stimulation

The more channels through which a message is received the more memorable it is. A message received through all six senses is optimally memorable, especially if the input is synchronous and simultaneous. Sequential single-

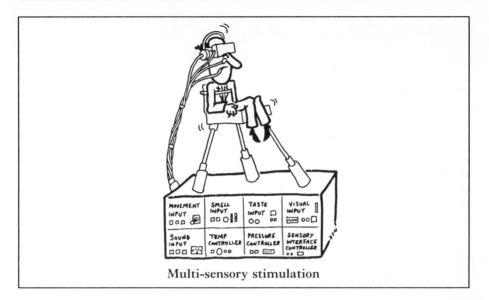

Multi-sensory stimulation

channel multi-sensory input can be extremely effective too, particularly if contextual transfer of the information is likely to be required. Or, in plain English: learning visually, physically, verbally... helps learners who will have to transfer knowledge from one situation to another.

Rhythm and rhyme

Have you ever noticed that you can remember large sections of songs, but virtually nothing of speeches or lectures or even poems? Songs are more memorable because the information has a predictable structure, distinctiveness, entertainment value, brevity, rhythm and rhyme. Make your training so.

Mnemonics

Mnemonics are useful for remembering lists (POP RIOT), or a large number of related facts. They are no substitute for understanding. Mnemonics are a useful prompt to the ingredients of understanding during the learning process. When full understanding is obtained, there is very rarely any need for mnemonics. In fact using mnemonics may be a sign that your performer has not yet reached a level of full understanding. Understanding allows the performer to make their own decisions, rote learning (as characterized by the use of mnemonics) is unlikely to result in independent decision making.

Use, understanding and learning

Understanding is central to learning, memory and performance. You wouldn't expect anyone to effectively use an understanding of something they couldn't remember. You wouldn't expect someone to remember and effectively use something they didn't understand. If they are helped to understand, and see the use and benefit of possessing that understanding, they will be motivated to devise their own structure for remembering the information.

Organizational strategies

One of the most effective ways of acquiring memory and understanding of complex issues is to organize the ingredients in a number of different ways. Organizing material helps you to see the interconnections in the material you are learning. If you were trying to understand financial accounting you might choose to organize the material into documents, format options, procedures, legal requirements, information in, information out, or in a hundred other possible ways. Any field of study can have its components arranged in any number of ways. The more meaningful ways the learner has organized the material, the greater will be their understanding and retention.

Multiple meaning/context

Any piece of information, fact or concept has a particular meaning dependent on the context in which it is viewed. The more different meanings given to a concept, the more memorable and understood it becomes. For instance, JIT (just in time) methods have a specific meaning in the context of manufacturing. Its meaning is slightly different from a management accounting point of view, and different again from the marketing angle and so on. The person with the greatest understanding of JIT is the one who sees it from the largest number of different points of view or in the greatest number of contexts.

The most effective training method in the world

'Give someone a fish and you feed them for a day. Teach them to fish and you feed them for life.' If you apply that truism to teaching, what would be the first and best thing you could ever teach someone? Without doubt it would and should be how to learn. But how many of us were taught how to learn at school? At college? Ever? Hmm. Never is most usually true. It is way past the time to change that. We should be teaching our children the educational equivalent of fishing. Or should we? Really it is up to the performer to teach themselves how they learn with the assistance of their coach or educator. How can the coach help? By asking the performer to explore how they learned a skill, or how they are teaching themselves the skills they are currently acquiring.

It can even be done hypothetically. 'How would you go about learning... boxing, song-writing...?' Choose something that is sufficiently unknown to the performer that they don't become involved in the technicalities. 'What stages of learning would you go through? Devise a plan to reach a certain level of competence.' The objective is to have the performer become aware of the process they use to learn. 'Distil the process so you can apply the learning sequence you have just devised to anything you want to learn.' Once recognized, they can then analyse and improve their learning process on a continuing basis. But above all else, the objective is to encourage the performer to take responsibility for their own learning and development. 'Teach someone a skill and you give them the possibility of a job. Have them teach themselves to learn and you give them a living for life.'

Learning styles

Most of us have adopted a complex mix of learning methods. Undoubtedly we favour some more than others. Equally certain is that the methods we choose as our favourites are the ones we enjoy most and which produce the best results. Each performer has their preferred method or mix of methods. As stated previously, they may know the method but have never articulated it to themselves. Knowledge of their preferred method will enable the performer to plan their learning and development more precisely and effectively.

Part of the coaching/mentoring role is to help the performer learn and develop in the way best suited to them, within the confines placed by the company. The coach should have at least a broad awareness of the main categories of learning style. They are:

- Experiential learning.
- Observational/vicarious learning.
- Theoretical/academic learning.
- Functional learning.

We will cover this material by adopting the following system:

- Description of characteristics of the style.
- People with this style learn best in/from...
- People with this style learn least well from...
- People with this style are best fitted to...

Experiential learning

Experiential learners learn best from experience in association with others. In graphic terms they are the people who get in there, roll up their sleeves and ride with the punches. They are, in entrepreneurial terms, those who've had a few broken noses, black eyes in the commercial ring, and they love it. They learn by trial and error and by real-life experimentation. They thrive on crises and are always on the lookout for the next great challenge or learning experience.

The learning activities most likely to be beneficial to experiential learners are those involving novelty, novel experiences, problem challenges and so on; challenges others would consider nearly impossible; situations where best efforts are praised regardless of outcome especially in relation to the previous point; fast-moving crisis situations in which a multitude of tasks and task skills are required; role playing; competitive teamwork-oriented, educational business games; any learning experience which requires activity.

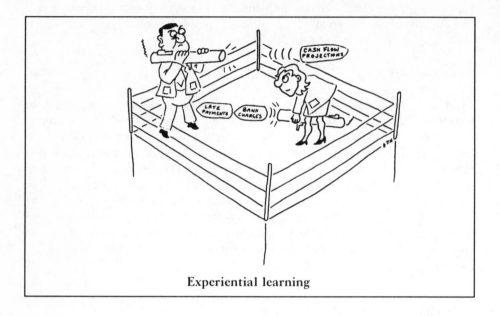

Experiential learning

They are least likely to learn from activities requiring detached analysis or requiring solitary effort; which involve any form of passive learning such as reading, lectures, and so on; requiring compliance with rules, or procedures; or involving attention to detail or 'trivia'.

Coaching don'ts: Do not ask the experientially inclined performer to state what they expect to learn, or assess what they think they have learned after the experience.

This is the learning style most preferred in sales departments. Coaching this kind of learner can be a nightmare. Despite your best efforts to encourage them to take responsibility for their learning, you will perceive them as being irresponsible about everything. Fortunately for the coach/mentor they are likely to be, or will be in the process of becoming, successful achievers or entrepreneurs. As such, they are rarely coached/mentored. They are rarely willing to put up with what they see as the stifling environment of the big company. They may, however, be your boss.

EXERCISE

Whom do you know who uses this learning style? Which of your performers or subordinates from the past used this style? Do any of your bosses have this style? What do you think would be the circumstances in which it would be best to deliberately adopt this style even though it is not the natural one for you? Conduct this exercise for the remaining learning styles.

Observational/vicarious learning

Wise folk, who choose to learn from the achievements and mistakes of others, learn best by drawing on their own and other people's experiences. Thoughtful, quiet, calm observation is their trade mark. They think through all the various ramifications of any issue before coming to any conclusions. They invariably take the overview before acting. They are the kind of person who sits through a long and unproductive meeting, saying nothing till the end. When they do speak they summarize all the issues and the logical course of action with such a ring of self-evident clarity, that it makes you wonder why it took everyone else three hours not to get there!

The observational learner is most likely to learn from activities in which they can assess what they would like to learn, plan it and assess what was actually learned afterwards; activities involving watching, listening or thinking; those which require a detached analysis of a situation; or requiring the detailed research and preparation of detailed reports or analyses; conducted in a structured (safe) learning environment; allowing them to think before acting; and any other activity in which the performer can passively observe, process, evaluate, plan and then act.

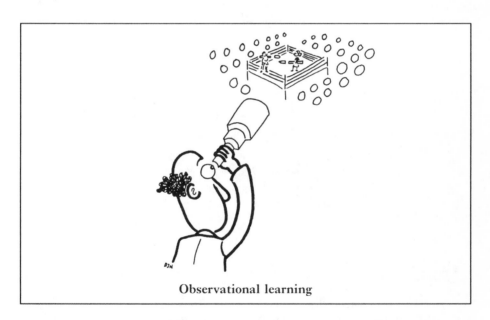

Observational learning

They learn least from activities requiring rapid action without planning; requiring insufficient time, information or resources; or requiring them to take the lead.

Coaching don'ts: Do not provide a group activity for this learner unless it is by prior arrangement and in a safe environment.

This is the learning style most preferred in commercial research or investigative activities. The coach/mentor whose learning style is one of the other three styles can become extremely frustrated with this performer. He or she will want to consider more than seems necessary. That frustration should not interfere with the performer's learning process. Accept that a great degree of pondering will occur before any decisions are made, accept that is how the performer learns best. Be prepared for long periods of silence, and requests to 'have a few days to think about it'.

Theoretical/academic learning

Highly logical, rational and sequential learners learn best by logically analysing on a rational step by step basis. They thrive in objective disciplines and are most uncomfortable with subjective or 'touchy feely' activities. Their rate of learning of cut and dried subjects is astonishingly fast, and in ambiguous, creative or opinion-oriented fields astonishingly slow – but not slow if they can find a way of applying logic, method and theory to the ambiguity-laden field. That can be achieved by the use of increasingly available, high powered computing.

Theoretical learning

The theoretical learner learns best from activities that are logically structured and have a rational purpose, that require understanding of complex issues, thinking in terms of systems, structures and theory, and an exploration of ideas and their interconnections; that allow an examination of the foundations and assumptions behind whatever they are learning; and by question and answer sessions.

They learn least well when there is no apparent purpose; decisions with no foundations are required; when the material or theory or methodology is half-formed (as is the case in many disciplines); and when they are surrounded by people of lower intellectual ability or by those with learning styles dismissive of theory, particularly the experiential learner.

Coaching don'ts: Don't offer half-developed anecdotal stories as sound theoretically-based advice; your credibility will drop faster than you can believe.

This is the learning style most preferred by the analytical and detail-oriented roles in organizational life. Mentoring this learner can be extremely taxing on a mentor/coach whose learning style is other than theoretical. It seems unnecessarily analytical to get the job done. Experiential and functional learners are most incompatible with the theory-oriented learner. These performers can unwittingly stifle the creativity of others by insisting on structured logical analysis of problems.

Functional learning

Like the experiential learner, the functional learner is concerned with results. If it works use it, if it doesn't, bin it or adapt it. The functional learner uses theory, but only if it works. They learn best by solving problems that have real-life practical applications. They continue learning by looking for improvements in their functional theories on an ongoing basis.

Functional learners learn best from activities which make clear the benefit to be gained from the new knowledge; involve 'how to' information; where they can test the advice offered immediately; taught by someone who can practise what is preached; which convey information that can be implemented immediately; presented in the form of tips, short cuts and improvements; involving practising the new techniques.

Functional learning

They learn least well when the learning experience has no immediate or obvious benefit; the method of teaching, or the teachers, are theory-oriented 'chalk and talk' types; where there is no opportunity to practise.

Coaching don'ts: Do not offer anything that has no real world use. If you do, your input will soon be perceived as being useless too.

This is the learning style most favoured in highly results-oriented production activities. The coach of this performer best not try any fancy untried theories if they want to have any respect. The test of whether or not coaching/ mentoring works with this type of learner is 'Am I improving faster like this than I would be on my own?' Coaches with an inclination toward theoretical learning are likely to be frustrated by the ruthless pragmatism of this kind of learner. Any pet theories offered as advice will be used if they work, evolved or dumped if they don't.

Combinations of learning styles

As we said, each of us has our own preferred mix of learning methods. The pattern is probably flexible between contexts. You might prefer to be a functional learner when you know the outcome of your actions will matter and a theoretical learner when abstract understanding is the end point of your learning exercise. Or you might prefer to learn theoretically in the early stages of understanding, and when theory gets to the point of sterility (academic debate), you learn functionally. Or perhaps you use all four styles by observing first, theorizing second, functionally experimenting next and fine-tuning your understanding experientially last.

In short, the coach should note that, while learners have a preferred style, they may use different styles in different contexts, different combinations of styles, different orders of the same combination, the style seen as most appro-priate or as most beneficial, or a style they actively dislike because they can see it would be the most beneficial.

Role-related developmental assignments

Central to successful coaching and mentoring is the provision of role-related developmental assignments – particularly if the coach or mentor is also the manager/director/supervisor. The use of role-related developmental assign-ments should be carefully planned and follow appropriate guidelines:

- Their purpose should be clearly defined and jointly understood.
- They should be useful and relevant to the performer and organization.
- They should be genuine and not 'dull labour' presented as 'development'.
- They should be challenging to the learner, but not overwhelming.
- And appropriate to the performer's learning style.

The purpose of a development exercise will always be generally to improve the performer's results or change their behaviour. An assignment may be aimed at increasing focus; increasing ownership; learning a new skill; creating an aware-ness that a new skill needs to be learned; practising or acquiring empowering attitudes; improving inner dialogue control; vicarious learning by observation; providing observation prior to theory formation, and so on.

There is often a genuine trade-off in the use of development assignments between the requirements of the task, the organization, and those of the learning performer. The ideal development exercise for the performer may be totally useless to the company (except in the medium to long term when the company will have acquired a more competent intellectual resource) but carried out none the less. The opposite should not be acceptable in the context of a development exercise.

What kind of role-related development assignments should coach and performer be choosing? Clearly those that match the objectives and learning style of the performer.

Here are some of the more commonly used developmental assignments: information collection, information analysis, thought experiments, project work, planning, problem solving, report preparation, verbal presentation, undertaking a different role, standing in for someone, observing someone, contact with others in other disciplines/departments/companies/industries, self-appraisal, self-appraisal by seeking opinion of those likely to have valid opinions, self-study or self-managed development, attending a training session, role-relevant exercises and so on.

EXERCISE

When you were an aspiring performer, what kind of developmental exercises did you most enjoy and find most relevant and most fulfilling? If you could have chosen developmental exercises yourself, what would you have chosen? How can your performers get to do the role-related developmental exercises they wish to?

Other development tools

Role play

Role playing can fulfil any number of functions, for instance, the performer may realize that a greater awareness of another party is required to improve their rapport. Pretending to be that person provides a chance to see the world more from their perspective.

Behaviour rehearsal

A new behaviour can be practised in a simulated environment as a way of learning the behaviour sufficiently well to at least stand a chance of success in the real world.

Puzzle provision

Involves presenting the performer with a puzzle or problem that requires the same thought processes/behaviours to reach a solution as the task for which they are being developed. This can be a safe, non-threatening way of developing a performer, particularly if the conclusion or skill required is one which is likely to be resisted or rejected by the performer initially.

Illustrations

Visual or other illustrations can completely encapsulate every aspect of a new/ improved behaviour or skill. It is hoped that the illustrations so far have achieved that for you. The method can be used by asking the performer to devise an illustration to summarize the desired achievement or outcome. Or by both of you devising one together (good for rapport development), or by you gathering a collection of visual illustrations for use with your performer to simplify and encapsulate the issues as they come up.

Exercises

The format of the exercises in this book are an example of what can be provided for the performer.

Debate and argumentation

Debate, argumentation, and the preparation of a presentation of any kind clarifies one's thinking wonderfully. Many writers report that they learn more from writing material than anyone could ever learn from reading it. The reason is that in the process of researching and developing an argument, an enormous amount of material must be considered, evaluated, structured, re-structured and discarded. The audience sees only the final output which may represent 15–20 per cent of that considered. By asking your performers to debate any issue, you facilitate maximal consideration and understanding of the relevant factors.

Self-debate

If time is pressing, the above process can be condensed by asking the performer to role play two separate roles debating the issue of concern. Alternatively the performer can be themselves but conduct a debate for and against a particular action, belief or stance. Or they could debate the relative merits of two competing courses of action.

List formation

List formation develops thinking too. The list can be of anything: elements of a skill, pros and cons of a decision, options for achieving a goal, choices of possible goals, and so on.

Structured thinking

Structured thinking is conducted by setting a format with which something will be examined, thought about, or carried out. The coaching, question asking, and other models presented so far are methods of structured thinking. By asking

Self-debate

your performer to devise their own structured thinking model you can increase their ownership much more than you could if you presented a model. Books are not very good at practising this principle but can go part-way by asking you to improve and tailor a model to suit your own situation.

Brainstorming

Brainstorming is a good way to encourage the performer to generate a large number of ideas in a short space of time, without having to prompt or draw out ideas.

Brainstorming

Teach me...

'You teach best what you most need to learn' and 'Teachers learn more than students' are absolutely true. Ask your performer to teach you or someone else about the thing they think they most need to learn. They'll learn more from teaching than they ever would being taught by you or anyone else.

Give it to me from another perspective...

We know that acquiring multiple meanings assists learning. This can be achieved by asking your performers to provide a different perspective from the one they currently hold.

Tell it like a story...

As with 'Teach me' and 'Debate', 'Tell it like a story' forces organized and clear thinking. Simply ask the performer to present the relevant issues in the form of a story.

Setting targets for role-related development assignments

Some task improvement targets can be hard to define. For example your performer has decided that he or she wants to improve the safety record of the company. The role-related development assignments to achieve that goal would probably go through several draft stages before an acceptable and workable version was found.

Fewer accidents is one of the goals, but what will achieve that? Better safety procedures? Possibly. Greater safety awareness? Perhaps. But how are they achieved? More safety education, more safety notices, and so on? The assignment should be specified to the degree that the outcome can be measured.

To summarize: the assignments should be challenging, assessable, possible and appropriate to the role.

EXERCISE

Here is a role-relevant exercise for coaches. Compile a list of which role-related development exercise and tool types would be appropriate for which learning styles within the confines of your likely coaching/mentoring. Use the information provided in the learning styles section.

Concluding comments and summary

The advanced development skills involved in coaching and mentoring consist of:

- Facilitating the self-managed development of performers.
- Using optimally effective training methods if training is what the performer requests.
- Providing assistance in whatever way the performer learns most effectively.
- Providing role-related developmental assignments to help performers develop in their post.

7

ASSESSMENT AND ANALYSIS

The following assessment and analysis tools can be used at several stages of the coaching sequence. They can be used during the performer's assessment of the here and now; designing of the bridge; building of the bridge... In fact there are circumstances where each can be used in every stage.

- Situational analysis.
- Skills analysis.
- Performance assessment.
- Personal paradigm analysis.

Let's examine each in more detail.

Situational analysis

What is it? The term situational analysis may give the impression that there is one way of analysing a situation. There are any number of ways. It is the general term for the process whereby performer and coach examine the environment in which a proposed achievement is to take place in order to devise an achievement plan. Situational analysis is mostly used as part of the designing a bridge stage of the coaching process. Once the objective is set, the means of achieving it are analysed.

When is it used?

When the achievement environment is not clear or simple. For some objectives, the outcome of situational analysis will be obvious, simple or self-evident. For more complex objectives or those being achieved in a more complex or politically involved way, situational analysis is a must.

Who does it?

It must be the performer; the coach or mentor can help with the provision of an appropriate structure.

How is situational analysis conducted?

The factors to be considered are:

- Hard resources: time, money, premises, equipment.
- Intellectual resources: knowledge and information, behaviour and skills.
- Relationship and influence resources: authority, team relationships, contacts and influence.
- Barriers to objectives.

Time, money, premises, equipment

Draw up a 'resources profile' of the objective. Create a 'needs list', and a 'would be nice' list. What hard resources are required to achieve the objective? What is available? What is the bare minimum with which you could achieve? How can you make up the shortfall? How can you borrow, trade, 'acquire' or otherwise gain access to what you need?

Knowledge and information

Draw up a 'knowledge profile' for the objective. What knowledge is required to achieve the goal? What information would affect your decisions? What information would help and hinder your objectives?

Behaviour and skills

Draw up a 'behaviour and skills profile'. What behaviours will be required to achieve the objective? When will you be required to behave in those ways? What skills will be required? (See skills analysis section.) What creativity, initiative, or other behaviour, thinking or skill can be used in place of other resources?

Relationships

Who can help? Who has control of resources which are essential for the achievement of the objective? Who controls those which would be of use? Who will help willingly and who can be persuaded? Who has information that could help? Who has control of any timing factors that could be of benefit? Whose influence would suppress an opponent's desire to block you? What debts can you call in? What favours could you trade to obtain what is desired? What favours could you withhold if necessary?

Group and team analysis

What are the likely behaviours of team members? What will be the interaction between team members regarding your objective? Who is motivated to what end? How can you harness those motivations? How can you obtain support? How can you minimize or negate resistance? (For more see the 'team coaching' section.)

Barriers, human, organizational and personal

What will be the barriers to your objectives? How can you overcome them? (See Chapter 12 for more information on what the barriers are and how to overcome them.)

Superficial or meticulous?

Situational analysis can be as detailed and meticulous a process as indicated by each of the above. It can also work well if a superficial 'gut' assessment is made of the environment in which the achievement will be undertaken. Whatever depth of analysis is conducted, situational analysis will happen by design or default.

Skills analysis

What is it? It is a thinking structure. It is the process whereby the skills required to complete any objective are deduced from an intellectual or physical examination of the tasks being carried out.

When is it used? It is most often used by the training or personnel functions to determine which people to recruit or what training to provide for those already recruited. For the performer and coach, it is an integral part of the achievement repertoire. We have already alluded to skills analysis on several occasions. Let's look at it in more detail now.

How is skills analysis conducted?

1 Define the objectives: what is the achievement target?
2 Take an overview of which skill areas will be required (physical, intellectual, people, technological and so on).
3 Identify the sub-goals and the sequence of tasks/stages required to achieve the objective.
4 Estimate which skills and to what level they are required to complete each sub-goal/task.
5 Verify your conclusions (by asking existing performers of the role, by questionnaire, by observation, by desk-based/library research).
6 Identify the relevant skills possessed by the performer and establish to what level.
7 Decide how to raise the level of any areas of deficit.
8 Undertake the development.
9 Evaluate and modify as required.

Remember from the skill acquisition section (pages 29–31) that skill consists of several components. The skills analysis should specify the knowledge, beliefs, attitudes and behaviours that define the skills concerned.

Who conducts skills analysis? Ideally the performer. It will maximize their ownership and responsibility for their self-development. Ultra-high achievers do so, and since that's what you're trying to develop that is what should happen. The coach may have to help the performer conduct the analysis first time round, or perhaps provide the steps of the analysis and support the performer in carrying it out. How can you make the skills analysis process more exciting and interesting for the performer?

Performance assessment and observation

- *What is it?* It is the observation and assessment of the performer's achievement level conducted with the use of realistic, available and reliable measures.
- *When is it used?* As part of the here and now assessment and/or during the final assessment stage of the coaching process.
- *Who does it?* The assessments can be conducted by the coach, performer, both, or some uninvolved outsider.
- *How is performance assessment and observation conducted?* There is a large number of methods available. Information can be collected from: peer group assessment, significant other assessment, supervisor assessment, subordinate assessment, customer and supplier assessment (both internal and external to the organization), output/outcome assessment. Other assessment methods available are in the section on System monitoring and evaluation (page 264).

Job description fulfilment

Where qualitative measures are not accurate or 'inappropriate', the performer can be assessed in terms of whether or not the requirements of the job description are fulfilled (mentioned earlier).

Real-time performance assessment

Assessment of real-time performance can be achieved by video or audio recording.

Observation forms

Forms with appropriate criteria for a 1–10 assessment are distributed to and collected from those able to assess the performer. The forms are either viewed individually or the assessment scores can be averaged to obtain an overall picture.

Questionnaires

Can be a more scientific and rigorous version of the above where the criteria of evaluation have been validated over a reasonably sized sample given the size of the company and the costs involved. Or an open-ended assessment where written comments on the performer against appropriate criteria are requested.

Appraisal history collation

The trends in the performer's appraisal forms are extrapolated to deduce performance at the time of assessment. Although it sounds inaccurate, this method can be remarkably predictive, mainly because past behaviour is the best predictor of current and future behaviour.

The accuracy and level of detail in each of the above assessments will vary depending on the method and the person or persons offering the assessment. The immediate superior probably has a detailed appraisal system which breaks the job performance down into detailed components. Customers and suppliers will be able to offer judgements on the performer's interpersonal skill performance, follow-up integrity and administrative efficiency and a few other performance ingredients depending on the role concerned. Subordinates will be able to assess the leadership and motivational skills. Superiors will be able to... and so on.

EXERCISE

Using the above methods conduct an assessment of yourself. Which do you think are the most cost- and time-effective of the suggested performance assessment methods in your organizational context?

Personal paradigm analysis

A paradigm is a system or a model. Each of us has a model of the world in our heads in some form. Our personal paradigm affects the way we act and react to the world. The model takes the form of a collection of beliefs. Some of the beliefs are consciously known and others – called epistemes – are held without awareness.

The personal paradigm is formed throughout our development and continues to evolve. As long as a paradigm proves to be useful it will continue to be held. If it appears to be breaking down it will be modified or in some cases, completely replaced. A paradigm can be thought to function effectively even though it is to others destructive, unrealistic, or downright silly. For instance, a man was spraying rattlesnake repellent on his clothes when a friend asked,

'Why are you using rattlesnake repellent?'
'To keep the rattlesnakes away!' replied the man indignantly.
The friend rejoined, 'But, there are no rattlesnakes in the UK.'
'See! It works!'

Self-satisfying paradigms

If the holder of a paradigm can see evidence that the paradigm is working, they will continue to hold it. Even if their behaviour towards the world causes the response they predict by the world. They expect certain behaviours from others and act in such a way as to give people good reasons to behave in those ways. Even when the expected response doesn't occur, it is perceived to be repressed or suppressed by others. In other words the paradigm allows the perception that is expected even if the reality is totally different.

Self-satisfying paradigms

Empowering and disempowering paradigms

Empowering and disempowering paradigms are best distinguished by the way they cause their holders to look differently at the worldly things that affect us all. Problems in the world, for example, are perceived and interpreted in terms of the paradigm through which the world is viewed. The holder of a disempowering paradigm will attribute all sorts of negative and destructive motives to a problem or the people associated with it. The holder of an empowering paradigm will view the problem as a challenge, as a foil against which to improve, as another good reason to continue with self-development, and so on.

Identifying the paradigm

Your paradigm is most easily visible at the extremes of its operating range – specifically, when it produces something really good or really bad, or when it appears very successful or very unsuccessful. Detecting the paradigm is a slow process requiring a large degree of honesty by the paradigm holder and a substantial amount of sincere feedback from trusted others. Paradigm analysis consists of trying to identify the beliefs behind observed behaviours, emotional reactions and assessable outcomes. There are several pointers or signposts to lead you to your own or your performer's beliefs:

- Inner dialogue.
- Emotional reaction.
- Weaknesses and other problem areas.
- Strengths.
- Opportunities seen and desired.
- Other observed behaviour.
- Perceived threats and motives of others.
- Expectations of self.
- Estimations of own capabilities.
- Estimations of others' capabilities.
- Plans for behaviour.

Inner dialogue

Inner dialogue is the conversation most of have going on in our heads. The mental reaction to some outside event follows a predictable pattern: comprehension (during which the event is filtered through the belief system); inner dialogue reaction; emotional reaction; behaviour and ultimately the end-results. By analysing what a performer says to themselves in response to some event, they, and you, can infer what their paradigm is.

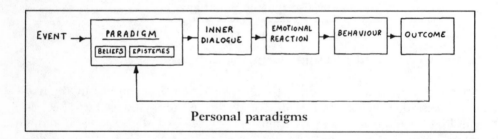

Personal paradigms

Emotional reaction

Emotional reactions are good indicators of underlying belief. Explore the beliefs surrounding incidents in which the performer feels a strong emotional reaction or generates a strong emotional reaction in others.

Weaknesses and other problem areas

Identify the areas of performance in which the achiever feels he or she is weak. Similarly examine the beliefs behind any areas in which the performer has problems.

Strength areas

Strong performances indicate the presence of empowering beliefs as part of the overall paradigm. Identify the areas of strength and infer the underlying beliefs. The empowering beliefs in this context may be transferable to assist in areas of poor performance.

Opportunities seen, opportunities desired

The visibility of opportunities is a reflection of the individual's mind-set or beliefs. Establish what opportunities the performer can see in various contexts, departments, in relation to various objectives and so on. Then try to tease out, or infer with the performer, what beliefs lie behind the identified opportunities. Find out what opportunities your performer would like to have. These will be very revealing. They will express what is important to the performer as effectively as any other method, if not better.

Other observed behaviours

This involves behaviour as reported by others (as gathered in the performance assessment stage). Take the information as gathered and establish agreement that the reporter concerned has good reason to say what has been said. Essentially you are establishing that the behaviour as reported actually occurred. Ask the performer why they behaved in that way. What did they hope to achieve? What were they trying to express? Then ask them what inferences they can make about their beliefs from that conclusion.

Perceived threats posed by others

The perceptions that performers have of others reveal their beliefs too. Establish what threats they see being posed against them.

Perceived motives of others

As above. And identify the beliefs behind assuming these motives.

Expectations of self

The expectations that we have of ourselves directly reflect what we believe we should be doing and achieving – which in turn directly exposes our beliefs and paradigms.

Estimations of own capabilities v. reality

By comparing the performer's estimations of their abilities against those as reported by others, inferences can be made about the range and accuracy of the performer's beliefs about themselves.

Estimations of others' capabilities v. *reality*

As above, except what is detected here is the gap between the performer's estimations of the capability of others and the reality of those capabilities. That can reveal numerous beliefs about others, and ourselves in turn.

Plans for behaviour v. *actual execution of that behaviour*

Often in cool, calm planning sessions we decide to take one course of action or enact one set of behaviours. When it comes to the crunch we do something else. Why should we have done that? What was our motive? What did we believe?

Process structure for paradigm identification

The process of identifying a paradigm can be structured as follows:

1   Identify suitably revealing behaviour, emotional reaction or outcome.
2   Agree that it occurred.
3   Explore motives for it.
4   Explore the inner dialogue associated with the motives.
5   Infer and examine the beliefs behind the inner dialogue and motives
6   Continue 1–5 above, until:
7   You have built up a list of beliefs, then:
8   Pull them together to form a first draft paradigm.
9   Test the paradigm by predicting how the performer would behave in particular situations.
10 Loop 1–9 until assured you have the correct paradigm.

EXERCISE

Conduct a personal paradigm analysis on yourself. Provide five reasons the performer should conduct their own paradigm analysis. Compile a checklist of your likely input to the performer's paradigm analysis.

Paradigm change

Having identified the paradigm, what next? If it is empowering, make the choice between leaving it alone and enhancing it. If it is disempowering, the decision to change to an empowering paradigm must be made. How is that change to be achieved? The following can be an effective process:

1   Identify the cues and rewards that maintain the disempowering beliefs and subsequent behaviour.
2   Explore the options for change.
3   Decide on the most empowering beliefs to be adopted.
4   Decide how to obtain rewards, internal and external, for those beliefs.

5   Decide what will be the internal and external cues for the behaviour.
6   Strengthen the belief by use of reference experiences.
7   Mentally and actually rehearse the new belief structure/paradigm until it is automatic.
8   Keep your guard up against the re-emergence of the previous paradigm.

In the chapter on barriers to achievement (chapter 11) the above list is elaborated, and there is more detail on how to change disempowering paradigms.

As we have said on numerous occasions, the coach/mentor should not subject the performer to a process; they should help the performer to either devise their own process or provide one which the performer can alter and use, or simply accept and use.

EXERCISE

Having conducted your own paradigm analysis, which parts of it do you think are disempowering and are likely to restrict your achievement? Use the above eight-stage paradigm-change sequence to improve your paradigm. You may have to read the section on handling performance problems (pages 139–142) to be able to do so fully.

Summary

During the assessment of the 'here and now' and the planning of the 'there and then', the performer has to consider several factors. They can be systematically and realistically considered using the analysis and assessment tools provided. Each of the methods enables consideration of one of the key areas on which successful planning and ultimate achievement depend. Success can be achieved without the use of these tools – indeed many high achievers will never have heard of the methods presented. They may not have a name for what they do during the planning stage, but usually consider the same factors. Using the analysis and assessment tools will help performers learn about the ingredients they should consider to achieve their goals, even if the method of consideration is personalized after the cessation of coaching. Indeed it is better for performers to adopt their own system of assessing and planning their routes to success.

8

INTERPERSONAL SKILLS

The following topics will be discussed in this chapter:

- Follow-up, feedback, appraisal, praise and criticism.
- Communication styles.
- Persuasion, influence, diplomacy and negotiation.
- Peak motivation methods and self-motivation.
- Handling performer failure and under-performance.

This section is mainly aimed at the manager/director/supervisor acting as mentor or coach.

Follow-up, feedback, appraisal, praise and criticism

Follow-up

For decades commercial training has been under-achieving. The shared un-spoken assumption (episteme) was that if training was provided, learners would implement the skills taught. They don't. Or at least if they do, it is for only a short period until the enthusiasm for the ideas has worn off or the first major obstacle to their implementation has been encountered. Follow-up was lacking. Follow-up designed to boost enthusiasm, to personalize, modify and integrate the new knowledge or skills into the learner's environment, working methods and so on was lacking.

Coaching and mentoring, if properly structured, provide continuing follow-up. That is one of the reasons it can be so successful. Follow-up can be provided in several ways: by identifying the obstacles to implementation early on; by providing feedback on the achiever's performance; by offering support during skills acquisition which is an integral part of coaching and mentoring; or by setting some form of, and time for, assessment of the newly acquired skill. A little rule might help here. When a new skill or new knowledge is to be acquired, when a target for performance is agreed, set a date and purpose for an appro-priate kind of follow-up as well.

Feedback

Honest feedback is so rare as to be positively priceless when found. Be a priceless coach. Honesty means not shielding the performer from the truth, it means helping them decide how they can improve. It may mean being very delicate, but delicacy should not become deceit. Honest feedback should focus on the positives, on what the performer must do to advance. Negatives can be provided, but the performer should invite them.

Feedback should be:

- Specific.
- Descriptive.
- Focused on improvable behaviour.
- Invited, not offered.
- Timely.
- Checked for accuracy with the performer.
- Checked with others.

Feedback should ideally not be:

- General.
- Evaluative.
- Focused on non-improvable behaviours.
- Imposed.
- Out of date.
- Unverified with the performer or others.

Appraisal

For the good combined coach/manager, appraisal is not something that happens bi-annually or annually; it is a continuing process. But it should never become a bureaucratic burden or a banal bore. In an ideal world it should be conducted every two weeks on a formal basis and daily on an informal basis. Continuous appraisal can be used to complement an existing coaching programme, or it can be conducted as part of the programme. Indeed the appraisal meeting is a great vehicle for introducing coaching to the performer. After the strengths and areas for development have been identified the coach/manager can discuss the possibility of using coaching or mentoring, in its many possible forms, to help the performer develop. The guidelines for successful appraisal are similar to those for feedback.

Appraisal interviews should be conducted:

- With the relevant performance information to hand.
- When, and not until, both parties understand and are committed to the purpose of the appraisal meeting.
- By systematically reviewing performance against agreed criteria.
- By both parties keeping the meeting on track.
- By providing constructive criticism – and ideally by encouraging self-assessment.
- By discussing future, training, remedial or performance enhancement action.
- By honestly discussing how the performer's future is anticipated in terms of promotion and advancement.
- By avoiding the common faults which follow.

EXERCISE

Be honest now: in your capacity as a manager, supervisor, director, how often do you conduct appraisal sessions? How many of what you describe as 'appraisals' would your staff describe similarly? Have some impartial outsider anonymously ask your staff how often they are appraised. You might be surprised at the answers. When was the last time you asked your staff to assess you? And the last time you asked for anonymous assessment by your staff? Is a regular appraisal of you set up as standard procedure? If not, why do you think it would be a good idea to do so? What questions can you ask performers to help them improve their appraisal frequency? What questions would help them seek appraisal from their staff and others?

Common appraisal problems which can be easily avoided include:

- *Not listening* – making hasty conclusions, expecting too rapid a change, making unfulfillable commitments, causing avoidable conflict, being too soft or harsh with judgements.
- *Similarity errors* – judging those similar to you more favourably, giving similar grades to apparently related criteria, overrating or over-emphasizing performance on dimensions that you value in yourself,

failing to spot defects in performance because they are similar to your own, judging similar staff as being of a similar standard.

- *Dissimilarity errors* – judging those dissimilar to yourself more harshly, being unable to assess objectively those you disapprove of or cannot understand.
- *Spread errors* – judging favourably overall because of one excellent dimension, judging badly overall because of one very poor dimension, judging items next to each other on the appraisal document in the same way, making decisions for the present based on past appraisals.
- *Easy life errors* – judging only on the easily assessable criteria, avoiding judging negatively for fear of the consequences that would follow.
- *Prejudging errors* – accepting the views of others prior to the appraisal, prejudging an overall performance increase and increasing the ratings allocated to all individual dimensions to fulfil that judgement.
- *Timing errors* – judging favourably or unfavourably because of coincidental factors, placing excessive emphasis on recent events or events occurring just after the last appraisal that ran contrary to the assessment.
- *Consistency errors* – not judging consistently within the appraisal exercise, not judging different members of staff consistently, allowing judgements to be affected by the day-to-day ups and downs of business life.

EXERCISE

Which of the above errors do you think you may have fallen into in the past? Devise a checklist against which you can compare your judgements for some of these errors, and which will guide you in avoiding them in the first place. Devise a series of questions that will help your performers to see the benefits of knowing the potential appraisal errors, and to devise a system designed to prevent their occurrence.

Praise

The outcomes you should expect are the outcomes you should reward. Praise is the most effective immediate reward a manager or manager/coach can offer. Done well it can boost performance for weeks; done badly it can demotivate in seconds. So how is it done well? As briefly as possible without being hurried. There are several components:

1   Create an expectation of performance feedback – tell them you're going to tell them!
2   Give praise immediately, as soon after the successful behaviour/outcome as possible.
3   The praise should be highly specific, the performer told exactly what they did right.
4   Express your emotions about the success.

5 Explain how it helps the department or organization.
6 After you've made the point, shut up, and let the performer savour the moment.
7 Make it clear that more and similar successes are desired and welcome.
8 Depending on your culture, make some form of physical contact – a hug, a handshake, a slap on the back.

Criticism

The outcomes you rebuke may be the outcomes you receive if the only way of getting your attention is to 'misbehave'. In other words using criticism exclusively, not using praise as well, will attract the behaviour you least desire. Criticism done well can increase desire to perform well, particularly if you make it clear that the behaviour is being criticized and not the person. Criticism done badly can make an otherwise good performer lose respect for the critic, and faith in the organization. So how do you reprimand effectively? In virtually the same way as offering praise, and with equal speed:

1 Create an expectation of performance feedback – tell them you're going to tell them.
2 Give criticism immediately, as soon after the undesired behaviour or outcome as possible.
3 The reprimand should be highly specific, the performer told exactly what they did wrong.
4 Express your emotions about the undesired behaviour.
5 Explain how it hinders or harms the department and organization.
6 After you've made the point, shut up, and let the performer feel your displeasure for a moment.
7 Encourage them to improve their behaviour or performance.
8 Explain that you value them but disapprove of the performance or behaviour.
9 Do not offer any physical contact. The performer must in no way think the behaviour is being rewarded.
10 When the reprimand is finished, normal relations should be resumed.

The coaching way to handle criticism, praise and feedback

The above procedures for praise, criticism and feedback or variants of them are those which are used by the most highly skilled leaders and managers. They seem to work. Or at least they seem to work with those people who are prepared to give up their self-responsibility to their superiors.

Ultra-high performance and the giving up of self-responsibility are incompatible. Criticism, praise and feedback should all be conducted in the way that maximizes ownership and self-responsibility.

In strict coaching terms the procedure for 'criticism' is as follows:

Coaching: praise, criticism and feedback

1 Create an expectation of performance feedback – tell them you're going to ask them.
2 Ask performance evaluation questions immediately after the undesired behaviour or outcome.
3 Ask questions that help the performer focus on what was constructive about the performance, what could have been better, and what actively hindered their performance. The coach should continue questioning until the performer has told them exactly what they did wrong.
4 Ask for an expression of their emotions about the undesired behaviour or poor performance. Be silent for a while for motivation-enhancing frustration to build up.
5 Ask for an analysis of how it hinders or harms the department and organization, if such an analysis was not provided under point three. Encourage the performer to wish to seek a solution.
6 Ask the performer how they think they can best seek to improve, plan the improvement, and agree to follow up the changes with you.
7 Paraphrase, summarize and check your understanding.
8 Support the performer's improvement planning with empowering questions.
9 Be responsive to their improvement plan during implementation.

The key issues involved in the coaching way of praise are ownership and self-responsibility:

1 Create an expectation of performance feedback – tell them you're going to ask them.
2 Ask performance evaluation questions immediately after the successful behaviour or outcome.

3 Ask questions that help the performer focus on what was constructive about the performance, what could have been better, and what actively improved the performance. The coach should continue questioning until the performer has told them exactly what they did right.
4 Ask them how they feel about the success.
5 Ask them how it helps the department and organization.
6 After they've made the point, shut up and let the performer savour the moment.
7 Ask the performer how they think they can maintain, enhance or build on the performance.
8 Support the performer's improvement planning with empowering questions.
9 Be responsive to their ongoing improvement plan during implementation.

EXERCISE

Using the above guidelines for praise and criticism, how do you think feedback should be handled in an ideal coaching situation? Draw up a list as above. When you try this method for the first time, after it is completed ask your performer for feedback. Ask them which method they think they are most likely to respond to.

Communication styles, diplomacy, persuasion and negotiation

Communication styles

Much of the information required to understand the variety of communication styles and their implications for coaching has already been covered in other sections, specifically in the Listening skills section and thinking styles as covered in the Coaching styles section. Refresh your memory by skimming the appropriate sections (see pages 57–59 and 46–48).

From the point of view of the listener there are only two styles of communication: effective and ineffective. Several varieties of effective style exist. Each of us has our own expression of whatever style we habitually use. Our styles are based on, and reflective of, a number of contributory factors. Upbringing, beliefs, thinking style, educational level, mood, attitude to self and others all play a part. Communication styles are in particular closely related to thinking styles.

Non-verbal communication provides enormous scope for individuality. The relative mix of verbal and non-verbal components in our communication is fairly stable. Approximately 80 per cent of meaning comes from signals other than the content of the words we utter. Most of our meaning is transmitted in our body language and the non-word components of our voice. There are many good books on non-verbal communication and you may benefit from reading at least one. If you do, don't fall into the trap that newcomers to 'body language' frequently fall into – that is, making the assumption that the successful interpretation of one particular body language message gives you the meaning of the total communication. Making that assumption would be like assuming that because you know the meaning of one word in the paragraph of a foreign language text, you understand the whole paragraph. Be careful too to avoid over-analysing the performer's body language to the point where you become paralysed by analysis.

The dangers of focusing on body language

Be aware of body language, but don't let it occupy the foreground of your thinking for long. You've managed until now processing body language on a semi-conscious basis; don't lose your ability developed over decades by being fixated on articulating something that need not be articulated.

As a developing coach or mentor it is useful to become aware of the effect your particular communication style will have on interactions with your performer. Try to define your communication style along the following dimensions. Those on the left are the best ways not to communicate; those on the right are best possible communication styles.

Non-verbal (physical)

Relatively motionless	High levels of gesticulating
Tight, closed body signals	Open, receptive body signals
Fixed facial expression	Variable, interested facial expressions
Little eye contact	Pleasant, interested, reassuring eye contact
Body pointed away	Body facing direction of listener

Non-verbal (vocal)

Voice unclear	Voice clear
Vocal pitch constant	Vocal pitch varying
Pace of communication steady	Pace variable for added interest
Emotionless voice	Emotion appropriate to communication
Negative attitude	Positive attitude

Verbal

Formal	Informal language
Complex	Simple language
Disorganized presentation	Organized presentation
Lack of knowledge	Knowledgeable but not pompous

EXERCISE

What additions could you make to the above list? A clue: there are several factors listed under What puts people off listening? and What makes people listen? (pages 58–59). Convert those into communication style dimensions.

Matching, pacing and leading

As we said in the rapport creation section (pages 53–57), skilled communicators match and pace the other party's communication style. What we didn't say is that there is a stage beyond that, namely, leading. When two people have been communicating in perfect harmony for some time, there is a natural tendency to want to continue that process. The skilled communicator can harness this tendency by testing to see if the listener will follow any changes made to the collective communication behaviour. If they do, the leader can then exert some considerable influence. The more willing the new follower is to do so, the more influence the leader acquires.

EXERCISE

Choose a safe person with whom to practise matching, pacing and leading. Find out what the limits of leading are. What exercises could you use to help your performers to learn matching, pacing and leading techniques?

Persuasion and influence

There will inevitably be occasions when the coach or mentor will have to be persuasive and influential toward the performer. The means of doing so will be considered under the following headings:

- Influence styles.
- Influence factors.
- Influence planning.
- Rapport and listening as an influence tool – matching, pacing and leading.
- When to use influence in coaching/mentoring.

Influence styles

There are as many variations of styles of influence as there are with coaching, mentoring, communication, thinking and virtually every other human inter- or intrapersonal skill. There is a variety of influence styles. Incidentally, there is a close overlap between the styles of any one individual. One's thinking style is similar to one's communication style, is similar to one's influence style, and so on. In many skills, style can be considered synonymous with strategy. That is certainly the case with influence, as will be seen next.

Visionary style   A user of this style will present a common vision, designed to appeal to the sense of hope and purpose we all need. They will use emotional rather than logical arguments. The images used will be colourful, the language vivid and the rhetoric powerful.

Visionary style

EXERCISE

Who do you know who uses this style? When would you choose to use it even if it is not your natural style? When would it be most beneficial to ask your performers the same questions? Repeat this exercise for the following styles.

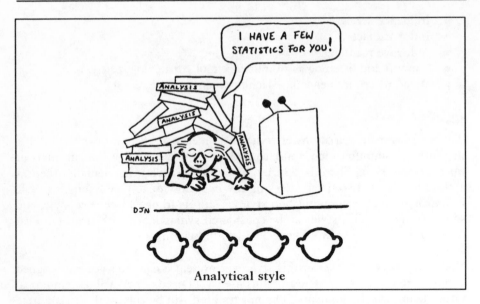

Analytical style

Analytical style The analytical influencer uses logic, reason and evidence rather than emotion. Their arguments are highly structured, organized and make a clear connection with the expressed views of others. They tend to appeal to our sense of order, structure and safety.

Realist style Realist persuaders make reference to higher authority. They state their objectives and purposes then offer rewards. They bargain and negotiate to achieve their objectives. They also spell out the likely outcomes of not pursuing 'their' way. Realists appeal to our sense of greed and of fear.

Realist style

Responsive style   Responsive influencers use interaction, flexibility and the suggestions of others. They intently listen to the goals of others in terms of what is said and what is done. 'Responsives' change their views to integrate those of others. They appeal to our need to be involved and to be considered.

Responsive style

Conservative style   Conservative influencers use inconsistency, viability and feasibility arguments to destroy the aspirations of other persuaders. They instinctively challenge any proposals as being shaky in theory and unworkable in practice. They appeal to our sense of maintaining the status quo.

Conservative style

Sales style Sales persuaders seek to satisfy needs by providing the ideal benefit for that purpose. They are highly interactive. They ask for small commitments to be made, one at a time, where the next is barely any different from the previous one, but the first is a long way from the last. They seek to 'help' the listener with their decision making, and handle any objections raised. They seek to appeal to our need to make decisions rationally.

Sales style

EXERCISE

Place the above styles in the order in which you most use them, or most identify with them. Which do you think would be most effective in the range of contexts in which you operate? Ask your performer to do the same.

When to use influence in coaching or mentoring

The glib answer is when persuasion will not detrimentally affect the performer's level of ownership. That is likely to be rarely. As usual, reality is much more complex than that.

On occasion, it may be appropriate for a coach or mentor to persuade the performer towards or away from something or other. Such persuasion is more likely to be acceptable and consistent with a mentoring position than with coaching. However, there will be times for both parties when the best course of action will be to cease being non-directive and performer-centred. The question then is how to do it in such a way that the performer's sense of ownership experiences minimal damage.

Influence factors

In any style used, there are three factors which will determine the outcome of the persuasion attempt, namely:

- The source or persuader.
- The message.
- The listener, receiver or audience.

Source   The factors associated with the persuader which influence the outcome of attempts have been consistently found to be expertness, trustworthiness and attractiveness. Expertness is attributed when the individual is articulate, understandable and knowledgeable. Trustworthiness is attributed when the speaker makes their motives known, and when they reveal something that would not have been in their best interests to reveal. Attractiveness is attributed when the individual is humorous, human, approachable, has the same needs, fears and aspirations for their loved ones as us, and when their facial and physical appearance is used attractively.

EXERCISE

What can you do to make yourself more credible as a source? Ask your performers the same question. From what other sections in this book can you obtain information to answer this question?

Message   To some extent the message will be organized in accordance with the influencer's style. The style can be made maximally effective if it has:

- An organized and clear structure.
- Information of relevance to the receiver and the relevance is clearly shown.
- A language and style appropriate to the audience.
- An element of interactivity which enables the speaker to demonstrate that they are responsive to listeners.

EXERCISE

How can you make your messages more persuasive? Ask your performers the same question.

Audience   Listeners are most persuadable when:

- Not pre-warned that persuasion is about to happen.
- Involved and interested.
- Committed to achieving a goal.
- Relaxed, but not passively so.

- They perceive themselves to be similar to the audience.
- They think their peers and significant others are likely to agree with the message.
- They stand to benefit, or avoid being harmed if the proposal is adopted.

EXERCISE

How can you optimally prepare your audience for maximum persuasion effect?

Influence planning

The obvious way for you and your performers to plan a persuasive message is to do so by considering the above factors, and how the source, message and audience factors can best be used to achieve the desired result. The best way to do that is to use – a friend of ours, not mentioned for some time – the question. What do you want the message to achieve? Who is/are the audience? To what are they most likely to respond? In what way do they want to hear the message? How can you get them involved? In what way can you show the importance of the message for them? How can you ensure they are relaxed? How can you ensure that they see the benefits of co-operating and the risks of not? How can you make yourself appear to be optimally expert, trustworthy and attractive to that audience? Where would be best, who (if not you) would be best, and when would be best to persuade the listener? And so on.

If you do have to use persuasion in coaching, prepare and plan it properly.

Rapport and listening as influence tools are regularly under-estimated, particularly listening. People tend to listen to those who listen to them. People are more receptive to persuasion by those with whom they are in mutual listening arrangements, that is where rapport is good. If you are going to have to persuade someone, or think you might at some stage in the future, Machiavelli would advise you to spend the time establishing a good rapport. Naturally, I could never make such a comment.

EXERCISE

Devise an exercise that your performers can use to test the above principles safely.

Diplomacy

Diplomacy is to truth and falsehood what grey is to black and white. Use your diplomacy palette wisely. Call something grey when it's clearly black or white and you're down. Call something white grey, or when it's black grey and you're shaken. Call it greyish when its greyish and you're OK. Don't lose your ability to paint in pure black or pure white by contaminating each with the other. If you must be diplomatic, know you are doing so.

Diplomacy is a much revered and much reviled skill. It is essential for peaceful coexistence, yet when practised badly it is seen as the two Ds: duplicity and deceit. Too little diplomacy and our performer can feel disregarded, with obvious effects. Too much diplomacy and the performer may make attributions about our Ds, or at the very least may think we are more concerned with protecting their emotions than facilitating the birth of a momentous achievement.

What are the principles of diplomacy as they apply to coaching? The cynic would reply 'diplomacy has no principles'. But every art has some guidelines.

- It is better to remain silent than to offer criticism.
- It is better to ask a question than to damn with forced silence.
- Avoid becoming involved with disputes between your performer and others, unless you are the other, or you are the coach/manager and the dispute affects your patch.
- You can't win arguments with those you seek to inspire; you might win the battle of the mind but you'll lose the campaign for the heart.
- Try to see the world through your performer's eyes.
- Tact is the art of making the performer feel comfortable without being too tacky.

EXERCISE

What do your performers define diplomacy as being?

Performer's diplomacy

Appreciate that your performer may be diplomatic with you. They may have their own rules of diplomacy which may include 'If you are better than your

Possible performer's diplomacy

coach or manager, use your talents with discretion. If you are really intelligent, feign a more acceptable level of grey matter capability. Before you speak, assess how the other party will react. If you are accidentally tactless, evasion is preferable to an apology which is likely to make the situation worse. If you are going to be more successful than your coach or manager, give them an emotional investment in your success, involve them as much as possible, and make them feel it is their doing. Give your boss what they want, tell them what they want to hear in the way they want to hear it. Always attribute the most desirable motives for your behaviour, whatever your actual motives are.'

You could find yourself dealing with Machiavelli reincarnate. How you choose to handle that must be your decision. I couldn't possibly comment!

EXERCISE

Assume that your performer has asked you to help them learn to be more diplomatic. How will you go about doing that?

Negotiation

Much of the material written on negotiation concerns itself with dirty tricks and ways of undermining, off-balancing and otherwise emotionally or intellectually beating the opponent into submission. That is completely inappropriate in the coaching/mentoring context. Some coaches in the workplace and non-workplace sector conduct what I've heard referred to as 'Terror Talks' where the sole objective is to terrify the performer into achieving out of fear of being dropped. A coach or mentor who had no other responsibility for the performer is unlikely to use such methods but a pressurized, frustrated coach/manager or mentor/manager may be tempted. Don't. It never works in the long term. It may work, but only long enough for the performer to seek alternative employment.

Such aggressive negotiating techniques should never be used where you expect any contact with the other party or any influence by the other party in the long term. You may win at the negotiating table, but if both parties don't walk away happy with the deal, you might find yourself defending against the commercial equivalent of a long term terrorist campaign. Since you can't predict who will be in a position to influence your future or who will have access to those who do, you should not use the aggressive methods advocated elsewhere, even with people you expect never to deal with again.

Negotiation is most likely to occur during the period when the achiever and coach/manager or mentor/manager are establishing the objectives of performance enhancement. Negotiation at this stage would not be conducted by the coach, operating in the strictest definition of the term; the performer should set the goals.

In practical terms, the coaching or mentoring manager will have no choice but to seek a negotiated balance between personal and organizational needs. The performer should be invited to find or propose an appropriate balance point.

In addition to the methods suggested to establish good rapport, the coach/manager can use the process of negotiating the objectives the performer will pursue to enhance their relationship. There are four main negotiating styles along a continuum which includes being conciliatory, co-operative, forceful and aggressive. (There is more information on negotiating styles in the section on conflict, page 227.) The extremes of the continuum are not appropriate to a meeting of people seeking to achieve the same ends. The mentor/manager is most likely to obtain results by negotiating in a co-operative way.

The negotiating behaviours most likely to generate results are the following. Create empathy and rapport. Establish co-operation as the means to the end, establish the desire for a win–win outcome. Humanize the proceedings. Establish what your performer wants. Establish what you want by putting forward your proposal in the form of seeking the performer's opinion. Negotiate complex issues by breaking them down into small parts. Build agreement by small advances, in small increments. When you reach a blockage, pull back to a position of common ground, then work together to find a route to progress. Should that not work, appeal to morals or ethics, ask for sympathy, or have a third party decide (but don't overdo any of those). Make it easy for your performer to compromise. Accept that no policy or position is absolutely immutable. Above all, show respect and trust in the performer.

EXERCISE

Devise some exercises that you can use with your performer to practise negotiation skills. Which negotiation situations could you use for role playing? What could you draw from the kinds of negotiations that we all have to engage in?

The aggressive negotiator as performer

Some potential coach/managers may be wondering how they can be expected to show respect, trust and co-operation with a performer who chooses to be hostile, manipulative or negotiates aggressively on a continuing basis. The ultimate sanction is to refuse to offer any further coaching until their behaviour changes. Or, less drastically, to establish unilaterally the goal for the first coaching session as examining and resolving their counter-productive attitude. Less drastically still is to let them blow off steam, to literally sit there in silence until either they realize their current approach is going to get more of the same, or they ask you why you are not replying to their demands. You can then ask how they would feel if they had just been spoken to in that way, and if they think that there are better ways of dealing with people than those they have demonstrated. It's painful; it's time consuming; it's hard work; but by jingo it works!

EXERCISE

What other methods could you use to deal with a performer who adopts an aggressive negotiation stance? In what roles would you expect a performer to be an aggressive negotiator? Should the above management strategies be used with someone who needs a tough negotiating style for their role?

Peak motivation methods

Having already covered motivation, what can be left to say? Some obvious things and some shocking things. Let's handle the obvious first. Motivation will peak and remain high when all demotivators are removed and all possible relevant motivators, internal and external, are in place.

The ideal motivation conditions are:

1   The business should be fun.
2   Rewards should be almost immediately available, or at least immediately visible.
3   There should be a high degree of glamour and social status with the job.
4   The rewards should be high, and the effort expected to gain them intense.
5   The individual should have total responsibility for their performance.
6   There should be no interference, no boss. They should be their own boss.
7   Business as a career should have been a matter of choice.
8   The area of performance excellence should be chosen.

EXERCISE

Ask your performer which of the above are available in their role? Which are available in your job?

As we all learn over the years, the real world version of most ideals is less than ideal:

1   Business for many roles is often dull, repetitive, and singularly boring. Yawn!
2   Rewards are long-term; the immediate rewards are survival salaries for most.
3   There is little glamour, and many people in most societies are deeply distrustful of business people.
4   Rewards are big only for a few, and usually late in life.
5   The individual has only partial responsibility for their results...
6   ... because of interference from the boss, shareholders, customers, national and world markets, the demotivating tax burden, regulatory officials, employees, unions, and on and on and on...

7   Business as a discipline is not a matter of choice. For most it was the job that just happened to be available when they realized that they didn't fit into the professions encouraged at school or college.

8   The choice of area and performance, if it occurs, is usually at the boss's behest.

Gosh, after reading that list I'm starting to wonder why I went into business, or why anyone bothers to. Replies on a postcard to:

The Constant Challenge of Business,
Unbelievable Diversity of Roles,
PO Box I Can't Imagine Anything More Fulfilling When It Goes Well,
Everycity,
Worldwide.

Seriously, though, with all the negative motivations it really is amazing that normal people regularly perform at the most supra-ordinary levels. More would, more could, if companies tried to turn the factors in the second list into the factors in the first list. An idealistic dream perhaps? Perhaps not!

There is a company in which the workers make most of the decisions. Staff set their own salaries, performance targets, and performance bonuses. Everyone has access to the company books on a continuous basis. There is no formality. 'Face time' is a thing of the past. There is a horrifyingly low level of administration, memos, meetings, checks and approvals (I can hear the average job-conscious bureaucrat plotting counter-arguments already). There are no internal hierarchy walls. Contrary to what might be predicted by some, workers do not vote themselves huge pay rises. As a group they act in a highly self-restrained manner, with the vast majority voting down the greedy few wishing to bite the hand that feeds them. Staff appraise and are involved in the selection of managers, any consistently not measuring up are effectively fired by their subordinates. Is your hair standing on end yet?

The company is striving towards full commercial democracy. The leaders of this company fully acknowledge that commercial democracy is hard work for them, but the returns are phenomenal performances from the staff. The staff turnover ratio reads like a fraction too small to measure, the sickness rate or lack of it would make most CEOs as sick as a parrot, and the growth rate reads like a fairy story, like an idealist's dream.

The dream is a reality. But where? In a stable mature western democracy? In a country with an economic stability that would put the Swiss to shame? No, in a South American country, ravaged by up to 900 per cent inflation, with a history of extreme political instability, and still only forming its democratic wings. The company is Semco, the country is Brazil. Those of us who feel inspired and humbled by that knowledge should now raise our hands. Hey, wait for me! More information is available in Ricardo Semler's book, *Maverick*, details of which are in the Bibliography.

EXERCISE

To enhance your performer's thinking about decision making, and in whose hands each decision is best made, ask them to devise a theoretical commercially viable company operating on the principle of commercial democracy.

Self-motivation enhancement techniques

Motivations can be altered and improved by the use of self-motivation techniques, which include:

- *Motivational dualling*:   Setting up patterns of behaviour that satisfy more than one motivation.
- *Motivational reciprocal empowerment*:   Setting up patterns of behaviour that increase motivation.
- *Self-rewards*:   Rewarding oneself for the achievement of little sub-goals.
- *Self-fulfilling prophecy*:   Decide that your motivation is high to make it high.
- *Self-deceit and self-manipulation*:   Tell yourself whatever you need to hear to motivate yourself.
- *Mental rehearsal*:   Rehearse any of the other strategies here.
- *Mental imagery*:   Regularly picture yourself being highly motivated.
- *Goal value reinforcement and affirmation*:   Continually re-affirm your belief in your objective.
- *Conflict resolution criteria*:   Resolve any conflicts in a way that maximizes motivation.
- *Mutual motivational support*:   Form a motivationally nurturing relationship with another.
- *Inoculation against demotivation*:   Saturate and surround yourself with motivating things/thoughts.
- *Inner dialogue control*:   Control what you think to favour maximum motivation.
- *Thought empowerment*:   Think motivationally empowering thoughts.
- *Adoption of empowering beliefs*:   Believe whatever maximizes your motivation.
- *Reference experience re-interpretation*:   View your life experiences to maximize your motivation.
- *Increase control over motivators*:   Gain more control over the things that help motivate you.
- *Emotional mastery*:   Control your emotions to assist your motivation level.

EXERCISE

What will you add to this list?

Handling performer failure and under-performance

Reasons for under- or non-performance

There are four reasons that a performer being coached/mentored can fail to, or under-perform:

1   A coaching/mentoring system failure has occurred.
2   Factors outside the performer's control.
3   Factors within the performer's control.
4   A combination of the previous three.

Coaching system failures

The most likely problems with the coaching or mentoring system are errors being made at one of the four main stages. It is possible that the 'here and now' was not realistically assessed, thereby having detrimental effects on the subsequent stages, and ultimately the outcome of the performer's attempts. At the bridge design stage it is not uncommon for objectives to be set in a way that is not clear, or for apparent clarity to dissolve in the face of unforeseen variables. The bridge construction phase can suffer the same fate: the methods chosen to achieve the objectives may be unworkable, or not workable at realistic costs, or workability may not prove to be as controllable as the performer had foreseen. Finally, it is possible that the performer's achievements were poorly measured giving the impression of non-success, or that there was an unanticipated, delayed outcome effect which rears its head after the performer has been judged to have under-achieved. Despite the apparent implausibility of the last effect,

Coaching system failures

it occurs regularly in business and in politics: the successor frequently basks in glories that were set running by the so-called unsuccessful predecessor.

The remedy for coaching system failures is to reassure the performer, modify or improve the process if that is appropriate, or to ask the performer what system they want to use or devise. What will you ask performers to help them reassure themselves that the coaching/mentoring system, while flawed, is workable?

The performer as the customer   Coaching failures can be handled effectively if the coach/mentor views the performer as a customer. Customer service-oriented companies communicate with their clients every so often just to check everything is OK. Those companies keep their customers involved. They provide an atmosphere in which any concerns can be raised and addressed before they can become big issues. By doing so they build up a positive balance in their 'goodwill account'. That balance can be drawn on to cover the costs of the inevitable mistakes which are made in any business relationship. If you have made goodwill deposits with your performers you can afford the occasional withdrawal without going overdrawn. If you have no balance, your request for a withdrawal will be denied; the customer will take their business elsewhere. But performers don't have the same degree of choice. It takes a while to find a new employer. They can't readily go elsewhere in body, but they can in mind. Build up a positive balance by helping your performers in unexpected little ways. The same principle applies to employees generally; build up a goodwill balance to cover the cost of the inevitable withdrawals. Compile a list of goodwill deposits you could make.

Failure caused by factors outside the performer's control

Where unforeseeable events caused the under-performance, performer and coach have to do their best to cope with and learn what can be learned from the experience. On a personal note I have learned a great deal from reading the biographies of successful people and particularly from their amazing abilities to cope with failure and carry on. I'm not sure where the following quotes came from, or which are from my own inner dialogue, but they've helped me in the past.

'The brightest dawn comes after the darkest night.'
'Most people give up a maddening few steps from their goal.'
'The only failure is someone who has given up.'
'Forget the failure; learn from the mistakes.'
'You stand a good chance of finding the route to success in a routing failure.'
'With every failure comes the seed of opportunity.'
'If you do happen to have invested good effort in a mistake, you owe it to yourself to salvage from it what knowledge you can.'
'Never, never, never give up.'

'Keep on keeping on.'

'The biggest battle when you fail is in your own mind.'

'Find the empowering message in the disempowering emotions initially associated with failure.'

EXERCISE

Early on in your coaching sessions ask performers how they have coped with failures in the past.

Failure caused by factors within the performer's control

The decision-making diagram shown in the figure will prove useful in determining quickly whether the performance problem is caused by lack of competence, motivational difficulties or some blockage. A 'No' response in any of the 'A' boxes indicates that training, practice or self-managed development is appropriate, unless any of the 'B' boxes have a 'No' response – in which case the reasons for the reluctance to acquire the knowledge, attitudes, or behaviour should be investigated and, if appropriate, rectified. Once all 'A' boxes can be completed with a 'Yes', any 'No' in the 'B' boxes indicates a reluctance to carry out the required skill or a component of it. To a lesser extent it indicates that a performer is so blocked that they are reluctant to even bother trying. In either case the reluctance should be investigated. A 'Yes' in box 'C' indicates a motivated, but blocked, performer.

SKILL COMPONENTS	YES/NO	MOTIVATED TO ACQUIRE/USE	
		YES	NO
KNOWLEDGE (KNOW HOW IN THEORY)	A		B
ATTITUDES (HAS NECESSARY ATTITUDES)	A		B
BEHAVIOUR (CARRIES OUT NECESSARY BEHAVIOUR	A		B
HAS ALL 3 ABOVE BUT DOES NOT USE THEM		C	B

Decision-making diagram for analysis of performance problems

To analyse and overcome blockages the reader is referred to Chapter 11 on coaching and mentoring for barriers. To rectify a competence deficit, refer to the section on acquiring new skills (page 29) and the skills deficit section (page 184) of the chapter just mentioned.

EXERCISE

Ask your performers what they think is the most empowering way to cope with self-caused failure.

Summary and concluding comments

Both coach and mentor require a range of advanced interpersonal skills to effectively help their performers. The extent to which each of the skills covered is required is determined by the exact role, combination of roles, industry, position of coach/mentor and so on. The skill required will also vary from circumstance to circumstance and from performer to performer. A coach or mentor in constant development uses whatever opportunities they can to improve their effectiveness. That will include regularly asking performers for feedback and assessment.

9

TEAMS AND ORGANIZATIONS

The same principles which apply to individual coaching apply to team coaching and mentoring, with one difference – the whole group must be involved in all the decision stages. The team as a whole will create a rapport with the coach, establish outline goals for the coaching process, lay the ground rules for coaching, assess the here and now, determine the detailed targets, and the means of achieving them, implement the plans, assess the outcomes, and modify the plans, targets or methods if necessary.

What affects team performance?

There are numerous factors. Assuming the obvious has been attended to (we all know how dangerous assumptions can be), the most important factors are the level of genuine co-operation and honesty between all the members of the team, and the individual performance of the team members towards the goals of the team. But most of all, the factor which determines high team achievement is purpose. Teams that have a clear, shared and powerful vision or purpose are enormously effective. High-performing teams, like high-achieving individuals, have 'direction'. (Other team success factors are mentioned in the healthy team behaviours checklist, page 157.)

Coaching a team, therefore, is most productively aimed at achieving a powerful sense of purpose, true team co-operation and mutual support, and coaching individuals to improve their team-oriented achievement behaviour. We will cover team coaching under the following three headings, providing suggestions for effective coaching at the appropriate point.

- Understanding team/organization formation.
- Team analysis.
- Applying the coaching sequence to teams.

Understanding team/organization formation

Although the formation of a group may appear to be a fairly smooth, gradual process, for the purposes of understanding what is going on it is best to consider the event in seven distinct stages:

1 Decision to create group: formation
2 Inclusion.
3 Influence establishment.
4 Norm formation.
5 Performing.
6 Evolving and self-regeneration.
7 Termination.

Formation

The decision to create the group may be made by one or two individuals in an organization who may or may not be involved. If they are, it is likely they will go on to lead the group. The group may be newly founded, or formed by giving new purpose or powers to a long established group, or have evolved from some previous organizational entity.

Coach/mentor input If the group is to be newly formed, the coach's main responsibility is to ask questions aimed at helping those establishing the group to provide a clear statement of purpose and remit. Devise some such questions.

Inclusion

Inclusion is primarily a self-selection and fitting in phase. Each individual decides whether or not they want to be, or are willing to strive to be, a team member. This is an apparently non-productive phase when individuals are too insecure, anxious and introverted to think of much beyond their own inclusion needs (see below). Those passing this stage quickly are in a better position to adopt early leadership roles. I say 'apparently' because, although it appears nothing is being achieved, the foundations for future achievement are laid at this stage.

Coach/mentor input Conventional training methods to ease the inclusion phase are regarded as 'petty and inappropriate little games' by some. The coach can best help during this phase by asking the members of the group how they would like to get to know each other. Be wary of following the first suggestion by the most forward member of the group; they may not – no, will not – speak for the others. Asking the group how they wish to conduct the induction process sets the precedent for later levels of group involvement and co-operation.

Influence

During the influence phase there is an intense but subtle struggle for position in the group hierarchy. There is much boundary marking and power play. This phase can be highly destructive. Potentially good working relationships can be destroyed and much distrust can be created, by even a mild level of over-enthusiasm for dominance.

Coach/mentor input – damage limitation Training methodology has much to offer here. Team development exercises can allow the dominance struggle to take place in a relatively safe emotional environment. It is debatable whether conducting the exercises does anything other than provide a referee in the form of the exercise leader or coach. But if that is the only benefit, the exercises are worth their weight in platinum: a referee's presence will enable the formation of a hierarchy without the destruction of potential working relationships before they start.

Norm formation

The norm formation stage involves the laying down of ground rules. Very often they are built up during the last two stages. There is a continuous process of norm establishment and norm maintenance throughout the life of the team. Group norm formation, if left to its own devices, occurs by a process of gradual accumulation of unspoken, mutually understood rules. The most effective teams develop norms to a level of absolute co-operation, mutual support and total trust, even when there is disagreement. Most teams do not reach this level of norm development.

There is often a period of dissatisfaction in the norm formation stage. The initial level of enthusiasm fades, the normality of the new colleagues becomes evident, and the size of the task becomes apparent.

Coach/mentor input There are many team exercises and games available in books aimed at helping groups develop and establish their norms. Groups can establish their norms fastest by deliberately setting out to do so – that is, the coach will ask the group how they wish to form their norms. (That is a leading question. It assumes the group should make such a deliberate attempt.) There is another appealing advantage: structured norm formation prevents or minimizes the likelihood of inappropriate, unfair, divisive and demotivating norms emerging. Norms that seem almost acceptable if unspoken, when verbalized appear ridiculous and inequitable. 'It's acceptable for John to challenge the chair, but not Jean.' Or 'It's all right for Mary to be late but not Paul.' Verbalizing norms as they are formed, and continually as they evolve, prevents any creeping inequity from growing into a full-blown demotivator.

The coach can also harness the sense of emptiness created by the period of dissatisfaction by encouraging the team to 'fill the gap' by making the development of a shared purpose their interim goal.

EXERCISE

Devise some questions aimed at helping the group see the benefits of deliberately forming their norms. Generate a method to use purpose formation as the focus for norm formation.

Performing

The group tends to carry out its work in the form of a repetitive cycle consisting of four stages:

- Preparing.
- Energizing.
- Activity.
- Rest and recovery.

Preparing

Preparing involves mutual support, nurturing, and sharing. This is the stage when group identity is reinforced and bonds are strengthened.

Coach/mentor input   Ask questions that will help the group focus on these issues.

EXERCISE

What questions will you ask? Compile a list.

Energizing

Energizing involves proposing, debating, challenging, constructive argumentation, planning, decision making, enthusing, and group self-motivation building. In fact the energizing process is a clone of stages three to six of the coaching process, or vice versa. Most of what has been said about stages three to six applies to the process of energizing. The group applies the sequence in an abbreviated way:

3   Assessing the 'here and now'.
4   Deciding on the 'there and then'.
5   Choosing a bridge between 'here and now' and 'there and then'.
6   Building the bridge.

Coach/mentor input   Ask questions which will help the group focus on how to conduct these processes more effectively, and questions aimed at increasing their collective ownership of the processes and their efficiency. Conduct the previous exercise by applying it to this section.

Activity

Activity involves activating plans, implementing decisions and providing mutual support and assistance to progress the objectives.

Coach/mentor input   Help individuals to increase their ownership of and focus on their part of the objectives, and to be responsive to the support needs of other members of the team. Conduct the last exercise.

Rest and recovery

Rest and recovery (R and R is a military term) involves recognizing the end-point, finishing the odd bits and pieces, celebration of the achievement, expressions of gratitude and thanks, or expressing gratitude for the efforts each contributed and taking a break before deciding how to learn from a non-achievement. Like the preparing phase, rest and recovery is important for group bonding.

Coach/mentor input   Ask questions which help the group appreciate the need for and take action towards a distinct period of R and R. That is especially important in a group of high achievers who may wish to start planning their next achievement on completion of the last. Conduct the last exercise.

Evolving and self-regeneration

The group must continually move with the times to survive. It must also be able to continue uninterrupted should any one member need to be replaced for any reason. It usually plans for the succession of its own members in some way.

Coach/mentor input Ask questions aimed at focusing the group on longevity issues. Conduct the last exercise.

Termination

Every group eventually breaks down. Even at a societal level. Few society structures survive more than ten generations. Most companies are lucky to survive one. If a group was set up to achieve a specific project and terminates on completion, there should be provision for the members to celebrate their existence and mourn their loss.

Coach/mentor input The provision of coaching in the termination of a group is unlikely unless it is a project team or some other deliberately short-term team. The most likely scenarios are company reorganization and liquidation. It may come as a surprise to some readers that receivers are not particularly interested in team coaching. Whatever the scenario, the involved coach can ask questions aimed at facilitating emotional expression. Conduct the last exercise. What questions could you ask? Compile a list.

Team analysis

Group performance will now be examined (under the following headings) in more detail by giving an overview of group dynamics, the means by which a coach can analyse what is happening, and the means by which a coach or mentor can facilitate group performance based on the information obtained.

- The power of purpose.
- Purpose evaluation.
- Individual needs.
- Norm analysis.
- Group participation patterns.
- Leadership analysis.
- Role analysis.
- Team self-assessment.
- Checklist of healthy team behaviours.
- Checklist of unhealthy team behaviours.

The power of purpose

In many ineffective groups, purpose is not defined, not understood, not shared, and not achievable because there are no clear targets. For example, a group may be set up to make decisions about something or other but, on closer inspection it may turn out that one, or a small number, of the group make the decisions prior to the meeting and the remainder of the group rubber-stamps the decisions. The role of the coach in this scenario is to alert the group to the long-term consequences of such a situation – more importantly to help them adopt the elements of purpose contained in the list of questions below.

The sad reality is that most employees in most companies all over the world have little idea of their company vision or strategy. Lack of shared purpose is one reason a single entrepreneur can regularly achieve more than the combined resources of huge multi-national organizations. No individual is more effective than a team working well; but most individuals are more effective than all teams working badly. The number of successful entrepreneurs testifies convincingly to the validity of the following: common purpose creates colossal power.

If the team coach does nothing more than create a shared vision, she or he will have given the team a powerful advantage over its competitors.

Purpose evaluation

- What is the declared purpose of the group?
- Judging by their activity, what is the real purpose of the group?
- How much of a gap exists between the last two answers?
- How clear is the purpose of the group?
- Is it defined in terms of scope and outcome objectives?
- Is it clearly defined in terms of the methods used to achieve it?
- Is each member of the group clear about and committed to their role in the objective?
- Do those objectives have clearly defined criteria for achievement?

EXERCISE

Distil the above list of questions into a set of criteria that should be satisfied if a group is deemed to have a clear and specific purpose.

Coach/mentor input Use the conclusions of the last exercise to decide what questions the coach should use to increase the group's focus on, and ownership of, the team's purpose.

EXERCISE

Ask your performers to evaluate the purposes of their current groups.

Individual needs

For successful group participation, each individual member has three needs which must be satisfied:

1 Inclusion.
2 Influence.
3 Affection.

The precise nature of the needs and the route to their satisfaction is as follows.

Inclusion

The individual determines whether they have a sense of similarity to the others, makes the choice to self-include or not, is included by the others or not, is included by the leader individual or not, engages in self-including behaviour or not.

Coach/mentor input   Team inclusion is a process and decision that individuals conduct mainly without support. There are at least two ways that the processes can be conducted with minimal threat to the participants. First, the coach can ensure everyone present knows what is going on. Second, some ice-reaker games can get the process started. How can you ensure that everyone knows what is going on? Should the team be invited to suggest its own ice-breakers?

Influence

The individual has a desire to influence, and needs the leader to respond to their influence attempts; need to be supported in those attempts by at least some of the others; does not feel, justifiably, that their inclusion is dependent on the outcome of the influence attempts. Each member of the group should feel they are empowered by the group and within the group. They should feel that essential resources are available for the pursuit of their part of the common purpose. They should feel that the organizational or team procedures do not block their attempts to achieve on behalf of the team or organization.

EXERCISE

What questions should you ask to determine if each individual's influence needs are sufficiently satisfied to enable performance?

Coach/mentor input   Ask questions of individuals designed to focus their attention on how to increase their influence abilities and skills. And on how the group can optimally empower each member of the team. What questions will achieve this?

Affection

The individual needs to feel liked, experience delight in the achievements of the others in the group and have others delight in their achievements; be willing to express their affection to others; be liked by the leader; like the others in the group; feel a variance of views is valued; and feel that openness and honesty are the norm.

EXERCISE

What questions will you ask to determine if each individual's affection needs are sufficiently satisfied to enable performance?

Coach/mentor input   Ask questions of individuals that require focus on the positive aspects of other group members. Ask questions requiring focus on the achievements of others. In fact asking any question that will facilitate the above affection elements will help. What questions will achieve this?

EXERCISE

What questions should you ask of your team leading performer to help focus their attention on the three individual needs of their team members?

Norm analysis

Every group forms a set of shared and agreed values. In the same way that an organization's recruitment policies are best assessed by the profiles of existing staff, a group's norms are best assessed by what is actually done, not what is said to be done. The norms can be inferred by observing and listening for answers to the following questions:

- What is the apparent priority given to things like facts, statistics, emotional expression, vision, political issues and so on?
- What is the decision-making style? Is it autocratic? Democratic? Laissez-faire? Or anything in between? That is, does the leader appear to conduct a democratic process, but overrules the outcome if it is not as he or she had expected?
- Is the decision-making process consistent? Or does it vary depending on... depending on what?
- How are conflicts handled?
- What is the reaction to lateness, non-achievement, failure to carry out an agreed action, challenging the head of the hierarchy...?

Coach/mentor input   Ask questions designed to have the group think about its norms, to identify those which are empowering and disempowering. Ask the group to choose, to adopt and enact empowering achievement-oriented values.

EXERCISE

Is the pattern of exercises becoming predictable? If so, you will know what comes next: what questions can be asked to help the group analyse its norms and choose to adopt empowering norms?

Group participation patterns

There is considerable overlap between norm analysis and group participation analysis. In fact the actual group participation patterns are revealing of the norms active in any team; they are separate but linked. The participation patterns are to norms what symptoms are to disease: they are the manifestation not the mechanism, the consequence not the cause. Analysing group participation patterns will give the coach a rapid way to understand the function of the group. They are uncovered with the use of appropriate questions:

- Who speaks, when, and in what order?
- What is said and by whom?
- Who are the highest contributors?
- Who are the lowest or non-contributors?
- What kinds of contributions are made by the contributors?
- Who are the most frequent targets of each contributor's offerings?

Coach/mentor input   Ask questions designed to focus the attention of the group on the group participation patterns, and then learn from those observations. Ask questions that enable the group to make inferences about and then improvements of the underlying norms, the decision-making methods, the communication patterns, the conflict resolution methods, the... whatever problems need to be addressed. The coaching input for norms applies from then on. What questions will you ask?

Leadership analysis

Leadership is a funny business. The nominal leader of a group may not be the actual leader. In some countries, the President or Head of State actually functions in that capacity; in others they are figureheads obliged to stay out of management affairs. The same applies in groups of a smaller nature. All types of leaders can be official or unofficial, that is functioning as recognized by some higher authority, or not recognized but operating in that capacity. There are three leadership roles in any group. Some leaders combine the roles and fulfil them, others delegate them by design or default. The roles are:

- The accountable leader.
- The effective leader.
- The emotional leader.

To determine who fills what role, ask yourself or the team members questions like:

- Who will be called to account if things go wrong?
- Who most guides the group in its decision making?
- Who most keeps the discussions on track?
- Who most supports, reassures and encourages members of the group?

EXERCISE

Expand this list of questions.

When the roles are accidentally or deliberately split, much of the performance of the group will be dependent on the co-operation between the three leaders (or two if one person combines two of the roles). Leadership analysis can be extremely difficult. The skilled leader can facilitate a team's self-leadership efforts, to the point where their presence or non-contribution is hardly noticed. The highly skilled, effective leader is invisible except when the group is going off track. That can result in inaccurate judgements being made about the leader's ability. It can be assumed that they are not leading effectively. Their skill can be detected by their strategic overview inputs, by observing the leader making statements that are directed at explaining, analysing the overall process, or by seeing them asking questions that enable the group to realize that a wrong turning has been made – alerting them that a distraction has inappropriately turned into a major issue.

Leadership can also be analysed in terms of the three functions required of it, namely, to fulfil the purpose of the group, to maintain group cohesion and address team development needs, and to satisfy individual needs of team members. A skilled leader blends in and continues working to find the common ground in the three needs. He or she may place different emphasis on one of the three areas for a period to ensure that the total mix remains in a functional balance.

For a greater understanding of leadership generally, and the three needs of leadership specifically, the reader is referred to what, after several years, I still consider the best book on leadership ever written – *Effective Leadership*, by John Adair.

The effectiveness of leadership can obviously be measured in terms of output; it can also be measured in terms of the leadership processes:

- To what extent does the leader ensure fulfilment of the needs of individuals as outlined above?
- To what extent does the leader ensure the group follows its purpose?
- To what extent does the leader satisfy the needs of the group?

Coach/mentor input   Ask questions aimed at focusing the group's attention on the way it leads itself, at raising awareness of the assignment of the three leadership roles, at having the group decide how best to lead itself. Ask questions of the leader(s) aimed at focusing their attention on how they can satisfy the three needs of the team, the individual, and the objective more effectively. In what ways will you ask those questions? Compile a list.

Role analysis

There is a large number of roles that could be played in any team other than the constructive, supportive, dedicated team member, or one of the three leadership roles. Some of the more common are The Scapegoat, The Rebel,

Role analysis

The Abominable No Man/Person, The Yes Person, The Bully, The Pedant, The Critic, The Timekeeper, The Referee/Umpire, The Saint.

The roles, and more than one may be adopted per person, are best analysed by examining actual behaviour as opposed to the claimed behaviour of team members. The most common behaviours in meetings follow, as does the next exercise.

EXERCISE

Match each of the behaviours in the list below to the most appropriate role above.

EXERCISE

Organize the following behaviours into two types: empowering and constructive, and disempowering and destructive. Then further break down the empowering and constructive team behaviours into three categories: those that best satisfy individual needs; group functioning and cohesion needs; and task/purpose achievement needs.

Some role-determined team behaviours

- *Bringing in*: Involving another member of the team, inviting their contribution.
- *Building on*: Taking a contribution made by another and enhancing it.
- *Stimulating*: Presenting a statement or question aimed at starting team thinking about an issue.

- *Proposing*: Putting forward a proposal of some kind.
- *Accepting person, not idea*: Where an idea is disagreed with, but the person and their offering are accepted.
- *Inclusion*: Including a person's contribution in the developing proposal.
- *Clarifying*: Seeking elaboration or explanation of a contribution.
- *Simplifying*: Taking a complex contribution and distilling its essence.
- *Enlivening*: Making a good idea, badly presented, more lively and therefore acceptable.
- *Initiating*: Proposing without the need for a contribution, starting or re-starting the ball rolling.
- *Testing understanding*: Asking questions to determine the level of individual or shared understanding.
- *Consensus testing*: Asking questions to find out what the level of consensus for any item may be.
- *Information seeking*: Obvious.
- *Information provision*: Obvious.
- *Summarizing*: Providing frequent summations of the proceedings so far; keeps the team on track.
- *Unifying*: Making a statement; asking a question; reminding the team of common purpose.
- *Expressing emotions*: Expressing the feelings of the team in response to any issue.
- *Harmonizing*: Reconciling or demonstrating the common ground between members in dispute.
- *Compromising*: Accepting/encouraging acceptance of a non-ideal solution to make some progress.
- *Gatekeeping*: Controlling who contributes next in discussions.
- *Supporting*: Offering support to a person or a position.
- *Habitual supporting*: Offering support to a person whatever they suggest.
- *Blocking out*: Refusing to discuss an issue.
- *Shutting out*: Responding to a question aimed at someone else.
- *Picking*: Taking major issue with someone over a tiny detail.
- *Hurrying*: Either finishing others' sentences, or expressing impatience as the point develops.
- *Disagreeing*: Taking issue with a point made.
- *Habitual disagreeing*: The standard response to all suggestions is 'No'.
- *Attacking*: Attacking an idea is rarely genuine; it is more usually a cover for personal attack.
- *Habitual attacking*: Using the slightest provocation to attack weaker members of the group.
- *Defending*: Responding to an attack by accepting, or not pointing out the personal element.
- *Scapegoating*: Consistently blaming one person for all that goes wrong, or could have gone wrong.
- *Knee-jerk objecting*: Consistently taking issue with any and every decision taken by the group.

- *Burden sharing*:   Agreeing to share others' responsibilities.
- *Burden shifting*:   Refusing to accept responsibility, especially when blame is involved.

EXERCISE

What could you add to this list?

Coach/mentor input   Ask questions of those team members who engage in disempowering or destructive behaviours, questions which are aimed at, first, helping them to become aware of such behaviours, and second, aware of the consequences of those behaviours. It is better to help the maladaptive performer see the consequences of their behaviour and to develop their own motivation for change than to point them out. The coach should also ask questions aimed at encouraging others to resist the impact of inappropriate or destructive team behaviours in others. Further questions can be asked of the group to encourage them to ask questions aimed at helping the maladaptive team member become aware, and take responsibility for, their behaviour.

EXERCISE

How can you encourage the further development of constructive team-role behaviours?

Health checklists

The atmosphere during a team's operations is a very accurate predictor of the

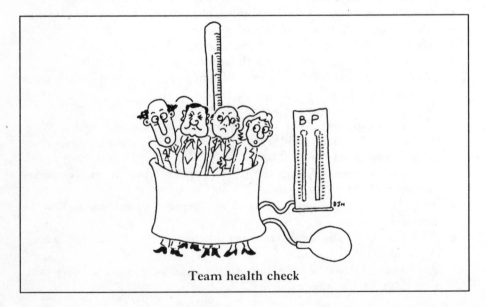

Team health check

health of its functioning. Below are two lists, one of healthy team behaviours and the other a list of terminal symptoms.

Checklist of healthy team behaviours

- Common purpose.
- Established organizational structure.
- Membership criteria agreed.
- Continuity of group.
- Growth and adaptability.
- Free from cliques.
- Individual freedom and acceptance.
- Willingness to accept discontentment.
- Willingness to resolve conflict internally.
- Decision-making methods agreed and flexible.
- Absolute co-operation with, and faith in, team.
- Mutual support, acceptance and recognition.
- Group supports individuals, individuals support group.
- Group is mostly self-leading.

Checklist of unhealthy team behaviours

- Scapegoating.
- Excessive compliance.
- Personality clashes.
- Destructive competition and conflict.
- Politics comes before purpose.
- Apathy, lethargy.
- Inappropriate dominance by clique.
- Group irresponsibility.
- Disorganized, moving structure.
- Risky shift (a group taking a decision more risky than any individual in the group would take alone).
- Reduced commitment and persistence.
- Creativity stifled.
- Individuality stifled.

Applying the coaching sequence to teams

Now let us turn our attention to applying the seven-stage coaching model outlined earlier (page 39) for individual coaching to a team setting.

Assessing the team here and now

The toughest part of assessing teams is getting the members to be honest. In the same way that 98 per cent of drivers think they are good drivers, 99 per cent of team members think their team is the best and they're just waiting for the chance to prove it. Ho, hum! Asking the team if it functions well is like asking the fox if it guards the hen-house well. It will: it won't let a single chicken escape! So, how can you obtain an assessment? By asking the team to compare its results against quantitative measures, and by self-assessment aimed at detached analysis.

Assessing the team

Team assessment

Compare the team's performance to that of other teams, departments or industries. This sounds remarkably easy, and it is for the top team, the board of directors; financial and other performance factors like labour cost, return per employee and so on are readily available. For non-top teams the objective performance figures are a little harder to obtain. They can be deduced by breaking down the elements of the company's overall performance into departmental contributions. For instance the performance of the finance department can be assessed by comparing the ratio of finance labour costs to total expenditure or to total labour costs against another company's performance on the same ratio.

If the group decides that they will assess themselves on objective measures, they should decide what measures and how to compile them. The performance of every group can be measured, despite what some will try to tell you. For some, like public sector employees, it may be harder to measure performance but 'harder' is no excuse not to. On the contrary, 'harder' is even more reason performance should be measured: if it is difficult to quantify then there is more scope for poor performance to go undetected, and universal experience of human nature is that what is inspected is to be expected – and what is ignored will be neglected. Excellent performance will also go undetected, with the consequence that there can be no rational basis for deciding who is performing well enough to be likely promotion or bonus material. This begs the question: how do public sector bodies which resist performance assessment make promotion decisions? It can't be on the basis of performance because they tell us that can't be measured! I can hear alarm bells ringing. Oh, it's the bullshit detector going off again.

If the team resists quantitative performance assessment it is the coach's responsibility to diplomatically raise awareness and seek team ownership of the notion: the only way to improve is to know how well they are doing, what their starting points are and what their weaknesses are. The only way to have that accuracy of information about a group is to use impartial assessment measures. Plan how you would help the group arrive at, endorse and act on that view.

Team self-assessment

On what bases should a team assess its own effectiveness? The two most frequent subjects for assessment are process and outcome. Outcome self-assessment involves examining the perceived achievements of the group in numerical terms along various, not quite objective, dimensions – 'not quite objective' because the means of measuring the performances are entirely within the team's control, or within individual members' control. There may be the occasional group or group member who will try to pass off self-assessment measures as quantitative assessment data. Of course this is very rare(?) and in your entire coaching career you will be most unlikely to witness this in business in or politics! How will you help the group to see the self-defeating consequences of pretending they are doing well by reference to supposedly impartial favourable data?

Outcome self-assessment   The specific outcome of each group will vary depending on its purpose, industry type, economic cycle and so on. In principle each group can assess its outcomes on the following bases:

- Ratio of objectives set to objectives achieved.
- Ratio of objectives achieved on time to objectives achieved late.
- Achievement of objectives set: the percentage of objectives completed totally, satisfactorily, barely.
- Initiative: number of assignments undertaken by group not prompted by higher or lower teams.
- Problem anticipation: number of problems anticipated and pre-resolved to number not anticipated.
- Crisis management performance: time elapsed

  - from point of crisis to point of detection.
  - from detection to point of action.
  - from first action to successful resolution.

EXERCISE

What other general outcome measures could be made?

Process self-assessment   The process of each meeting will be determined by the purpose. That is rather simplistic: process is determined by the current priorities of the team in terms of group, task and individual purposes. Whatever the purpose, the efficiency with which the process is carried out can be assessed. Coaching a team involves encouraging the members to improve their team activity effectiveness. The best way to do that is to monitor whatever measures would be constructive. For instance

- Number of meetings.
- Time taken to reach decisions.
- Number of decisions per meeting.
- Number of issues covered per meeting.
- Information exchanged.
- Length of meetings.
- Number of ideas generated during meeting.
- Percentage of time wasted, not concerned with process or outcome planning.
- Number of irrelevant or side issue discussions.
- Percentage of attendances.
- Punctuality of attenders.
- Number of meetings per outcome achievement.
- Number of action points/objectives set per meeting.
- Percentage of action points from previous meetings completed.
- Percentage input per attender per meeting.
- Agenda set at conclusion of previous meeting.
- Minutes available how many days after meetings?
- Number of conflicts.
- Number of conflicts resolved by mutual consent.
- Number of conflicts 'resolved' by agreeing to disagree.

EXERCISE

What other general process measures could be made?

Coaching for team cohesion

Some trite phrases sum up the best courses of action in team coaching. One in particular works well: 'People who play together stay together'. They stay together not just in terms of proximity but mentally too. Suggest and discuss the possibility of the team members having some kind of social time together. The bonding process would also be helped if they engage in some kind of group

Coaching for team cohesion

learning experience, or in some kind of charity event during which they could work together for the benefit of others.

At some stage in team coaching, the group should have a chance to learn about group functioning, particularly about healthy and unhealthy group behaviours. If the whole team knows the most effective team-process behaviours, they will subtly expect each other to behave in those ways. Since we know people tend to rise to fulfil high expectations, the whole team performance can be enhanced by virtue of mere common knowledge and shared expectation. What can you ask to help teams want to explore effective team processes with you?

Coaching the organization

The most effective way to achieve any change in an organization is from the top down. To set up a coaching culture in the whole organization the top team should set an example, and set the precedent. Even if there is no systematic attempt to introduce or push coaching company-wide, there will probably be a natural spreading of coaching. There will be an active 'pull' by staff as a result of the trickle-down and boss-mimicking effects. Corporate culture reflects, and often exactly mirrors, the culture displayed by the top team. What the team above or the top team has, everybody wants. Resistance to coaching is likely to be minimal under those circumstances. How can you maximize the appeal of coaching as adopted by the top team?

An organization can also be encouraged to introduce coaching by virtue of the 'critical mass' effect: where sufficient people in the organization, at whatever level, engage in coaching or mentoring, whether or not with official approval, the whole organization will eventually adopt the practice. If the top team have not yet realized the benefits available from treating staff as valuable intellectual resources, you can implement coaching in your own department. Others will gradually notice the results obtained and want to copy you. The process will eventually be so widespread it will achieve a critical mass and become a *de facto* policy, whatever the top team says.

Coaching individual team members

We have noted in passing, but not stated explicitly, the goals of coaching teams as they apply to the individual. There are two distinct purposes in coaching individual team members:

1 To improve their team-oriented achievement behaviour. This might include:

  - Team participation skills – influence skills, presentation, argumentation, negotiation, assertiveness – and so on.
  - Personal paradigm analysis in relation to the team, an analysis of their empowering and disempowering beliefs vis-à-vis the team.
  - An analysis of the individual's motivations toward the team. People at different stages in the personal motivational needs hierarchy will be differently motivated towards the group.

  Someone whose security is under threat as a result of marital problems will be unlikely to be optimally motivated towards the team, unless they then seek companionship in the team. Someone who is already a successful member of one team that satisfies all their needs may be involved in a second team in body and mind, but not in spirit. Suffice to say that the coach should explore and seek ways of enhancing motivation with the individual team member.

2 To improve individuals' role performances so that their contribution to the team is greater. Improving the performance of individual team members is achieved using the same process in teams as is used in individual coaching/mentoring. That is, their individual contribution to the team effort is coached as if it were an individual effort.

EXERCISE

At what stage in the team-coaching process should the coaching objectives regarding each individual be made clear?

Coaching the team to coach the individual members of the team

The ultimate level of team functioning is total co-operation. Teams having reached this ideal coach themselves and their individual members. One of the devices that can be used to reach this level of co-operation is to ask each member of the team to rate themselves on how they think they have performed in terms of their role, and to specify where they can improve. The team then offers honest, constructive feedback, support, and advice on the self-rating and the proposed improvement methods. The beauty of this system is that everyone can help everyone else. A genuine air of mutual support develops quickly because of the trust necessary to conduct the exercise without injuring the feelings of others. One will, after all, be next on the chopping block if one has not been helpful and supportive!

The coach has at least two choices with such self-coaching devices. He or she can introduce self-coaching methods when the team is functioning well and is ready for self-coaching, or introduce self-coaching as a rapid way of bringing the team to the highest levels of co-operation.

EXERCISE

By drawing on the material covered so far, what other team self-coaching devices can you pull together? Clue: any suggested team coaching question can be turned into a team self-coaching method.

Coaching logistics

If you remember our discussion on individual coaching, we emphatically stated that observation and analysis ought to be two separate processes. The same applies to team coaching. There should be separate meetings for the purposes of coaching (analysis) and group performance (observation). That is not to say the coach should not be present. He or she can obtain the most accurate observational information about team functioning from meetings where performance is the purpose. Meetings where coaching is the purpose are likely to encourage members to be on their best team behaviour, thereby making analysis of the process by the coach more difficult. Separate coaching meetings will address the issues of performance raised in this chapter, and should be complemented by individual meetings for the purpose mentioned above.

EXERCISE

How frequently should coaching meetings be held? How frequently should individual coaching sessions with team members be held? What factors should you consider in answering the previous two questions?

Concluding comments and summary

Coaches and mentors can help team performance in several ways:

- By helping the formation of the team to be as beneficial as possible for future working relationships.

- By helping individuals fit into the team.
- By helping the team to analyse, understand and improve its own functioning.
- By helping individuals to support the team and the team to support its members.
- By helping the team to adopt the characteristics and sense of direction necessary for high achievement.
- By helping individual members perform as effectively as possible in their individual contributions to the team effort.

In principle the coaching or mentoring of teams follows the same sequence of events as coaching an individual performer. The main difference is the number of voices with which the performer speaks.

Part III

Dealing with problems

10

PEOPLE PROBLEMS

Coaching and mentoring for people problems involves the following:

- People problem knowledge.
- Defining people problems.
- Coachable problems.
- Stress, eustress, causes, handling it, preventing it.
- Counselling skills.

People problem knowledge

Do you think more coaching and mentoring time will be taken up with planning achievements, helping performers acquire skills, or sorting out problems and barriers? Yes, that's right: problems – or more accurately helping your performers to sort out problems. Since that is the case, you might reasonably assume that some background knowledge of people problems will be useful.

Defining people problems

What are 'people problems'? The term seems user-defined and in the workplace context can include:

- A belief that an associate is under-performing or is being disruptive or difficult.
- Being disappointed with someone's actions.
- Finding someone's actions inexplicable.
- Finding their actions explicable but unacceptable.
- Stress-related behaviours and responses.
- Failing to meet deadlines.
- Failure to negotiate extensions on deadlines despite it being obvious to all that the deadline will be missed.
- Failure to put in the extra effort required to meet a deadline.
- Producing substandard work.

- Being inconsistent and unreliable.
- Resisting change, even change to the benefit of the resistor.
- Claiming credit for others' achievements.
- Being pedantic.
- Refusing to attend to detail.
- Being passive or aggressive.
- Failing to communicate.
- Being spiteful.
- Being too demanding.
- Covering up mistakes.
- Blaming others for mistakes.
- Being too reactive.
- Being under-responsive.

EXERCISE

Add your most frequent experience of people problems to this list.

In fact anything one person does not like about another can be perceived as a people problem. Often it will turn out to be the person making the complaint who has the problem; at the very least they seem unable to control what they think, feel or do in relation to the stated source of aggravation.

Coachable problems

The above are coachable. Problems with their foundations in mental or physical ill health or in addiction should not be addressed by the coach other than to alert those who need to know, that is, assuming that such a disclosure would not breach the confidentiality arrangement with the performer. As a coach or mentor, your reputation and trustworthiness will be in tatters if you breach confidentiality, even once; it always seems to get out. The most appropriate course of action for the uncoachable problems is to ask questions that will help the performer (or non-performer in this situation) to see the benefits of addressing and solving the problem of their own accord before its continuance leads to dismissal or worse. However, the law in many countries is based on the principle that statutory intervention is required if someone's behaviour or likely behaviour is seriously harmful to themselves or others. You may, in such rare circumstances, be helping the person by breaking their confidence. The law in many countries makes it illegal for individuals to not immediately pass on information about actual or possible criminal activities received in the course of a professional and otherwise confidential meeting. Faced with such a dilemma, a coach or mentor should consult their company lawyer.

But how can a non-physician, psychiatrist, or addiction specialist know what they are dealing with? You can't, and that is exactly the point: if the problem is beyond your understanding in your capacity as coach or mentor, it is a good indication that other courses of action are required. Be cautious of using any knowledge you may have acquired in these fields. If you overstep the bounds of the coaching relationship and start dabbling in 'therapy' (however meaningless that may be) you leave yourself open to all sorts of accusations.

Now back to those areas in which we can offer assistance.

Stress

Next to AIDS, cancer and heart disease, probably the most talked about malady of the late twentieth century is stress. A book on coaching and mentoring without a section on how to coach stress problems is simply inconceivable. So here goes.

Stress, eustress, control and causes

What is stress? Perhaps it can best be defined in terms of what effect it has. There is a fairly wide consensus that it costs about 10 per cent of the gross national product of most western economies. In the UK alone around 90 million working days a year are lost. Economies as a whole bear the cost, but companies specifically are hit hardest. To some extent the cost may be self-inflicted.

Companies are increasingly finding themselves held liable for causing their employees stress. At time of writing, industrial stress injury claims are starting to gather pace; large sums of money have been paid to employees emotionally damaged by stress factors in their workplace. Employers in some parts of the world are expected to provide a safe workplace both physically and mentally. Failure to do so can be a costly oversight.

EXERCISE

What do you, your performers, and your staff find stressful in your workplace?

That's the picture on a macro scale, what of the micro? For the individual, stress is a subjective experience with physical manifestations. While everyone instinctively knows what it feels like, stress is very hard to define for the purposes of communication. Does the following definition work? 'Stress is an unwelcome and unpleasant mental, emotional or physical strain or tension'. Some stress can be very pleasant and highly exciting, a roller-coaster ride for instance. Another complementary term is required: eustress, that is, stress which is welcome, desired or even enjoyed. In terms of the superficial measurable reactions, stress and eustress are indistinguishable. But inside, subjectively, one feels light while the other feels heavy. The same external experience can be perceived by two people entirely differently. One may experience stress while the other thrills in eustress. The differentiating factor seems to be 'control'.

People at high levels in organizations experience and report less stress than those in lower positions. The higher ranking personnel have more control over their environments, actions and outcomes. The lowest levels in most organizations have least control and greatest stress. Stress in society seems to mirror commercial stress. The most successful entrepreneurs thrive in environments that would worry many people to death, yet they report enjoying their hectic lifestyles. By stark contrast, those with least control – unemployed unskilled workers – report very high degrees of stress. At less extreme points there is a marked difference in the stress level between employees of small private sector companies and large, public sector organizations as measured by the level of absenteeism. Even when the small private companies are operating in the same industries, or in direct competition with the public sector employees, there is a lower rate of stress, a lower rate of absenteeism. The issue again – control.

EXERCISE

When have you been at your most stressed? Was it when you had least control? Those factors you identified in the last exercise, were they those which caused most stress, the ones you had least control over?

Causes

So what are the specific causes of stress? 'Control' is not the only factor involved. Stress occurs when there is a mismatch between the challenge faced by that individual and their perceived ability to cope. That is, stress will occur if the performer is either over-stretched or under-stretched. The perceived ability to cope can be affected by many factors: belief system, the expectations of superiors, and so on. A performer can become completely burned out through too much challenge or, perhaps surprisingly, too little. Potentially extremely high achievers can fail to cope with trivial demands because of long-term under-stimulation, long-term non-availability of serious challenges to their abilities. Many people who go on to amazing successes have failed dramatically in roles in which it would be assumed someone of such stature should have succeeded.

EXERCISE

Ask yourself and your performers when you/they have failed at something incredibly easy for them.

Symptoms and stages

As you will see from the graph opposite, there are six stages in which stress can be thought of as having an effect on performance. (Have you ever noticed that when people like me present any explanation of any phenomenon it

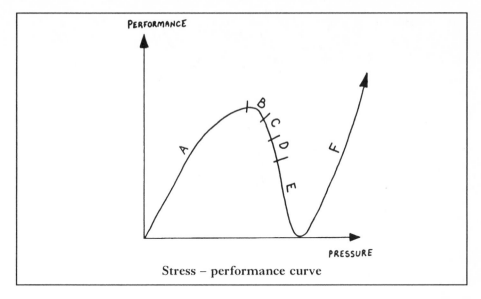

Stress – performance curve

conveniently occurs in stages, usually between three and seven? Ever wondered why?)

In stage A the performer feels a sense of excitement and challenge and responds favourably to pressure whether it is internally or externally applied. Stage A is normally experienced as eustress, it's the roller-coaster ride of the business world. Ask your performer to describe what stage A feels like so they will be more aware of when they are moving out of it.

In stage B the performer is energetic, enthusiastic, over-stretched and having doubts about coping while still managing to do so. The performer and coach can be alerted to problems at this stage by observing expressions of frustration with work of a standard that is more than satisfactory; refusal or reluctance to take time off; apparently too busy, but unable to refuse more work; less time being spent with hobbies, friends and family; and what time is spent with them is overshadowed by the ever-presence of the work taken home.

EXERCISE

What will you ask performers to increase their awareness of their stress levels if they look as though they have entered this stage?

In stage C achievers start to blame others, experience feelings of fatigue, anxiety, irritability and of being in a rut. The alarm signals are the expression of any of the items from the list just given, plus poor time management, 'grasshopper activity' (jumping from one job to another, trying to get them all done but completing few or none), working long unproductive hours, continuing to make too many commitments.

Grasshopper activity

EXERCISE

As the previous exercise.

In stage D the performer is discontented, angry, resentful, apathetic, bitter, feeling guilty, losing self-respect and showing signs of emotional distance. The alarm signals are manifestations of the points just made, and particularly the expression of lowering commitment to work and family, extremity in positions taken, extreme and visible fatigue, low quality of life, and taking themselves far, far too seriously. The time for asking questions to raise awareness is probably past. The cold hard realities of the situation must be pointed out in as compassionate a way as possible. How can you do so?

In stage E the non-achiever has totally lost their grip: they are withdrawn, in much emotional pain, experiencing extreme feelings of personal failure, and probably well down the road to developing some form of physical or mental illness. In short, they are burned out. The identifying signals are alcohol or other substance abuse, regular physical illness, voluntary and involuntary isolation from previous colleagues, reluctance or outright refusal to communicate and, most obviously, high absenteeism. Another sign is panic paralysis. Panic paralysis is often seen in companies that are having difficulty. The senior management are so stressed out, they can see no way of solving the situation. Instead of seeking ways of finding solutions, they do nothing. It is quite common for receivers or liquidators to go into a company and find months of unopened communications, bills, orders and so on.

EXERCISE

What can you do to encourage communication? Ask questions? If

Stage E

they have entered panic paralysis, an astute and detailed analysis of their predicament is the last thing you can expect in response to a probing question. Assuming you are coaching such a person, how will you explain what has happened to them?

In stage F a most peculiar phenomenon can occur, namely, if some short-term life-threatening event occurs – perhaps a car crash or a serious accident of some sort – the performer can perform at remarkably high levels, where the word 'superhuman' is not an exaggeration. It is almost as though, for the performer,

Stage F

danger and personal risk are not an issue. Perhaps they see a quick and easy route back to self-control, success and self-respect and are prepared to risk everything to achieve it rather than continue in the burned-out state. For other people, having been through the burn-out mill is not a requirement to reach stage F; some people simply don't perform at all until the rewards, pressure or stakes are amazingly high. Then, and only then, do these people achieve at an incredible level.

Handling it, preventing it

There are numerous causes of stress which are totally outside our control: death, ageing, the meaning of life's irresolvables, government policies, all forms of taxation, cultural expectations, prejudices, crime, local government and other regulatory interference, organization problems, interpersonal problems, and so on. All are out of our control, or are they? Is it empowering to assume they are out of our control? No! They may be out of our control in terms of how we can change them, but not in terms of how we process them, what and how we choose to think about them – that is if we choose to think about them at all. So what is an empowering way to think about the factors that could cause you and your performers stress?

1   Ignore, don't think about, or have someone else think about those stressors you can't control.
2   Choose to take absolute and total responsibility for those things you *can* control which are: your beliefs, thoughts, attitudes and behaviours.
3   Choose to think, feel and behave in ways that will increase, reduce or maintain your stress (eustress) level at the point that reflects your performance aspirations.
4   If your aspirations are too high or too low and are causing stress, either alter the aspiration or acquire better coping skills.

And what can be done to help your stressed performers or subordinates?

5   Give your stressed subordinates 'time out'.
6   Discuss a change of job function.
7   If the stress is caused by under-stimulation, explore the creation of new challenges.
8   Give them more control over targets and resources (but don't let 'not coping' become a method for your subordinates to coerce you into giving them their way).

That makes stress management sound simple. It is simple: stress like everything in life (finance, emotions...) is either controlled by you or will control you. A clear unambiguous choice. Those are the empowering thoughts behind stress management. What actions are available?

The actions implied in the factors listed under The principles of performance and achievement (pages 10–16) can be used by you and your performers. They are summarized as follows:

- Head–on stress management.
- R and R (again).
- Substitution and distraction.
- Self-pampering.
- Emotional release.
- Emotional self-management.

Head-on stress management

View stress as any other problem you choose to solve. A sequence of decisions leads to a resolution:

1   Become aware of and acknowledge the existence of stress as a problem.
2   Decide to take control of and responsibility for the stress problem.
3   Define and clarify the exact nature of the stress.
4   Identify and verify the causes (internal and external).
5   Explore possible solutions (those following this paragraph).
6   Decide what defines an acceptable solution.
7   Evaluate the alternatives; choose a solution to the stress.
8   Devise and implement the stress-busting action plan.

The hardest part of managing stress, like life's other problems, is recognizing it, admitting it, and taking responsibility for it. Once that is done, the rest is a mere formality. Perhaps I overstate the case slightly, but one must be allowed a little exaggeration for the purposes of explanation!

EXERCISE

What questions can you ask to help your stressed performer to see how to go about solving their stress difficulties as they would any other business problem, that will facilitate awareness of their stress if they haven't admitted it to themselves yet?

R and R options

Stress is frequently caused by insufficient rest and recreation. R and R is also a great preventer of stress. Here are some issues you could explore with your performer to establish in their minds whether or not they are firing on all cylinders in their rest and recreation engine.

What are they doing for their rest and recreation? How often do they engage in R and R? How often during the working day do they take a break? Do they really relax during their breaks or do they spend them chatting to colleagues? Do they know how to totally relax their body? Are they aware of how to use the body relaxation methods available?

R and R options

Several methods are available, for instance, starting at the neck and working down to the feet, gradually tense and relax each major muscle group in sequence: neck, tense and relax shoulders; shrug up and relax, shrug forward and relax, shrug back and relax, shrug down and relax, and so on down the arms, forearms, hands, abdomen, buttocks, thighs, calves, ankles, and feet.

How often during the day do they take a micro break, a 15- to 30-second pause during which they take slow deep breaths, change body position, look at something else, take a short walk round the office? How well do they plan natural breaks into their work? To what extent do they recognize the perform-ance enhancement effects of a short break?

Do they accept that while relaxation may take some time, it saves time because of the increased efficiency and energy levels which are maintained through regular breaks? Ask them what benefits they think can be had from regular breaks.

EXERCISE

Some of these questions have deliberately been phrased in a way that breaks our established guidelines. Decide which they are and then re-phrase appropriately.

Substitution and distraction

Many people cope with their very high-stress jobs by engaging in high-risk activities. The rationale is that by engaging in high-risk, high-stress pastimes, there is little possibility of being able to think about the stresses of their working roles. They block out high stress with a different but even greater stress. The distraction needn't be outright suicidal, dangerous or illegal, but every so often high-level politicians are found engaging in activities that seem so risky to their careers as to be almost stupid. To them it is not stupid. On the contrary, it may be one of only a few ways of dealing with such pressure. Taking and managing such extreme risks makes the pressure of the job seem more manageable in comparison. What stress distractions could you safely admit to having engaged in? This method doesn't work for everyone, but your performer would be best served by exploring the more sensible distraction options available.

Self-pampering and self-enhancement

Another way to cope with stress is to engage in self-pampering. Take a hot bubble bath, have a massage, sauna, manicure, pedicure, have your hair re-styled, or get fitted for a new hairpiece, buy some new clothes, have clothes tailor-made, have some off-the-peg clothes altered to suit you... in other words, do something that has no purpose other than to indulge yourself.

Self-pampering

EXERCISE

Ask your performer when they last indulged themselves. How often do they engage in activities purely for the pleasure they give?

Emotional release

What does your performer do as a means of emotional release? Do they engage in art, poetry, reading, writing, music, acting, comedy, building or making things, working out? Are their emotional release patterns constructive? (Not 'constructive' in the sense of having a measurable production outcome, but constructive in the sense of not having a destructive effect on themselves or others.) How regularly do they engage in emotional release?

EXERCISE

Compile a list of as many emotional release options as you can think of in ten minutes.

Emotional self-management

As you've probably gathered by now, I advocate thought and belief control for emotional and behavioural self-management. For those not willing to be so coldly rationalistic, there are other ways. As you could, no doubt, anticipate, the method can be expressed in five neat and tidy little stages.

1 Temporary containment.
2 Acknowledgement and recognition.
3 Expression.
4 Release.
5 Re-direction.

Temporary containment   There are numerous self-containment methods which can be learned and improved (try adding to this list):

- Good old fashioned 'tongue biting' is still widely practised, good news for oral surgeons and dentists everywhere.
- Deep breathing, meditation and relaxation techniques. Caution should be exercised using this method; breaking into your favourite mantra during a run-in with your CEO may dent your credibility slightly!
- The chicken reaction: get out of the situation before you say something you'd regret. Clucking all the way to the door is not advised, but collecting yourself on the other side of it is.
- The boxer's side-step: move out of hitting range, change the subject to something you feel more comfortable with for long enough to compose yourself, then pummel the issue into throwing in the towel.
- Roses in horse dung: concentrate on the positive smells (aspects) no matter how overpowering the surrounding odour.

Acknowledgement and recognition   Having contained your emotions, move on to the next stage. Accept that emotions are natural and assume that the best way to manage them is to be honest with yourself; admit you have them. Become aware of how your emotions affect yourself and your performers. Encourage your performers to observe the effects their emotions have on their behaviour.

Emotional expression 'You foul-mouthed, pickle-brained, half-witted, loathsome offspring of a camel turd' is not quite what we have in mind! (Even if it is true!) The reader in doubt is referred to the section on diplomacy (page 132). Practise expressing your emotions with others; express the positive feeling first, and as you get to know the person better, tell them if you feel uncomfortable with their current behaviour. If you feel troubled, tell someone; don't require them to help (unless that is what you want). Just ask them to listen, to hear you out. Show interest in how other people feel. Listen to them, and they'll probably want to listen to you too. Develop a mutual confiding relationship with another person.

EXERCISE

What exercises can you ask your performers to do to enhance their emotional expression capabilities?

Release   This part is good. It's a licence to behave like a spoiled brat and be praised for it! Scream and scream and scream until you're sick! Kick, shout, punch, bite, tear, smash and otherwise go berserk. Do all of these things and more – in private, on your own, preferably in a padded cell, and to some safe inanimate object which is owned by you and unlikely to retaliate. It feels wonderful! The sound of smashing crockery is music to frustrated or angry ears. If by chance you are caught behaving in this way, there's no use blaming me. I'll say it was a printing error and suggest you be contained for your own safety!

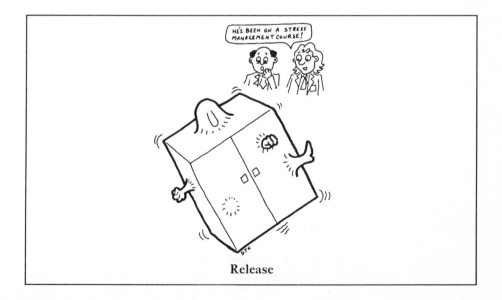

Release

Ask your performers to compile a list of safe ways of releasing stress, frustration and anger with the intensity and satisfaction suggested above.

Re-direction   Some people choose to harness their stress and frustrations by re-directing them. Some of the world's best creative works owe their existence to talented people using this method. Ultra-high achievers seem able to convert their stresses into action. Instead of worrying about producing something on time, they use their anxiety to motivate their production effort. Work stress is not the antidote to work stress for everybody. Outside of work, some are prolific writers, others create music, some direct their frustrations into sport. It has been suggested that the reason there are a disproportionate number of successful black athletes in some western countries is a manifestation of racial prejudice in which the victims re-direct their frustrations and energies into something which secures the indisputable recognition of their performance.

EXERCISE

Ask your performer how they could re-direct their stresses in such a way that it helps their performance.

Counselling skills

What are counselling skills? Do you need to spend years in training? The shocking answer is NO! There are numerous studies which show that untrained counsellors (and other psycho-blah-blah-ists) are just as effective as, and totally indistinguishable in practice from, their trained counterparts. Some studies have actually found that those on the receiving end of counselling (unknowingly) prefer the supposedly untrained counsellors and may in fact benefit more from such people. Shock! Horror!

What has this to do with coaching? Well, remember we talked about 'the technically ignorant coach' doing a better coaching job than the 'expert in the field coach' because they are forced to focus on the performer and not the performance? Yes? Well, the same seems to apply to counselling. The fact that you know little about counselling should not put you off counselling in the workplace; it should encourage you. It is likely that you'll do as good a job, if not better, than the so-called professionals. You've already had a lifetime's experience in the field, actually practising your counselling skills with friends, relatives, lovers, parents, children (shall I go on?), work colleagues, sports colleagues, social colleagues...

With skills picked up over such a long period and practised so regularly, there is little need to understand theory. Most well-adjusted people have a pre-articulate, high-level, automatic expertise in counselling. It could be that formal training in counselling-related fields interferes with automatic skills to the point of reducing effective performance below the level of the supposedly untrained. So, if you want to maintain your skills, I suggest you skip the remainder of this section. As a qualified psychologist and psychotherapist, it's already far too late for me!

I am not saying that counselling provides no benefit – quite the contrary. We know that counselling within three days of a trauma can be extremely effective in preventing the later emergence of post-traumatic stress disorder. (Incidentally, that is the first firm finding of benefit directly attributable to counselling.) If you were a 'counselling professional' how would you present that information? 'Professional counselling help is essential for preventing post-traumatic stress disorder. Buy my services today.' Yes? Yes! But what you won't be told is that PTSD can be prevented by virtually any form of counselling provided by virtually anybody. The essential ingredient is that the victim has a chance to express their feelings and explore the event with a supportive other person, preferably someone known, trusted and respected, and ideally, someone who has had a similar experience and coped successfully.

There are eight predictors of counselling success; you might recognize them from elsewhere. If you provide each of the eight in some way, you will function as an effective counsellor. 'Some way' is used deliberately; there are more than 250 approaches to counselling taught world-wide. All claim some scientific evidence for success. The obvious explanation for different methods being equally effective is that the methods used are irrelevant; what matters is not what is different about them but what they have in common. The following are the relevant common factors:

1   Give the performer support and reassurance.
2   Have a good relationship with the performer (see the Rapport creation section, page 53).
3   Be interested, genuinely listen to the performer, pass no judgement. (See the Listening skills section, page 57).
4   Provide them with a plausible explanation for what has happened and, if asked, a feasible solution.
5   Give them an opportunity to express their emotions (see the stress management section, pages 174–180).
6   Give them an opportunity to experience success within your interaction to boost their confidence.
7   Encourage the adoption of empowering beliefs, attitudes and behaviours.
8   And most of all, give the performer a sense of positive expectation and hope.

EXERCISE

Invest some time in working out how you should provide each of the eight ingredients. You already have all the information in this book to do so.

Seriously valuable tip: do not slip into 'counsellor's voice'. That's the warm, syrupy 'I really relate to you', soft, patronizing, gooey, 'I'm so sorry, my dear' voice which induces instant and prolonged nausea in everyone this side of the Milky Way. A more effective communication barrier has yet to be invented.

Concluding comments and summary

Both coach and mentor will be confronted by a large number of people problems as part of their roles. Many problems will be everyday disputes between members of staff; some will be more serious than others. The really serious problems should be left to those who specialize in those areas. However, since most successful people in business have developed highly sophisticated people skills, they usually have first-rate counselling skills without even knowing it. Providing good counselling for performers is a simple task which can be learned from scratch (if it needs to be learned at all) and performed competently by following only eight guidelines.

Stress is the serious people problem coaches and mentors will encounter most often. Performers can best be helped by facilitating recognition of the indicators and by being encouraged to take responsibility for altering or rectifying the situation. There are numerous stress management strategies available to performer and coach alike.

11

BARRIERS TO ACHIEVEMENT

The obstacles to achievement are much more abundant than the ingredients available for achieving. For the purposes of clarity and simplicity, obstacles can be thought of as being personal, organizational and environmental. In this chapter we will look at personal barriers to achievement. We will identify and explore ways of overcoming the barriers to achievement and present an organized system for managing barriers, as follows:

- Barriers as skills deficits.
- Barrier management principles.
- What are the barriers?
- Specific skills deficits.
- Belief/paradigm obstacles:

    - The main types.
    - Disempowering belief barriers.
    - The effect beliefs have on relationships.
    - Personal obstacles as organizational barriers.
    - The reluctant performer.
    - Self-imposed barriers and self-sabotage.

- Coaching to overcome belief/paradigm obstacles:

    - Factors forming beliefs.
    - The dimensions and intensity of beliefs.
    - Expectancy.
    - The importance of beliefs illustrated.
    - Empowering beliefs defined.

- Belief change method.
- Identifying the disempowering:

    - Analysing and inferring beliefs.
    - Explore the options for change.
    - Decide on empowering alternatives.

- Exploring the options for change.

    - Establishing the empowering replacements.

- Rewards.
- Cues.
- Establishing the foundations.
- Rehearsing.
- Self-defence against the disempowering.
- For the really entrenched.

Barriers as skills deficits

If achieving is a skill, then some barriers to achievement are manifestations of skills deficits. There are at least three overlapping ways in which achievement can be blocked: specific skills deficits; disempowering beliefs or paradigms; a lack of barrier management skills.

Achievement is a super- or meta-skill. On a personal and organizational scale, the ability to achieve is a skill in its own right; it is a super-skill made up of several component skills. If the necessary mix of skill is not available, either partially or completely, there will be no achievement. The role of the coach or mentor is to help the performer or organization to identify the lack of which specific skill is causing obstacles to achievement. To do so, knowledge of the likely skills deficits and knowledge of the benefits and drawbacks of this approach is required.

There are distinct benefits to thinking of obstacles as skills or belief deficits. Doing so empowers the blocked person or organization. It allows them to think of the barrier in a way that implicitly assumes a way round. Put simply, seeing obstacles in terms of skills or belief deficits provides an explanation of the problem and solution in one manageable package. The 'barriers are skills deficits' assumption encourages self-responsibility. It makes the performer more likely to look to themselves first as the cause of non-achievement. Only when there is nothing that can be done should external factors be examined.

EXERCISE

What other benefits are there in viewing some barriers as mani-
festations of skills deficits?

There are problems as well as benefits in choosing to think so simplistically. For instance some people may try to surmount a barrier that is insurmountable by improving their skills; they may take personal responsibility for a non-achievement that is beyond their control. That would not be desirable; it would lessen the performer's confidence in their ability to control outcomes. Such a situation is unlikely to be a real worry since most people look for external reasons for why they cannot or have not achieved. Most will blame external factors for failure even when there is no rational basis for doing so. When a genuine barrier does emerge, taking personal responsibility for overcoming it is essential for achievement, whether or not the means of surmounting it is acquiring the relevant skills.

What should we as coaches do if we assume barrier management is a learnable skill? Do we encourage the performer not to blame external factors? No, we encourage performers to improve their barrier management. We encourage them to take control of the barriers or the barriers will control them. We encourage ownership of the means of overcoming the barriers.

Barrier management principles

Barrier management is conducted in several stages. There are three occasions in the coaching or mentoring process during which barrier management will be used: at the objective setting and planning stages, and during the implementation phase when the inevitable non-anticipated barriers emerge. The essence of barrier management is contained in the following general principles.

1   Become aware of and/or acknowledge the existence of the barrier(s).
2   Decide to take control of and responsibility for the barrier(s).
3   Define and clarify the exact nature of the barrier.
4   Identify and verify the causes (internal and external).
5   Explore possible solutions (for example, avoid it, use it or confront it).
6   Decide on which criteria define an acceptable solution.
7   Evaluate the alternatives.
8   Choose a solution to the barrier.
9   Devise and implement an appropriate barrier management plan.

Barrier management

10   If you change the achievement plan or method of implementing it, repeat
the above process.

EXERCISE

Make this list your own by abbreviating or condensing it.

Obstacles of all sorts can be handled in a large number of ways. For our
purposes there are three possible solutions: avoidance, use, and confrontation.

Avoid it

Avoiding an obstacle is often the smartest option if it is possible. There is no
need to manage or deal with a potential obstacle if it can be completely
sidestepped by achieving the desired objectives in another way. Most goals can
be achieved in any number of different ways. But planning and executing an
alternative which is more effort- and time-consuming just to avoid an easily
cleared obstacle is patently counter-productive. There is a small and dwindling
number of people who will go to extraordinary lengths to avoid using or
learning to use information technology. The effort that goes into avoiding this
'barrier' is hundreds of times greater than that which would be required to
overcome it.

Avoid it

EXERCISE

*Compile a first draft list of obstacles you think it would be easiest
to avoid.*

Use it

The perfect judo throw uses the opponent's attempts to throw or their attempts to prevent being thrown. Every barrier can be used to assist you in some way, if you can only find the way. The factors that motivate those people or events behind the barrier can, in many instances, be harnessed. Every strength is a weakness in some context and vice versa. You just have to find the context and create the situation in which the contextual advantage is on your side. You could also analyse the motives and find a way of satisfying them to the point where those behind the barrier actively want to help, despite their obligation to maintain the barrier. Or find a way of using the resistive force of the barrier to help you. For instance you may want to 'provoke' those behind the barrier into being so extreme and unreasonable that others sympathize with, and wish to support, your attempts to find a way round. I make it sound easy, eh? It's not. Using a barrier as an asset requires enormous thought, maybe so much that avoidance could be more time- and cost-effective.

Use it

Confront it

Handling obstacles can be like handling fear. Often the best way to handle fear is to face it head on. Control fear or fear will control you. Blast your way through the barrier, overpower it using reasoning, persuasion or whatever other

Confront it

methods you deem necessary. Find a way of rendering it impotent. In military terms you can surprise it, distract it, deceive it, cut off its supply lines, plan an attack in such a way that the line of retreat is determined by you, draw it in to what it thinks is an easy victory, spread propaganda and misinformation and so on. This applies to organizational as well as personal barriers. One of the best ways to handle the fear of public speaking is to distract your mind with such devices as concentrating on your breathing, or imagining you are talking to a collection of your best friends.

EXERCISE

What kinds of barriers are best overcome by confrontation?

What are the barriers?

As was said earlier, it is empowering to assume that a barrier is the manifestation of a skill yet to be learned. For the purposes of explanation, personal obstacles are organized into three sub-groups, the first of which straddles the other two: an absence of the success ingredients; specific skill deficit; a belief or paradigm problem.

Barriers to success can emerge from an absence or inadequate amount of one or more of the success ingredients:

- Direction.
- Desire and motivation.
- Self-image.

- Belief structure.
- Persistence.
- Willingness to learn.
- Support systems.

A description and explanation of each success ingredient can be found in Chapter 2. Success can be attained on the basis of a few ingredients which match the requirements of a particular success environment. It is not necessary to have all the ingredients in place. Ask your performer which they think are missing, if any, in their environment, and what they propose to do to rectify the deficit.

EXERCISE

Which of the above do you most need to address to heighten your level of success?

Specific skill deficits

A performer will simply be incapable of achieving results if they do not possess the skills to do so. In most workplace situations, the issue is not whether the performer has the technical skills (although at the lower rankings that is the case) but whether they have the necessary people, management and thinking skills to organize the achievement through others.

The most effective way to rectify the problem is to ask the performer to identify the skill deficit and plan and implement whatever self- or other-managed training or development they believe will rectify the deficit. Most of the deficits will be:

- Problem-solving skills.
- Creativity skills.
- Influence and persuasion.
- Team building and leadership.
- Training and coaching skills.
- Self-management.

Problem-solving/decision-making skills underdeveloped or absent

Does the performer: engage in information gathering about the problem, have suitable knowledge of problem-solving methods, convene problem-solving meetings, effectively lead those meetings, facilitate the problem-solving abilities of others, set criteria for an acceptable solution?

EXERCISE

What questions can you ask to help the performer find out whether this is the skill deficit responsible for the under-achievement?

Creativity under- or undeveloped

Management problem solving by the book goes only so far down the road of achievement; creativity is required to go the rest of the way. There must be a willingness to recognize, generate and capitalize on creativity, manage and harness the creativity of others, learn and use creativity techniques, set up a 'creativity is good' culture within their sphere of influence. I can heartily recommend a suitable text on this subject: *Opportunity Spotting: Corporate Creativity For Growth*, by yours truly, published by Gower, 1994.

EXERCISE

As the previous exercise.

Influence, persuasion skills; team building, leadership and motivation skills, under- or undeveloped

For treatment of these areas, see the appropriate sections of this book for information on the core ingredients of these skills (page 126).

EXERCISE

Refer to the appropriate section if necessary before conducting the exercise as above.

Training/staff development/coaching skills

A performer may be failing to equip those who need training with the appropriate skills to carry out the tasks required. Or they may not have sufficient coaching skills to bring out the best in their staff.

EXERCISE

What question will you ask to help your performer identify if this is the area causing the under-achievement? If they think it is, what should you ask to help them pinpoint exactly which skill is lacking?

Poor self-management

Poor self-management consists of inadequate emotional management, time management, stress management, energy levels management, self-motivation skills, knowledge management and so on. As an example, a performer may fail to transfer knowledge or skills from an area in which they have expertise to another in which those skills would be directly applicable.

EXERCISE

As the previous exercise.

EXERCISE

Devise a checklist or other system against which to encourage performers to consider whether or not their barrier to achievement is a skill deficit.

Belief/paradigm obstacles

The existence of a disempowering personal paradigm or belief can surface and show itself in apparently unrelated barriers. For instance, a belief that the organization does not tolerate failure could manifest itself in a fear of doing anything remotely risky. The method for overcoming belief and paradigm barriers is covered in detail in the section on handling belief barriers (page 197–209). But for now here is a list of those it would be useful to recognize.

The main types

- Fear obstacles.
- Reasoning obstacles.
- Conflicting interest barriers.
- Unclear belief system barriers.
- Disempowering belief barriers.

Fear obstacles

These include fear of failing; some of the implications of failing; appearing stupid or foolish; being laughed at; being thought odd; being different; being fired; some of the implications of succeeding.

Reasoning obstacles

These include the belief that analysis is superior to creativity, logic always provides the best solution; intelligent behaviour is always the most constructive behaviour; one must be capable of providing instant judgement; experts are always right; one's best interests are served by concentrating on the short term; and so on.

Conflicting interest barriers

Performers of all kinds have a constant battle to resolve conflicts which may interfere with their performance by acting as highly effective barriers. The conflicts include high-risk, high return versus low-risk, certain but low return; employer's interests versus employees' interests; honesty versus expediency.

Unclear belief system barriers

Belief systems can appear unclear because of conflicting values; inconsistent convictions; they have been suppressed; they are at odds with the organization's values but a disguise has been attempted; the person is a genuine nihilist. Often it is worse to have an unclear belief and value system than to have a disempowering one. With a disempowering belief, the coach has something on which to work with the performer, but with an unclear system, it is difficult to know where to start. Having said that, it can be easier for the farmer of achievement to work a green field than a scarred landscape.

EXERCISE

Which barriers have stopped you in the past? Which stop you most often and most effectively?

Disempowering belief barriers

Some irrational, disempowering workplace beliefs/paradigms include the following:

- One must be the best at everything.
- One's history is the absolute determinant of one's beliefs.
- Others should be dependent on one.
- One should be dependent on others.
- It is easiest to avoid difficulties.
- One should ruminate over worries.
- One's happiness is externally caused.
- One's performance is externally caused.
- Promotion and advancement have little to do with one's performance.
- One's superiors are capricious and manipulative.
- Others are leaders, one is a manager.
- One wasn't born with the right disposition to be successful.
- One must be loved and admired by all to be of value.
- One's bosses have all the answers.
- One's bosses think they have all the answers but really have all the errors.
- It's their fault I'm under-performing.
- If he or she wasn't working with me I'd be doing well.
- I must be seen in the right circles to get ahead.

- My face must be seen in the office late at night to get ahead (face time).
- I must sacrifice my life to the company to get ahead.
- I know plenty about my field but can't offer anything to any other.
- I know a lot about my field and bet I could do a better job at theirs too.
- If I don't agree with my boss I'll get fired.
- They'll laugh at me if I get it wrong.
- They'll reject me if I perform too well.
- I couldn't cope if I failed.

Long it may be, but an exhaustive list it is not. There are as many disempowering beliefs and paradigms as there are under- or non-achievers.

Some of these beliefs may not be irrational in certain companies: it may, indeed, be wise to hold such beliefs in some organizations. Any company set up in such a way that it is sensible for a sample of the above to be held by the staff won't be around for very long. If everyone refused to work in such an environment, the companies concerned would have no choice but to change their culture. By accepting it, you condone it and perpetuate it. It is no coincidence that the most successful companies empower their staff.

EXERCISE

Start a log book of the disempowering beliefs that you witness in yourself and others.

The effect beliefs have on relationships

The beliefs held by a performer about other people will ultimately affect their behaviour towards the performer, as can be seen from below. An empowering

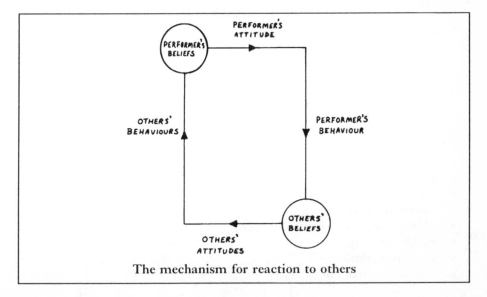

The mechanism for reaction to others

belief about another person is likely to create a positive effect while a dis-empowering belief creates negative effects. You may have noticed that some people are able to produce positive results from awkward people who seem un-manageable by everyone else. The explanation is that the beliefs held about people in general, and the 'awkward' person specifically, are empowering.

EXERCISE

What do you think the empowering beliefs are?

Personal obstacles as organizational barriers

A personal barrier held by someone in a position of authority becomes an organizational barrier to achievement. The coach can encourage the manage-ment of organizational barriers in the same ways that personal barriers can be handled, namely by avoidance, use or confrontation (confrontation also includes persuasion). The organizational and environmental barriers to achievement are almost identical to the barriers to coaching and mentoring, which will be covered in the next section. A brief list now will give a flavour:

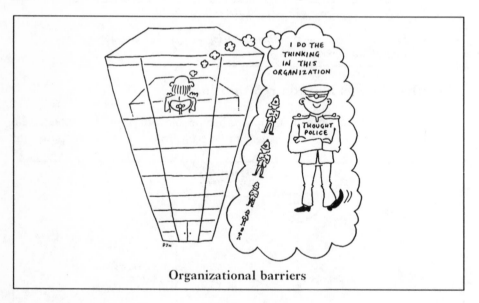

Organizational barriers

- Results pressure.
- Time pressure.
- Management autocracy.
- Shut up and listen communication.
- Rigid hierarchy.
- Rigid procedures.
- Over-burdening bureaucracy.

- Skills monopolizing.
- Information secrecy.
- Resource protectionism.

EXERCISE

What is the greatest obstacle to achievement in your organization?

The reluctant performer

There are several categories of reluctant performer:

- Performed well in the past but lost the motivation (demoralized).
- Have all the necessary skills, but are motivated not to use them (negatively motivated).
- Have the skills but are not motivated to either use or not use them (apathy).
- Have no skills and no motivation to obtain them (unskilled, unmotivated).
- Have the skills and the apparent motivation but seemingly sabotage their attempts (self-saboteurs).
- Have no skills and are sabotaging their 'attempts' to acquire them (self-sabotaging learners).

Obviously in real life, the divisions are not as simple as I have suggested, but even if they were, there are just too many causes of performance reluctance to even begin to catalogue them in a book on coaching and mentoring. There are as many reasons for wilful non-performance as there are reluctant performers. As you know, we are talking about big numbers here. After I've given some examples of the self-saboteurs, we'll explore the general principles that apply to handling reluctant and other under-performers.

Self-imposed barriers and self-sabotage

It may be unbelievable to you if you are a habitual achiever, but some people go to great lengths to prevent themselves achieving successful performance. Some people engage in what others would regard as self-sabotage deliberately as a rather bizarre self-protection mechanism, 'If I'm going to fail, I'll choose the how, why and wherefors'. Others self-sabotage accidentally; the successful thinking or behaviour pattern they have chosen to adopt in one situation causes non-success in another.

EXERCISE

Which of the following saboteurs have chosen their path and which are accidental self-saboteurs?

Self-sabotage

A self-sabotage menu

- *The 'big shot in words'* is too frightened to try, because if they fail, they have to admit to themselves and everyone else that they were full of hot air.
- The same motivation applies to the *'I could have made it if I'd wanted to, but I chose not to'* type of self-saboteur.
- *The 'I like me the way I am and if I become upwardly mobile I'll have to compromise myself and my principles'* type sounds like a genuine person; alas, we all have to compromise every day of our lives so this is a red herring. It isn't even a convincing colour of red!
- *The 'I want security'* type is probably the saddest case of all. He or she won't push and won't take the opportunity to perform because they don't want to take risks. Their philosophy is 'it's better to be a live bore than a dead adventurer'. The sad part is that not taking risks is the most risky option of all. When a company has to chop some staff, what staff levels usually go first?
- *The 'I fit in well as I am'* type is to be admired for not wanting to perform so well that they make their friends look poor, or at least that's what they think. What do you think?
- *The 'If it wasn't for my boss, my spouse, my kids, my... I'd be a success'* type always has a fine excuse to hand. Of course, by making and believing the excuse, they sabotage any chance they ever had to be successful.
- *The 'loser's limp'* type is probably the most credible and believable of them all. They have a genuine impairment of some kind which holds them back. Don't you understand? At the risk of sounding totally unsympathetic we could fill several books with details of high achievers who had

some kind of impairment. Many have terrible burdens yet continue to achieve year after year.

- *The 'fear of failure' self-saboteur*: the things we think about and dwell on are the things we attract to ourselves. If someone dwells on failure they can expect more of the same.
- *The 'grasshopper'* type wants success so much that they will jump into whatever seems to be the route to success. The problem is that the big thing today is often not the big thing for success tomorrow, as the landscape is always changing. The grasshopper doesn't stay in any one place long enough to achieve any serious results.
- *The 'sure thing only'* type suppresses their true desires because they can see more likelihood of success in other things. This form of self-sabotage is particularly cruel because the performer can never put their heart into the 'sure thing' to the extent they would have had they followed their passion. As a result, they get a fraction of the performance level from the sure thing than they would have from their passion.

EXERCISE

That's the starter course on the self-sabotage menu. Add the main course options and some desserts.

EXERCISE

Ask your performers which of the above they have used. Are the circumstances in which they did so likely to recur? If so, how will they stop themselves reverting to the tried and tested response?

Coaching to overcome belief/paradigm obstacles

The first assumption to make is that no one but the person concerned can change their undesired behaviour. Old jokes can often be instructive, in this case: 'How many psychiatrists does it take to change a light bulb? One, but the light bulb must really want to change', has a ring of truth to it. In short, the really reluctant performer, the seriously maladaptive belief structure is beyond cost-effective coaching. Coaches and mentors are wasting their time with such people. Time is better spent with the frustrated but willing under-performer, the motivated but blocked non-achiever (the performer who wants to achieve but can't overcome whatever is blocking them), and the unwillingly reluctant performer (the performer who recognizes and does not like their under- or non-achievement.).

So how do you help these performers? Before we look at a suitable procedure, a little background information on the nature of beliefs is required. You will be better equipped to handle and rectify disempowering beliefs if you know how beliefs are formed, along which dimensions they vary, how their level of intensity varies, how they affect a performer's expectancy of a particular outcome, and what effect expectancy has on performance.

Factors forming beliefs

Beliefs are formed and changed on a continuing basis. Virtually every aspect of life has an input to our belief-formation process. The most important factors influencing the formation of our beliefs are:

- *Reference experiences:* Experiences we choose to refer to in the formation process (more later).
- *Habitual questioning*: The questions we ask determine, and are dependent on, what we believe.
- *Global/human norms*: The beliefs that all humans hold.
- *Societal norms, morals*: The beliefs predominantly held in our society.
- *Local/familial norms*: The beliefs held by our peers, bosses, friends, families and so on.
- *Concurrent emotional state*: The emotional state at the time of an experience influences belief formation.
- *Vocabulary and language*: The words we use influence what we believe.

EXERCISE

What other factors do you think influence the formation of our beliefs? Choose one of your own beliefs; analyse what led you to adopting it.

The last point is worth exploring further. Our words affect the way we think. If we describe something as horrible when it is merely inconvenient, how is that likely to make us feel? We often use words inappropriately, like 'terrible' and 'awful'. Describing what is seen in a particular way will determine what is subsequently seen. What you say you see makes you see what you say. You will see something when you believe it, and believe it when you see it.

It makes sense for you and your performers to deliberately choose to believe you will be a success; you will then be able to see how you can achieve success. Your performers will tell you much about what they believe from the words they choose to use. If you use language that is empowering and expectant of success, it influences your thinking in such a way that makes success more visible. Encourage your performers to use empowering, positive and expectant vocabulary.

The dimensions and intensity of beliefs

There are three dimensions of beliefs:

1   Permanent – transient: the object of belief applies – always/sometimes.
2   Pervasive – localized: the object of belief applies universally/only locally.
3   Personal – impersonal: the object of belief applies only to the holder/to everyone.

Beliefs that are at the left-hand extremes on all three dimensions are virtually impossible to deal with, certainly in the context of coaching. The more toward the other extreme, the more amenable to change they are. An ideal achievement belief is one that is permanent, pervasive, and impersonal, that is it applies everywhere all the time and anyone can adopt it to the same effect, if they so choose. Encourage your performers to develop their achievement-oriented beliefs in that format.

EXERCISE

Do all the beliefs outlined in Chapter 2 on the nature of achievement adopted by successful people conform to the permanent, pervasive, impersonal rule?

The intensity of beliefs

The intensity level and consistency of a person's desires and beliefs is highly predictive of the outcomes they will achieve in the future. The intensity of beliefs can vary along the following arbitrary dimension:

1   Casual opinion
2   Strong opinion
3   Conviction
4   Absolute fact

Most rational people know there is no such thing as an absolute fact. 'Facts' change depending on your point of view and the current state of knowledge. Fact: the earth is flat (then). Fact: the earth is a slightly misshaped sphere (now). It pays to allow yourself to believe in your goal as though it were an absolute fact even though you would rationally agree there is no such thing.

Expectancy

The dimensions and intensity of beliefs ultimately manifest themselves in the sense of expectancy that a performer has of success. We know the level of expectancy of success is a strong predictor of success. A strong expectancy creates a self-fulfilling prophecy. The more you anticipate it, the more evidence you see for it. Expectancy created by holding certain beliefs is a multi-dimensional phenomenon: it varies in level, magnitude and range. That is, the strength, and generality of an expectancy (how far it spreads) will determine, partially, the performer's likelihood of success. A strong expectancy helps one to see ways of fulfilling those expectations. By encouraging your performers to expect success, you will be helping them see the ways of achieving it.

EXERCISE

How can you encourage a high level of expectation in yourself and your performers?

The importance of beliefs illustrated

Probably the most effective way to demonstrate the importance of altering performance by addressing the beliefs behind the performance is to show the complexity of the process going on. As you can see from the figure, each of the stages in the behaviour sequence is affected by and has an effect on every other stage either directly or indirectly. Once the process has started it is simply not possible to analyse what is going on or to try to control it. It would be crazy to try to alter behaviour on its own while leaving the beliefs that cause that behaviour unaltered. The same applies to emotional reactions and inner dialogue and every other stage in the sequence. The only viable option is to change the outcome at the earliest possible stage in the sequence. The earlier in the chain of events a positive effect takes place, the greater the propensity for positive feedback to make the whole process self-supporting. Adopting empowering beliefs sets off a chain of events that enable fulfilment of those positive beliefs.

Empowering beliefs defined

The empowering beliefs of achievement should be permanent, pervasive and impersonal and held with the level of expectancy and intensity of an absolute fact. How can a performer adopt such an intensity of belief? By seeking confirming evidence, by deliberately ignoring contradictory evidence, by seeking support from remembered and appropriate reference experiences, by creating confirming reference experiences (engaging in training that will 'prove' one's belief). More on this shortly.

A disempowering belief is best challenged by asking questions that enable the performer to see the negative consequences of their belief, by seeking contradictory examples, by seeking out contradictory reference experiences, and so on.

Belief change method

Let us now pull all this information on beliefs and paradigms together into a structure. Beliefs are changed in two stages, i) identifying the disempowering, ii) establishing the empowering, which in turn are made up of further stages:

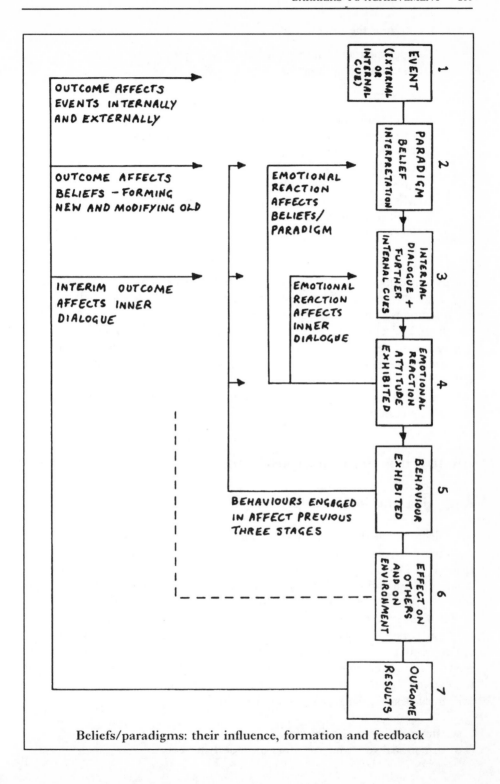

Beliefs/paradigms: their influence, formation and feedback

   i)   Identifying the disempowering:

      1   Analysing and inferring beliefs.
      2   Explore the options for change.

   ii)   Establishing the empowering:

      3   Decide on the most empowering beliefs to be adopted.
      4   Decide how to obtain rewards (internal and external) for those beliefs.
      5   Decide what will be the internal and external cues for the beliefs and behaviour.
      6   Strengthen the belief by use of reference experiences.
      7   Mentally and actually rehearse the new belief structure/paradigm until it is automatic.
      8   Keep your guard up against the re-emergence of the previous beliefs or paradigm.

Let us now explain in more detail how each of these is achieved. One last point before we do: you may remember in the section on paradigm analysis (page 112), I promised more details on how to help change to a more empowering paradigm, and elsewhere I promised that we would demonstrate how to help the reluctant performer. Here it is: the methods for handling a reluctant performer and helping to change a disempowering paradigm are the same. Reluctance to perform is based in the performer's belief repertoire; somewhere there is a disempowering paradigm lurking destructively in the background. First it needs to be identified.

Identifying the disempowering

Analysing and inferring beliefs

First, identify the cues and rewards which maintain the disempowering beliefs and their subsequent behaviour. Refer again to the section on paradigm analysis (page 112) for a full account of the process for identifying beliefs. If you have a fair understanding, a brief summary, which follows, will suffice. In this situation we are particularly keen to find disempowering beliefs.

Paradigm analysis (for identifying disempowering beliefs) consists of trying to identify the beliefs behind observed problem behaviours, emotional over- or under-reactions, or sub-standard outcomes. Beliefs generally can very easily be inferred from their most visible manifestations, those producing behaviours at the extremes of the value judgement range; good or really bad, successful or very unsuccessful. To recap, the most useful indicators are:

- Inner dialogue as reported by the performer.
- Emotional reaction indicators of underlying belief.

Analysing and inferring beliefs

- Weaknesses and other problem areas.
- Opportunities seen and not seen.
- Opportunities desired.
- Behaviour as reported by others.
- Perceived threats posed by others.
- Perceived motivations of others.
- Expectations of self.
- Estimations of own capabilities v. reality.
- Estimations of others' capabilities v. reality.
- Plans for behaviour v. actual execution of that behaviour.

The inference process can be conducted as follows:

1. Identify suitably revealing behaviour, emotional reaction or outcome (examples from above).
2. Agree with the performer that it occurred.
3. Help them to explore their motives for it.
4. Help them to explore the inner dialogue associated with the motives, the thoughts or self-statements they made just prior to acting on their motives.
5. Ask the performer to infer what beliefs must be behind the inner dialogue and motives.
6. There are usually several possible beliefs behind each action; ask the performer to suggest as many as possible, as in B1 to B ... below. Then choose the belief they think is held.
7. Continue 1 to 6 above until you and the performer have built up a list of disempowering beliefs.
8. Pull them together to form a first draft unifying disempowering paradigm.

9   Test the paradigm by predicting how the performer would behave in particular situations.

10   Draw conclusions from successful and unsuccessful predictions. Ask 'what would prove this hypothetical paradigm wrong?'

11   Loop 1 to 10 until confident that you have both identified the correct disempowering paradigm.

Analysing the beliefs behind a particular behaviour is conducted in the reverse order to which that behaviour occurs. The following version of the diagram 'Personal paradigms' (page 114) will help summarize the process:

Analysing and inferring beliefs					
Order of occurrence of behaviour	5th	4th	3rd	2nd	1st
Order of analysis	1st	2nd	3rd	4th	5th
	Outcome observation	Behaviour causing outcome	Emotional reaction	Belief 1 Belief 2 B 3 B 4 B 5 B …	Cue: Internal or external

---

EXERCISE

Identify one of your own and one of your performer's disempowering beliefs using the above process.

Explore the options for change

There are three points in the process which can be used to change the outcome: cues, beliefs, behaviours. There is little point in attempting to change emotional reactions; they are manifestations of belief. There is little point in trying to change outcomes; they are dependent on behaviour. Attempts to change behaviour without changing belief are notoriously unsuccessful. So that leaves cues and beliefs available as options for change. Trying to control the external cues that trigger behaviour is like trying to control the weather: you can shelter against it, you can hide from it, but you'll always be subjected to it and therefore, to some extent, controlled by it. Internal cues can be controlled but they are generated by one's beliefs. Thus the only effective way to attempt to change a disempowering paradigm, under-performance or reluctant performance, is to help the performer to seek out and empower their beliefs.

So in exploring options for change, the performer and coach/mentor should be looking for alternative empowering beliefs to replace their disempowering predecessors. An alternative to 'My boss never supports me' could be 'I regularly seek ways in which my boss will want to support me'.

EXERCISE

Generate a list of empowering alternatives to those identified in the last exercise.

Establishing the empowering replacements

Decide on empowering alternatives

You and the performer decide what is the most empowering belief to adopt by referring to the desired outcome and asking empowering questions like: What belief makes the outcome most achievable? What belief gives the performer the greatest sense of control? What belief gives the performer the greatest number of ways to feel good about their behaviour as well as the outcomes? What belief presents the fewest ways to feel bad or disempowered in the greatest number of operating contexts? What beliefs do successful performers in this skill area hold?

EXERCISE

What other ways can you and your performers use to determine the most empowering set of beliefs in relation to any desired objective? Decide which belief you or your performer are going to adopt.

Rewards: decide how to obtain rewards, internal and external, for those beliefs/behaviours

For any behaviour to be maintained and for any belief to be maintained, it must be rewarded, it must have its existence justified in some way. The rattlesnake repellent behaviour mentioned earlier was maintained because the holder of the belief had evidence (reward) that the belief and manifest behaviour were working. For a newly acquired belief and resultant behaviour to be maintained they must be reinforced/rewarded. The performer should decide how they want to see the belief as rewarding. They could praise themselves on a continuing basis as the results of the belief start to filter through; they could set up a self-reward structure for each time they behave in a way manifested by the belief; they could remind themselves of the immediate and future benefits of adopting the beliefs, and so on. There should be similar attempts to create an external reward structure. That may consist of setting up tangible rewards, or it may be as simple as the pleasure obtained in seeing how much others appreciate one's behaviour. Ask the performer to devise a reward structure for their new beliefs and behaviour.

EXERCISE

What reward structure are you going to set up to reinforce your newly adopted empowering belief? Ask your performers the same question.

Cues: decide what will be the internal and external cues for the beliefs and behaviour

The cue for applying the rattlesnake repellent may be the clock: 'I haven't used it for four hours. Time for another application'. The trigger cues for beliefs and their subsequent behaviours should be chosen by the performer. He or she should decide when it is appropriate to apply the belief. The belief should be firmly attached in the performer's mind to a range of contexts. For instance, one could believe that screaming 'NO' at the top of one's voice is a good way to prevent unwanted behaviour in others. It works well in confrontations that may degenerate into a threat to personal safety, but it's not so clever as a response to one's CEO habitually twiddling their wedding ring!

Newly adopted or modified beliefs must be anchored to, or married to, an appropriate context and to appropriate cues. To achieve 'belief-to-cue bonding' practise mental rehearsal as advocated in stage seven of the method (page 202).

EXERCISE

What cues will you and your performers use to turn your newly acquired empowering beliefs into an appropriate behaviour?

Establishing the foundations: strengthen the belief by use of reference experiences

We know that people react differently to life's experiences. Some are scarred for life by some harmful experience; others are invigorated, strengthened and developed by the same reference experience. The differential effect comes from the way the people concerned choose to look at and interpret the event. Habitual achievers make empowering interpretations; habitual failures make disempowering interpretations. For instance, someone with a newly acquired disability can ponder on what they have lost or on what they have gained. The outcome of that choice is more obvious than obvious. Our beliefs are, at least partially, formed by the way we choose to interpret our experiences. Our beliefs can be re-formed by the same process; we can choose to reinterpret our experiences in any way we wish. If achievement is the goal, then the sensible way to reinterpret experiences is to turn them into positive reference experiences that can reinforce our empowering beliefs. How?

By asking yourself, or your performer, to provide five reference experiences that will support the new belief; that may be sufficient to adopt the new belief, if not continue:

- By asking the performer to identify their significant shaping experiences.
- By separating them into empowering and disempowering interpreted experiences.
- By looking for ways in which the disempowering can be reinterpreted to support the desired belief.
- By looking for ways in which the empowering can be enhanced to support the desired belief.
- By deciding to interpret all future reference experiences in an empowering way.

The coaching input, after asking the performer questions to focus awareness on the potential contained in reinterpreting experiences, should be delicate and sensitive; it is a deep and very personal process. However you may want to encourage the performer to select shaping reference experiences drawn from working life in order to avoid having to go deep into their personal past. The reference experiences used to support the new beliefs are not as important as the level to which they are supported.

EXERCISE

Use the above process to strengthen the empowering beliefs adopted in the preceding exercises.

Rehearsing: mentally and actually rehearse the new belief structure/paradigm until it is automatic

As you will remember from an earlier section (see Chapter 2, The nature of achievement), the highest levels of performance come when, through practice, the skill is virtually automatic. The same applies to the use of beliefs. Beliefs are most effective when so strongly held as to be integral parts of us. The behaviour manifested from the belief becomes automatic with practice too. There are numerous ways in which the adoption of new beliefs can be practised, ranging from mental rehearsal to verbal affirmation. Decide how you are going to rehearse your new belief. And ask your performers.

Self-defence: keep your guard up against the re-emergence of the previous beliefs or paradigm

People behave more true to themselves as they become more stressed. In the transition period between holding the old disempowering belief and the new empowering belief, the performer is vulnerable to slipping backward, particularly when under stress. There will also be a period when the new belief feels unnatural, artificial and clumsy. During that period the old will seem more 'reliable' and 'useful'. The performer may be tempted to lapse back into 'what works'. The coach should alert the performer to those difficulties before they occur. Ask the performer to formulate and ask themselves questions that will enable them to maintain their new behaviours.

EXERCISE

Think about the circumstances under which your new belief will be difficult to sustain. Decide how you are going to deal with those eventualities. Ask your performers to do the same.

For the really entrenched

Some additional stages may be required for those who are really entrenched. Those who cannot see the benefits of changing, particularly reluctant performers, or for those whose disempowering beliefs are permanent, pervasive and personal. If the performer has not been able or willing to generate any alternative beliefs it is likely they still cannot or will not see the cost of holding their old belief or the benefits in the more empowering alternatives. It is also possible that they have not developed sufficient resolution or conviction to take the plunge into new intellectual waters. The following will help:

1 Ask the performer to list (on sheets of paper) the costs to them and others of their not changing their behaviour and adopting more empowering beliefs. Ask them to list the costs in terms of finance, career, peer acceptance, job satisfaction, respect, status and standing, and so on.
2 Ask them to list the benefits of changing in terms of the same factors.
3 Ask them to link huge amounts of pleasure to adopting the new belief.
4 Ask the performer to link huge amounts of pain to not adopting the new belief.
5 Ask them what will be the additional costs of not changing right now.
6 Ask them what will be the additional benefits in changing right now.
7 Ask them to make the change now.
8 If successful, continue the process of building the new belief. If unsuccessful repeat 1 to 7.

EXERCISE

Test the above on yourself by addressing one of your less desirable habits which you would like to change.

Concluding comments and summary

The number of manifestations of barriers to achievement are plentiful in comparison to the few ways in which achievement is possible. Barriers, although many, have only a few causes: they can be the manifestation of a skill deficit or a disempowering paradigm. The rectification of skills deficit barriers is relatively simple, but paradigm barriers to achievement require more work. The performer needs first to identify the problem beliefs and then to replace them with empowering alternatives. That is the start of the process; the performer must then rehearse, adopt and integrate the new paradigm. The degree to which the performer can see the value of adopting empowering beliefs, and their commitment to doing so, will determine their likelihood of success both in changing their paradigm and in achieving successful performance.

12

BARRIERS TO COACHING AND MENTORING

In this chapter, the following types of barriers to coaching and mentoring will be considered:

- Personal barriers.
- Organizational barriers.
- Environmental barriers.
- Process barriers.

Several factors will present barriers to coaching and mentoring. Most of the barriers are surmountable given forethought, planning and persuasion. The barriers are found in the same three areas as in the obstacles to achievement: personal, organizational, environmental.

Personal barriers

Most of the personal barriers to coaching and mentoring are the same as those to achieving. The difference can be defined as the different reasons offered by potential achievers and others for resisting the provision of coaching and mentoring.

Previous negative experience

Cynicism is regularly created by the frequent non-implementation of previous new initiatives. 'Seen it all before. We've had leadership, MBO, MBWA, excellence, functional analysis, critical path analysis, blah blah blah analysis, mission statements, quality circles, briefing teams, empowerment, yawn, yawn, yawn. You know what? They always sound good initially. Top management get all excited about it, and start to implement it. The great new hope hangs around like a bad smell for a while as it gradually goes sour, and a few months later you never hear another word. Coaching and mentoring are just the next in a long and continuing line. Oh, and one last point. You'll hear wonderful reasons why the latest initiative won't go the way of the others. "Coaching", we will be

Cynicism

told, "is the big one." We'll all smile, say "yes", wait for the nonsense to pass like an unwelcome rain shower, and carry on as before.'

Sounds familiar? Almost certainly. But how do you handle it? By pointing out that cynicism is a self-fulfilling prophecy: if you think something won't work, guess what happens? By pointing out that if everyone in the company believed the system would work, regardless of its intrinsic efficacy, it would work. By asking questions of the cynic that help them to see the disempowering consequences of holding such beliefs. The true cynic will have an answer for everything. If you realize you are dealing with such an individual, side-step them if required. You are wasting your time trying to help them. Some people will defend to the death their right to make a mess of their lives in whatever way they see fit, and that includes holding disempowering beliefs about methods which can dramatically improve performance.

EXERCISE

What questions will you ask to help the salvageable cynic see the self-fulfilling nature of their stance?

Resistance to change/fear of the unknown

Many people resist any change habitually – not because there is any specific problem with what is proposed, but because of the general problems with all propositions. These include the pain, inconvenience and effort of changing; the loss of the nice, comfortable operating pattern that has been set up and improved over several years; the discomfort in having to work hard to reach that comfort zone again. Worse still, it is almost impossible to tell how much

Fear of the unknown

extra work will be required. Promises of minimal inconvenience are not worth the gold they are written on. Most threatening of all, one has no way of telling whether one will be able to cope with the changes or whether agreeing to them is effectively signing one's own dismissal notice. Anyone suggesting that organizational changes could not lead to any of these fears coming true has not been living on planet earth for the duration of their lives. It won't be the first time a worker has implemented a new system only to be told on completion of the work that the new system has made them redundant at an age when they will never find work again. These fears regularly come true. They come true frequently enough to be justifiable, but not (just) frequently enough to be inevitable.

How do you overcome this obstacle? With honesty. Spell out the problems, tell people how difficult it's going to be. If it's going to make some people redundant because of the increased productivity of staff generally, say so. Don't be so unethical as to ask those likely to be made redundant to implement the system for you. There is no reason why staff should be made redundant because of increased performance; those extra person hours that become available can be directed towards the important tasks that are never achieved because they are always overshadowed by the urgent. Like product succession planning, regular systems improvements, interdepartmental communications improvements, and so on *ad nauseam*.

EXERCISE

Devise a systematic strategy to help people cope with their fear of the unknown consequences of coaching and mentoring.

Blocks in communication

Many of those resisting a proposed change will do so simply because they have not understood what is being proposed. That will be either because the message has not been presented properly or by virtue of the speaker's communication barriers. (See the section on listening turn-offs, page 58.) The best way to overcome these barriers is to ensure good communication as outlined previously, and to give the audience good reason for listening (that is, show them what is in it for them).

Attitude barriers to coaching and mentoring

There are several common attitudes that function as barriers to coaching and mentoring, they include the following:

'It's too time-consuming for the little return that may be possible'

This attitude is most clearly seen in the way resistant managers and others respond to the coaching methods for praise, criticism and feedback. There is no doubt the approach is more time-consuming in terms of the actual time spent speaking with the performer. But not overall. The skilled manager using conventional methods will spend some time preparing their criticism or feedback before they speak to the performer. If this time is included, the conventional method is more time-consuming. Why? Because with the coaching method, preparation time is not required. The performer does all the thinking which the manager would previously have done. What does that lead to? More self-responsibility, a better relationship, and most of all, effective self-evaluation and a plan for change that has the total commitment of its author – the performer!

EXERCISE

Ask anyone exhibiting this kind of resistance if they object to you anonymously asking their staff which approach they would prefer. Predict what kind of reaction this question would receive.

'Too costly, too risky, too many things can go wrong'

All of these are true if insufficient effort and commitment are put into making coaching work. As was said earlier, the effort and determination invested into making a theory or practice work is a greater determinant of the outcome than any intrinsic efficacy the theory may or may not have. In other words, a bad system applied by dedicated persistent personnel is more likely to work than a great system staffed by the half-hearted.

EXERCISE

Ask what those exhibiting this resistance would do to minimize the costs, risks and so on.

Lack of skills: 'I can't do it; it needs expert staff'

Did you know that there are approximately 100 operating rules for each of the professions – management, law, medicine, accountancy, and so on. (Incidentally, I know of only eight in the psychology of counselling and those you have already learned about in the counselling section.) That's right: only 100. How long does it take to learn that few? Even more shocking is the conclusion derived from a Pareto analysis of the application of those rules in practice: 80 per cent of all positive outcomes are achieved by applying only a 20 per cent core of the rules. What does that mean? It means that you could score four out of five on the basis of the possession of one in five of the rules. If you were passing yourself off as a physician using these principles, one in five of your patients would sue you, if they lived; the other four wouldn't be able to tell you from the real thing, as is evident from the numbers who practise fraudulently for years before being discovered. One wonders how many are never discovered.

Let's take a less contentious example, coaching. How much more than the competent amateur does the serious professional know, and how often does that knowledge show? Quite a lot and not very often are the answers. You can use the core principles to great effect in most instances from day one. As days two, three and four come, you will be acquiring more and more knowledge. In other words, once you have mastered the basics, get out there in the real world and continue your coaching education; you can only improve. Starting from a position of 80 per cent effectiveness is probably better than conventional methods.

EXERCISE

From the way the information has been presented in this book, work out what the core 20 per cent of practice rules are in coaching and mentoring.

Fear of poaching

'Why should I spend good money coaching people to high standards when we all know my competitors will come along and offer slightly better salaries and my prize people will be gone, taking with them all my training investment?'

Why indeed? Why should your staff stay if someone else thinks they are more valuable? If you fail to pay your staff what they are worth, that is inevitable.

'But that's not fair. I pay for their education and I have to pay them more for being more educated as well?' Yes, if they have increased their abilities you ought to be fully using those abilities; you have paid for them. The only way your competitors can offer more money for the same skills is if they can command a better return from them. Yes, I accept that some industries pay higher salaries for the same skill than is paid in other industries, but the variation within industries is usually very small. If your staff are leaving because of a small pay difference there is something else wrong. I suggest you find out what

Fear of poaching

it is. Do you conduct exit interviews? That's a good time to find the real reason why someone is leaving. If they are leaving because they have been offered a promotion then you have been under-utilizing their potential.

'Well in that case, I shouldn't have spent the money training them and coaching to the point where they were under-utilized'.

No, you should have used their skills more effectively.

'Oh, you will tell me anything to get me to accept this coaching idea, wouldn't you?'

EXERCISE

Devise a way of overcoming 'fear of poaching' resistance.

'Already doing all of that, thank you'

Have you ever met Mr and Mrs 'We're doing it already'? A charming couple. They were introducing empowerment while most of us were managing by objectives. They were also practising quality circles before the wheel was invented. Of course they provide good coaching: 'We do it every year during our annual appraisals'. Ugh!

EXERCISE

How will you persuade Mr and Mrs 'We're doing it already' that they may be doing something but it falls far short of what is recognizable as coaching or mentoring?

'They're all lazy so-and-sos'

This type of attitude shows no trust in performers to take responsibility for themselves or their work. It reveals a cynical view of humanity: 'These people don't want to work, they just want a fat pay cheque at the end of the week in exchange for as little as possible.' Not so, dear friend. Most of us need a sense of satisfaction in our lives. Most of us get that from our work. Most of us need the satisfaction from work well done for the sake of our mental health. If people are coming to work and not getting any satisfaction, then you ought to be doing something about it. Make their work varied, interesting and satisfying. Have productivity competitions with worthwhile prizes, 'most helpful worker of the week' awards, 'best improvement idea' prizes. Don't have people doing the same job on a production line week in week out; give them a chance to do other jobs. It's in the best interests of staff and the company for everyone to be able to do as many different jobs as possible. Large companies like Lucas received handsome returns from the early 1990s onwards by adopting flexible role systems.

EXERCISE

How will you persuade those who object to coaching on the above grounds that there may be another way? Go through the above sources of resistance to coaching again and generate another strategy for handling each of them.

'My staff perform, or they're fired'

Some take that approach. Probably the way to handle this barrier is to ask questions aimed at helping them to realize that they shouldn't expect any loyalty, any initiative, or expect staff to protect their interests; they shouldn't expect anything other than bare minimum compliance from their staff for as long as they can stomach management's attitude before they move on. Alternatively you could wish them 'Good luck. You'll need it'.

EXERCISE

How can you help such people see that their staff output would be higher and their turnover lower if they adopted other approaches?

'Being told works for me, not that non-directive, wishy-washy nonsense. My staff expect autocracy'

'Being told' is what most people have experienced. Most accept and even adopt 'being told', even though they don't like it; because it is so widespread they assume it is the standard, accepted and best management practice. They assume that since they gradually got used to the resentment created by 'being told' that others will too. They don't make the connection between how much better they respond to being consulted and asked in situations outside of work, how much more motivated they are in those circumstances, and how their staff might respond.

EXERCISE

How can you help them make the connection? What questions will you ask?

'That wishy-washy stuff will undermine my hard-headed image'

Why do some people assume that others respond better to fear than to vision, respect and mutual loyalty? Is being a hard-headed businessperson so fashionable that it overrules common sense? Or is the labour market such that people have no choice but to work for such people? Probably. Are the individuals who have no choice the calibre desired? Probably not.

EXERCISE

How can you help them make the connection? What questions will you ask?

'I already get results with other methods: I'm better at what I already do'

Yes, there is much to be said for this argument. Why fix anything if it isn't broken? Good point, except this is not fixing, it's evolving. We would still be living in caves if we had had this attitude as a species. Most of us have an

Already get results

insatiable desire to improve our lot, not just for ourselves, but for others too. We didn't leave our caves until we had built some alternatives. Keep your existing methods. Build your expertise in coaching and mentoring until the point has come where you feel it is time to leave the cave behind.

EXERCISE

That is my way of attempting to encourage change. How would you do it?

'The training department handles all that'

Did you know that during two separate strikes involving physicians (one in Israel, one in Canada) the mortality rate actually dropped significantly? So significantly that the press reported 'Death takes a holiday'. The explanation? Bad physicians? No! People tend to abdicate responsibility for their health to the medical professionals. No physician can ever replace the power of the body's natural defences, but some patients expect exactly that. The consequence is that some people die in medical care who might not have otherwise. The same applies to coaching. No training department, no matter how good, can ever replace the power managers have to improve their staff. The training department should be a resource for managers to use, not a means of abdicating training and coaching responsibilities.

Organizational barriers

Organizations don't intentionally put up barriers to the achievement of their staff, but they do put up barriers as an attempt to channel the efforts of staff in the direction desired by the company. Unfortunately, many of those boundaries and channelling devices also act as barriers to achievement. Some of those barriers exist by design and are necessary. Others exist by either lack of design or bad design. Some of each will be considered.

No example set

If your bosses don't value coaching, why should you? If you don't engage in mentoring your subordinates, why should they mentor theirs? The most powerful persuasion tool, when it comes to encouraging the adoption of new methods, is seeing someone else achieving better results by using the new methods. The most powerful verbal example is something along the lines of 'I've experienced it and it worked for me, but I must admit I didn't expect it to'.

Example setting need not only be from top down; there is every reason it should be from bottom up too. If you want to see the highest levels in the organization adopt coaching and mentoring company-wide, start by providing it for your staff. When others start to see the results, they will want to copy you, from above and below. Once set up and achieving results, how will you publicize your system?

The culture

Linked to the above, many companies have cultures in which coaching and mentoring would be virtually impossible to implement. Have you ever been in a meeting and raised a concept so new that no one else in the room could possibly know what you are talking about, yet heads nod in understanding? In such companies, ignorance is a crime as heinous as incompetence. One and all go to great lengths to appear totally knowledgeable about all issues. Coaching in that kind of culture is for under-performers. It is remedial treatment for those not quite bad enough to dismiss, yet. Naturally one should avoid being 'coached or mentored' in such a culture.

The obvious and best way to change such a culture is by example from the top. Occasionally an outsider can set an example. Let me start the ball rolling: I am ignorant of many business issues. Some areas of ignorance I know about and am addressing. In other areas, I am ignorant of my ignorance but am trying to reach awareness of those areas. How could you set an example?

Time pressure

Jobs that must be done today are always dealt with before jobs that must be done, but which could be completed any time. Sending that order out today is urgent. Implementing an effective coaching and mentoring programme is important, but not urgent. The organization should certainly channel efforts to where results are urgently required. But it should not impose so much time pressure that only the urgent is ever attended to. Time must be allowed for the important things that will allow improvements in the performance of the urgent tasks – important things like coaching and mentoring. How can you set the example with your staff and performers?

Budget pressure

A manager under heavy budget pressure will be reluctant to spend any money on something that does not promise an immediate return (enforced short-termism). Coaching and mentoring promise a high return but in the medium to long term. There may be short-term gains in morale but they take time to convert into results. Or do they? When has your output been highest? When you have a worthwhile goal and your morale is high? That's the case for most people. So it appears coaching or mentoring can produce a quick return by virtue of morale enhancement.

A small amount of budget pressure is probably a good thing as long as it is coupled with a realization of the returns available from enhanced morale. The kind of pressure which becomes a barrier to coaching is that which is so intense that it creates a stress response beyond the manager's tolerance. Clear thinking vanishes, stress-induced intellectual paralysis appears. An organization which imposes that much pressure should not expect positive results; it is creating an environment which makes coaching and mentoring a very low priority – not to mention the possible stress consequences to their staff. How can you help performers negotiate the appropriate level of budget pressure with their superiors?

Low skill – low expectation environment

'Our staff are poorly educated, just about semi-skilled, and certainly not motivated. We've tried everything to improve their performance. Alas, we have no expectation of any improvement in this industry.' It is widely assumed that the staff in some industries are not worth training. What chance does coaching have in that kind of environment? None; the staff are beyond training. That is true, if training is imposed on them by management. Coaching would have the same chances of success if imposed.

So what can be done to improve performance? Ask the people who know best, the performers. Ask them what they think would improve their output. What kind of support would they like from whom? Would they like to know about some of the available systems? What kind of coaching or mentoring would they like to know more about?

The key issue here is overcoming the barriers which organizations create to ownership and self-responsibility. If you hear the kind of statement given at the start of this section, you know someone somewhere in the organization is depriving performers of ownership of their performance. How will you persuade resistors/performers to let staff decide how to increase their performance?

Threat to management control: desire for autocracy

Encouraging the kind of ownership described above is often perceived as a threat to management control. There still persists a view of management that it is about being in control. It is not. Management is about encouraging performers to be in control. We know self-control, self-responsibility and ownership of performance leads to high achievement. Organizations of the future will be managers of intellectual resources; they will be 'led' by people whose job it is to ensure performers are not deprived of their ownership. The most powerful companies in the world will be those giving away most power to their achievers. Ask your performers what effect trust from their superiors has had on their performance.

Secrecy

Organizations frequently deny performers the tools to achieve by restricting the circulation of important information. Some even take pride in the efficiency of

Threat to management control

their 'need to know' information controls. Secrecy is important. Naturally they don't want their competitors obtaining trade secrets. But staff must have the information needed to perform as well as they can for the organization. By depriving staff of information, a company says explicitly 'We don't trust you with this information, so we are withholding it'. If the company does not trust the staff, why should the staff trust the company? If they have no trust, how can they be expected to feel secure and nurtured in their workplace? If they don't feel trusted and supported, why shouldn't they look for a place of work where they will be?

Secrecy

EXERCISE

Develop a system whereby staff can find out what they need to know to perform for the company.

Petty rules

The more petty rules a company has, the more likely the company is staffed by those with high levels of compliance and low levels of initiative. High achievers will not and do not have to tolerate petty rules being imposed on them. The kind of pettiness most frequently seen is being required to tidy your desk at the end of the day or, worse still, being required to keep a continually tidy desk while working. Such rules do nothing for output, although those imposing them will tell you things like 'a tidy desk represents a tidy mind', or 'it gives out the impression of our professionalism'! As a customer, if I see a tidy desk, I ask myself 'Am I paying for tidy pretension or for results?' As an employer I ask myself 'Do I want a tidy mind or do I want results?' The individual performer is most effective when left to do their work in their own way. If highly compliant staff are what a company or organization requires, then as many petty rules as possible should be imposed to drive away anyone who might ever think for themselves! Which companies do you know that seem to have such a policy? Which professions? If initiative and performance are what is required, try to avoid petty rules.

Already over-burdened with bureaucracy

Bureaucracy stifles and demotivates everyone except the 'admino-phile'. If you burden your proposed coaching or mentoring system with huge amounts of administration, don't expect anything other than resistance and resentment. The administration requirement should be the absolute minimum needed to assess the effectiveness of the coaching or mentoring programme. What do you think the minimum should be?

Its effectiveness can't be measured

The difficulties in assessing the efficacy of coaching and mentoring systems may present an organizational barrier. It may be claimed by those who oppose coaching that its effects cannot be measured or assessed. That's not true, but when did truth ever spoil a good argument? Coaching can be assessed, as will be shown later. The same people will ask, 'What organization will spend time and effort introducing any system that can't be evaluated?' The answer sought is 'None', but that is an answer that can't be provided. The answer which must be provided is 'Many'.

Many organizations blindly introduce systems without putting in place the means to assess their efficacy. Large numbers of companies have introduced psychometric testing of potential employees in an attempt to be 'scientific'.

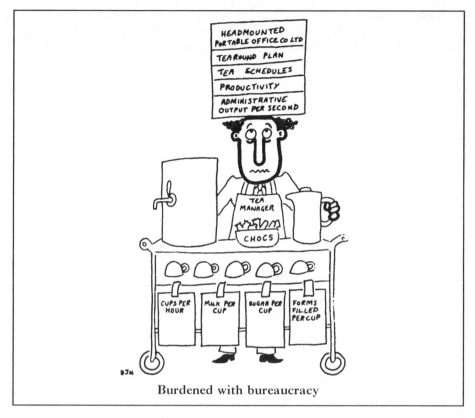

HEADMOUNTED
PORTABLE OFFICE CO LTD

TEA ROUND PLAN

TEA SCHEDULES

PRODUCTIVITY

ADMINISTRATIVE
OUTPUT PER SECOND

TEA
MANAGER

CHOCS

CUPS PER
HOUR

MILK PER
CUP

SUGAR PER
CUP

FORMS
FILLED
PER CUP

Burdened with bureaucracy

Psychometric recruitment systems have been introduced in many organizations without assessing independently the efficacy of the tests before implementation; or whether better employees were actually being recruited in exchange for the considerable expense. In short they adopt methods which are supposed to help, without assessing whether they actually do.

One controversial and slightly aggressive way to deal with the 'its effectiveness cannot be measured' barrier is to identify a system in the organization that has been implemented and/or is utilized without any form of assessment by the people making the objection. You can then assure them that coaching and mentoring is a system which will be implemented and assessed properly. Of course I advocate this approach with tongue in cheek, but the point is valid. How can you make this point in a diplomatic and persuasive way?

Formal training bias

The tried and tested methods are always preferable to new, uncertain, and more difficult methods. There is the possible misconception that either the status quo should be maintained or a new system should be adopted. There is a mid-ground. Using predominantly formal training methods does not rule out the use of coaching. Training and coaching can be conducted together as a performer-centred co-operative developmental venture. It is enormously hard work, and requires phenomenal degrees of concentration by the trainer. The benefit is, alas, not in direct proportion to the effort expended, and that observation is regularly stretched and used as a justification that performer-centred coaching does not work. It does, but not in proportion to the effort coaches have to put in; the law of diminishing returns applies. How can you persuade others that coaching and formal training are not mutually exclusive?

Resistance to self-managed development

How do conventional trainers react to self-confident, self-managed developers? You tell me. The answer is self-evident from a brief description of the behaviour and attitude of the kind of self-managed developer who becomes a successful entrepreneur or innovator at the coal-face of their discipline. Do they educate themselves through college or school? No. They may be forced there, in body, but the education of their mind takes place elsewhere. They don't appreciate being told how, what and when to learn, others guessing what they should learn, or being subjected to some arbitrarily devised syllabus which is designed more to fill three or four years with vaguely relevant material than to prepare future high achievers for their performances. They don't appreciate attending courses designed to partially satisfy all the needs of a large number of disparate people, or lectures which are more reflective of the interests of the lecturers than the needs of the developers; or long years of formal education which stifle their individuality. They don't appreciate long years of education at the end of which no more than 5 per cent is usable. 'Why', they ask, 'can't I get the relevant 5 per cent in a sensible time and move on to something significant? Why bother going through formal education, when I can drop out, get the 5 per cent in a fraction of the time, and move on to some serious achievement?'

Let's ask the question again: what is the likely resistance/reaction in lecturers and trainers to truly self-managed developers?

Coaching as assisted self-managed development – a 'threat' to the training staff

Training staff usually see self-managed learning as a threat to their jobs. You should expect resistance from that quarter. You should also expect a number of apparently convincing arguments against coaching and mentoring, particularly if the trainers are not to be the providers of coaching. Are coaching and mentoring really a threat to trainers? Quite the contrary! They are an opportunity to learn new skills, to support managers and coaches in new ways, to provide coach support services – both in terms of emotional support and training resource support. The company trainers can be called on by coaches and performers alike to provide what is required, when it is required. The training role can become one of the most exciting functions in the company. The training department can become the centre of coaching excellence. The

Coaching: a threat to training staff?

professional trainer committed to using whatever methods will achieve the best results will welcome the opportunity to be more effective which is provided by the self-managed development implicit in coaching.

EXERCISE

How will you encourage the support of the training function? How will you help them to see the benefits and exciting challenges that coaching and mentoring will provide?

Skills arrogance

'We, and only we, know how to achieve this or that.' Skills arrogance removes ownership and disempowers; it undermines those who are deemed, by the skill-arrogant, unable to perform whatever task is being discussed. Certainly there is a requirement in any organization for skill speciality, but that should not be used as an excuse for preventing others acquiring whatever skills they deem appropriate to improve their performance.

EXERCISE

In your company, when did the training or some other department last turn down a request for some kind of help with training because the person applying was deemed 'not to need the skills concerned and/or others were better placed to practise the skill'? How can you persuade others in your company that the performer is the best judge of what they need to perform?

Skills deficits

When there is no one in an organization who knows how to or has the practical skills to provide coaching, there is an organizational barrier. To a lesser extent the same applies to mentoring but, as has been said, few special skills are required to provide mentoring. If that is not known in the organization there will be an ignorance barrier.

Other organizational barriers

Anyone who believes they have something to lose will present resistance to coaching in proportion to the level of the perceived potential loss. Who do you think has most to lose from coaching or mentoring? How can you help them to see the benefits, for them and others?

Overlap of barriers

The individual barriers of the CEO and other senior staff become organizational barriers. One of the best approaches to handling organizational barriers to coaching is to determine whether or not the organizational barriers are the personal barriers of the senior staff. Do so by asking a chain of questions aimed at finding out what their objections are to coaching and mentoring. Ask them to reflect on whether or not those objections are converted into organizational policies or other instruments that create barriers. If so, was that what was intended?

Environmental barriers

The environmental barriers to coaching are those over which management has little control. For instance in the UK, owners/directors of a company cannot claim the costs of any training they engage in against tax. What message does that send? Clearly, if you own shares in the company you help to run, we, as the State, don't want you to try to acquire skills to improve your running of the company. Short of campaigning for change there is little that can be done against many of the environmental barriers. Others include legal constraints, liability implications, union restrictions and so on.

There have been some stunningly effective ways of handling these kinds of barriers in the last few decades, such as Rupert Murdoch moving to 'Fortress Wapping', and other international companies simply pulling out of a restrictive country *en masse*. At an individual level, top-flight scientists and other high fliers make the choice between campaigning for change over a long period, or emigrating to a country that doesn't put up environmental barriers to performance. The result is well known as the 'brain drain'. What other environmental barriers are there?

The process barriers to coaching and mentoring

Two main barriers can surface by virtue of the processes which take place during coaching and mentoring: conflict and frustration.

Conflict

An understanding of the causes, a possession of strategies for prevention, and an awareness of the methods of management of conflict are an essential part of coaching and mentoring. We shouldn't assume that all conflict is negative. Conflict can be positive:

- It can assist development – by debate and argumentation.
- It can facilitate open and honest discussion.
- It can enhance communication, or unblock communication.
- It can release blocking emotional build-ups.
- It can increase involvement and commitment.
- It can result in a problem being solved.
- It can result in any other kind of positive outcome.

EXERCISE

Under what other circumstances can conflict be positive? Under what circumstances may it be constructive to engineer conflict with your performer?

Of course conflict is usually negative, mostly when it leads to a breakdown in communication, leads to feelings of dissatisfaction, and distracts those involved from dealing with the really important issues.

What are the causes of conflict?

- Habitual disposition – by virtue of personality or job requirements.
- Personality clashes between coach and performer.
- Different expectation brought to the interaction by one's self and/or others, for instance, expectations about performance standards, rules and procedures, areas of responsibility.
- Different objectives for the coaching/mentoring sessions regarding outcome, process or methods used, resources used/available.
- Different perspectives of some or all of the involved issues.
- Misunderstandings or mis-communications between the parties.

EXERCISE

What other causes can you think of? Come up with, or ask your performer to come up with, an example of one conflict from their past based on each of the above.

Preventing conflict

Some people go through life seeming never to have any serious conflicts. Of course they do, but the way they handle other people ensures that disputes rarely develop from those conflicts. If one does, it is resolved quickly in a way which is acceptable to both parties. The techniques involved in conflict prevention include the following:

Sharing knowledge on the causes of conflict   It is difficult to imagine two people who know the causes of conflict allowing any dispute to get out of hand. Unfortunately for world peace, 'difficult' does not mean impossible. How will you share your knowledge of conflict causes with your performers?

Tolerance of individual differences   People who are tolerant of us are much more likely to receive our tolerance. The effect can be harnessed by choosing to start the process by being the person who shows tolerance.

Listen to what people are saying   Refer to the section on listening skills (page 57). Suffice to say here that we listen to those who listen to us.

Acquiring knowledge and genuine understanding of the people worked with   Refer to the section on influence (page 145). We know that those who influence us most are those we know best. Prevent conflicts by having a good rapport with those you coach or mentor.

Spend productive time in relationship maintenance   All successful relationships – those in which conflict is prevented or resolved readily – depend on both parties maintaining the arrangement at an appropriate level.

Honesty, both to self and others   Diplomats find their hair standing on end at this kind of advice, but we know that people who talk honestly with each other have deeper, more satisfying and longer-lasting relationships than those who operate at superficial or 'social inanity' levels.

Encourage others to express their feelings about various issues   When others feel safe expressing their views with us, it is easier to detect conflict before it has turned into anything serious, and can be dealt with rapidly.

Avoid feeling defensive when others disagree with your view   Behaving in a defensive way causes extremes of reaction in others. Some sense victory and become more aggressive to finish their opponent off. Others back off for fear of causing a serious conflict, but as is always the case when someone feels pressured, the conflict remains, simmers, and eventually comes to a much more destructive head.

Maintain an open mind, avoid automatic assumptions of right or wrong regarding self or others   People are most responsive to those who are most responsive to them. By maintaining and demonstrating an open mind, you tell others you are willing to listen to them, to be influenced by them, to accommodate and respect them.

Set an example, try to encourage others to manage conflict constructively   We know that people adapt their behaviour to fit those they are interacting with. People with a sophisticated conflict management style demonstrate the benefits of their skill to those they deal with on a regular basis. Most of us (if we allowed ourselves) would find ourselves being more confrontational with others who are conflict-oriented and more accommodating with those who are accommodating towards us.

EXERCISE

How will you share your knowledge of conflict prevention with your performers?

How should you handle conflict when and if it does occur?

1   Stay cool.
2   Seek understanding of the other's point of view.
3   Check you have achieved that understanding.
4   Demonstrate that you do understand.
5   Ask how you can help the other party.
6   Ask the other party if they wish to hear your point of view.
7   Know exactly what you need to resolve the conflict from your point of view.
8   Be flexible in achieving it.

Stay cool

9   Persuade and allow yourself to be persuaded regarding the ultimate resolution.
10 Have a cooling-off period before final agreement, to consider all ramifications.
11 Where possible try to create a win–win situation for both parties.

This method will work if both parties use it. Indeed, it is likely that any conflict management method will work as long as both parties are committed to it.

The possible ways of resolving conflict

There are several possible resolutions to conflict: winning, domination, suppression, denial, compromise, co-operation, capitulation, defeat.

Winning   As has been said elsewhere, conflicts are never won. The cost of 'winning' may not always be obvious. The penalty of victory may not be immediate. The price of glory may have to be paid in multiple painful instalments, over a prolonged period. Some industry leaders publicly advocate dismissing employees who disagree with them. They hold their success up as justification for continuing the practice. Word soon spreads. Would you, the intelligent, creative, results-oriented person you are, want to work for someone who'd fire you for disagreeing? Of course not. Which begs the question, what kind of people do want to work for such an ogre? Those with sparkling achievement records? Those with initiative levels beyond measurement? No? Or perhaps those who can't find employment with anyone else? Hmm! Sounds more likely.

Domination   One party imposes their authority on the other. In relationships where co-operation is required, this approach will backfire in the way described above. It will succeed where both parties have entered the arrangement by consent (note the kind of people prepared to do so, as above). Where both parties have agreed that in the event of conflict an impartial third party will arbitrate and their decision will be binding on both parties, domination works. But this is not really domination; it is more like co-operation.

Suppression   Suppression can work for small, insignificant differences, or where both parties agree that the issues are not worth disagreeing over. Pretending there are no difficulties may be essential for the more serious conflicts, or where neither party can afford a dispute with the other. So, in fairness to our colleagues in the diplomatic services, honesty may not always be the best policy. On the other hand, perhaps openly agreeing not to discuss certain issues is the most honest method of suppression.

Denial   Denial is a favourite method with politicians of all colours. The existence of any problem is denied in the hope that others will agree and not pursue the issue any further. Unfortunately denial as a conflict resolution strategy only works if both, or all, parties agree, and usually only when the issue is fairly minor. For other than insignificant problems, it is a strategy that is totally inappropriate in a relationship dependent on mutual trust for its success.

Compromise   By far the most commonly used conflict resolution strategy, both parties move a little towards some middle ground. While it may appear to be the best solution, it has problems. Each party has different constraints on how far they can move their position. If one party is pushed too far, their commitment to the 'agreed' solution may be less than absolute. If compromise is used, both parties must really be in a position to do so, freely and not feel obliged to do so. The greater the level of obligation toward compromise, the greater the resentment towards it, and the smaller the commitment to it.

Co-operation   The ideal but most ingenuously used solution is co-operation. Much lip service is paid to 'working out a solution together', when in reality people are positioning themselves for a victory. If both parties are genuine, the outcome of this conflict resolution method will be a strengthened relationship and an agreement to which both parties feel totally committed.

Capitulation   The opposite of domination is where one party gives in to the wishes of the other. The capitulator superficially accepts the resolution imposed by the other party but seeks ways of redressing the balance behind the scenes and over a period of time. Capitulation works if both parties have entered the relationship on a consenting basis where it is the method agreed for conflict resolution. However, company heads should not assume that all employees are willing to capitulate by consent. There will always be a few who don't want their particular jobs but are forced to accept them for financial reasons. People forced to accept a position and then forced to capitulate in that position can make vicious saboteurs.

Defeat   One party imposes a solution on the other. Many of the world's longest running terror situations were started using this approach. Don't expect anything less than the equivalent in a workplace conflict.

EXERCISE

Ask your performers to think of one example of a conflict being resolved in each of the above ways. Ask them what the longer-term outcome was for each example.

Handling (verbal) aggression

Most aggression directed at you will not be about the issue the assailant is presenting as the main issue. There is usually some deeper-seated problem. It may be the final stage in a progressive build-up and you may be witnessing the human equivalent of a volcano bursting. So where an everyday commercial conflict has turned into full-blown verbal aggression, how do you handle it?

Make a beeline for the stationery cupboard? Too late, I'm already in there! Now what? From the safety of my position I can offer some tips. Naturally, it will be up to you to decide which are useful and which will escalate the situation. The process is similar to that described above for handling conflict.

Once you have established that you are under verbal attack, take a deep breath and take on some positive inner dialogue. You can identify an attack by the presence of unpleasant words, bulging veins, foaming at the mouth, clenched fists, statements that call your parentage into questions, and comments that call your, no doubt purer than pure, motives into question.

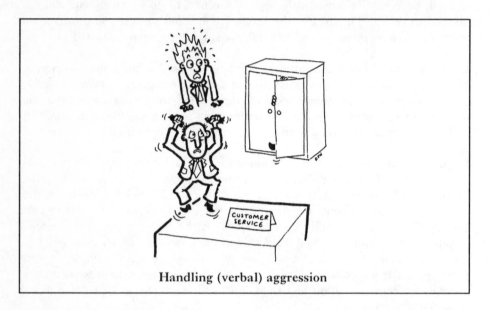

Handling (verbal) aggression

While taking care not to react to any of the personal attacks, try to discover what the assailant is concerned about. Show them you want to understand. When clarification has been provided, check your understanding. Seek confirmation that your understanding is correct.

Express your identification with the subject's emotional reaction to the situation (Yes, you do understand, and yes, you would probably feel that way too, wouldn't you!) and offer a way of resolving the problem, even if that way is only to sit down together and talk about it. Usually at this, or the previous stage, you will have seen the assailant warm to you. You are, after all, listening. You are, after all, taking them seriously! You are, aren't you?

If the aggression continues, repeat your expression of understanding and present your means of resolving the problem again. This is the point where many inexperienced conflict handlers lose control; they have been reasonable, they have been calm, they have tried to understand the person, they have offered solutions, and still they are being insulted and abused. The experienced conflict manager, for it really is just another management exercise – despite the emotional intensity involved – will calmly state how they feel being on the receiving end of this abuse and ask the assailant if this is really how they want to behave towards someone who is trying to help them. If the answer is 'no' they will usually calm down and apologize. If the answer is 'yes', then simply and calmly state what the consequences of their continued action will be.

A definition of stress may be helpful here: 'Stress is that which is experienced when one restrains one's self with one's mind from doing that with one's body which one's spirit and all of humanity would thank one for: that is, putting them out of your misery!'

If you have no consequences with which to 'cool' the abuser, or you have decided their use would be inappropriate, you have the option to terminate the interaction, refer it to a higher authority (not the higher authority implied in the above definition), or encourage them to vent their feelings. Even the most vociferous assailant will run out of steam fairly quickly.

A fairly high-risk strategy may be appropriate in some circumstances (where the aggressor is being extremely unreasonable and even irrational), namely to tell the aggressor that you are going to tape-record the proceedings. That will produce one of five possible responses: no change, a calming down, a withdrawal from the confrontation, a rapid and uncontrolled disassembly of your tape-recorder, or an addition to your anatomical apparatus. From the safety of my position in the stationery cupboard I'll let you decide whether or not to start taping.

EXERCISE

Ask your performers to remember a conflict they were involved in which degenerated into verbal aggression. After discussing the above ask them how they would handle it differently. How can you and your performers practise handling verbal aggression?

Frustration

What is it? It can be experienced with great intensity by those seeking, but failing to, complement your anatomy with various gadgets to which they may have a minor aversion. More seriously, it is experienced when attempts one feels should be successful are not, or when one knows what to do but just can't get it to happen. It can also be with other people. In short, frustration comes from a sense of falling short. But not totally failing.

Every negative and destructive emotion, to the high achiever, is a signal providing information about how to achieve results. The empowering interpretation of frustration is: one's mind has a powerful belief that one can achieve more than is being achieved. The way to handle it is to accept that your mind has alerted you to be more responsive to your environment, to be more flexible. You have been told you should start looking for other approaches, or to fine-tune your current approach. Do whatever it takes to generate some ideas on changing or improving your approach. Try to actually enjoy looking for improvements; you're bound to be more effective if you do.

Frustration

Share the negative. If your frustration involves another person, tell them how you feel. Don't cling to the negatives; agree that there is a positive side to the frustration, the empowering interpretation just mentioned. If you have been honest and positive with the subject of your frustration, there is a much greater likelihood that your next goal will be achieved successfully, in other words to jointly agree to act on the positive interpretation. Ask your performer to use this method the next time they experience frustration.

Ending the coaching/mentoring relationship

All relationships end. There is a sad inevitability about the fact that the passing of time always ends that which was once held so dear. Painful and uncomfortable as it is, it is best to view the coaching relationship as one that will inevitably end. It may be that mentor and mentored become friends and continue their association throughout their careers, but the coaching/mentoring arrangement *per se* must end at some point.

Wise partnerships are formed on the basis of a clear understanding of all the factors that will determine when and how the relationship starts, what its purposes are, how it will proceed and develop, and in what stages; how disputes, conflicts and other difficulties will be resolved; and when, how and under what circumstances it will end. The coaching and mentoring relationship should be set up on the same basis.

On a more upbeat note, coaching, at the height of its excellence, can be invisible. The highly skilled coach, like those at a similar level in all other professions, makes their art look effortless. The coaching relationship can be ended by the coach working themselves out of a job, by helping the performers to a point where they can self-coach as effectively and as invisibly as the original coach. The coach is then in a position to gradually fade into the background unnoticed. Discuss with your performers the intentions, logistics and conditions for ending the relationship.

No matter how well prepared we are, those of us in western cultures go through a predictable cycle of loss when we lose a friend or loved one. The stages are:

- Denial.
- Depression.
- Acceptance.
- Recovery.
- Post-recovery.

Denial is usually characterized by a combination of shock and various attempts to minimize or deny the loss. During the depression phase, there is an element of letting go and a deep sense of sadness at having to do so. In the acceptance phase, the worst is over and a period of discovery of the new self begins. The person experiencing the loss starts to test out new ways of living. During the recovery phase there is a period in which, gradually, full, normal functioning takes place, and finally in post-recovery, the loss is integrated into the person, it forms a clear part of their past, and they can look at the loss without being over-emotional about it. The whole process can be made less painful and faster by engaging in all of society's mourning rituals. What loss or mourning rituals will you plan for the end of the coaching or mentoring relationship?

Concluding comments and summary

There are four main barriers to coaching and mentoring: personal, organizational, environmental and process. Personal and organizational barriers are the most easily addressed. All barriers are best overcome by persuasion, education and example. You may, however, have to avoid, use or confront the human source of barriers. Even though the effort required to overcome the barriers to coaching and mentoring is great, the rewards are greater. But it is not as though the organization hoping to survive has any choice in the matter. The costs of not coaching and mentoring are high: a company failing to develop its staff always pays the ultimate penalty.

Part IV

Coaching and mentoring systems

13

IMPLEMENTING A SYSTEM

An overview of systems

Virtually any system that can be used in a mentoring context can also be used in a coaching situation. As such, the systems ought to be presented as being independent of the use they are put to. As you read through the various systems, keep your mind open for ways in which you can alter or improve them for use in your own company. Try to generate some new systems.

The influence of roles on systems

Coaching and mentoring systems adopted by organizations will depend on what objectives have been set. The objectives set will, to some extent, be influenced by the roles those setting the objectives perceive coaches and/or mentors can fulfil. The roles can be those of trainer, counsellor, guide, facilitator, role model, motivator, people problem troubleshooter, project guide, productivity enhancer, training liaison officer, cultural compliance officer, and so on *ad infinitum*. In other words the coach and mentor can be used for any purpose the organization chooses. The perceived role of coach or mentor can be as flexible as is required in the system.

Pure coaching systems

The ideal system in an ideal world is the pure coaching system with ideal performers and ideal coaches/mentors. Every performer is highly motivated and is an experienced self-managing developer, having their own assigned coach. Every coach is performer-focused, and available to the performer on a structured and spontaneous basis. Although the ideal is beyond reach, it gives us a benchmark or model to strive for.

Pure mentoring

The same applies to the ideal mentoring system. The highly skilled mentor is available for the highly motivated performer to learn from. The mentor's communication skills are better than excellent: she or he is able to convey information in exactly the way the performer will understand most rapidly, and most permanently. A mentor is available on a structured and spontaneous basis to every performer as and when required.

However, realism must prevail. The following systems are achievable, are tried and tested, and will work if the appropriate level of commitment is applied to them. Many can be used in conjunction with others. I'd suggest which could be combined but why should I do all the work? As you read through the systems, look for ways to combine them to produce improved derivatives.

Problem-focused

Coaches or mentors are often appointed to help individuals or teams solve specific problems. They can also be called on to help an individual with whom the organization is having problems: the under-performer, the reluctant performer, the self-saboteur, and so on. The arrangement usually ends when the performer is back on track. It is, however, unwise to end the relationship so soon or so abruptly. It is more likely to be of lasting benefit, in this instance, if the coach–performer contact is gradually faded out. That way the performer sees that she or he can function well with or without the coach or mentor before making the decision to end the relationship.

Project-focused

Project-oriented coaching and mentoring is aimed at supporting the performer's development throughout the period of a designated project. The coaching starts as the 'appointment' of the performer as project manager is made, or when appointments are made to the project team. The coach or mentor's work is done when the project goals are achieved or after supporting the team or performer when the project has either been abandoned or not gone to plan.

Training follow-up

Training which is followed up is much more effective than training that is not. If a company is going to invest in its staff, it is only reasonable to expect they will want to follow up that training to assess its effectiveness, and to reinforce and enhance the new skills. Coaching and mentoring can be used in the follow-up capacity. Done badly, follow-up coaching can be like the thought police coming to check you've done your homework. Done well, the performer will look forward to the chance to work through problems in implementing their new skills. Follow-up coaching and mentoring is done well by genuinely seeking to support the performer, and genuinely seeking feedback on the effectiveness of the training concerned.

Induction-focused

The event which lends itself most readily and most measurably to coaching and mentoring is the induction period. In some organizations each new entrant is appointed an 'induction friend' or an 'induction guide' or some other name with the same meaning. The multi-named single purpose is to help the new employee settle into the company or organization as quickly and as smoothly as possible. Of particular concern is overcoming the natural feelings of insecurity and inadequacy which exist when plunged into a strange environment. The handling of a new entrant and their resultant impression of the organization in the first few days will last a very long time. The better the induction the sooner and more effectively the performer will start achieving.

Qualification-focused

In many organizations coaching is directed towards helping the performer achieve a vocational or professional qualification. In many cases the coaching or mentoring procedure (although it may not be referred to by these names) is laid down by the relevant examining body. The company with such a system in place can widen its use to include general performance enhancement. If a qualification-focused system already exists, there should be little resistance to gradual expansion of the coaching or mentoring philosophy to cover all aspects of participants' performance, and eventually all aspects of all employee performance. Introducing a qualification-focused system may be the best and easiest way to introduce coaching generally to your company.

Peer group

Peer groups can be extremely effective at self-coaching and self-mentoring. In any group of people there will be a range of talents and abilities. If such a group is assembled for the expressed and agreed intention of helping each other develop, the peer pressure phenomenon will do the rest. Peer pressure will work in such a way as to place high regard on those skilled in one area helping others in exchange for help in their areas of weakness. If you are reluctant to entrust the outcome to peer pressure, you can apply the principles and practices of team coaching. If the resistance to introducing coaching is high, or the support for it is low, this method can be easily implemented. You and your coaching/mentoring supporters can start your own self-coaching peer group. Conduct the group outside of office hours if necessary. As your performance increases and word starts to get around you will find more and more people wanting to be involved. Accommodate their wishes as far as you can. At the point of there being too many people, ask new volunteers to form their own groups. Offer what support you can. As and if the process continues, it won't be long before coaching and mentoring are formally adopted by the organization.

Provision contingent provision (PCP)

PCP sounds more like a medication than a performance enhancement system. It does have a soothing effect on the introduction of coaching and mentoring.

The principle is that you can receive coaching and mentoring input if you are providing it. Anyone expecting coaching input from more senior levels would have to set it up for those in more junior positions. Coaching ability then becomes an issue. Is it wise to require someone who knows nothing (not even the 20 per cent core operating principles) about the techniques of coaching to provide coaching or mentoring to others? Clearly not. So some form of training or self-training is required (after an initial assessment of coaching skills, although as will be argued later, it may be more cost-effective to assume everyone requires training or self-training). Contingent provision of coaching must therefore require anyone who wants coaching to acquire the skills of coaching. The chain can be continued: those having received training in coaching can then make their first coaching sessions coach training sessions for their subordinates. Provision contingent provision therefore requires coaching one's subordinates to provide coaching for their subordinates and so on. PCP will only work if coaching is introduced to the company from the highest levels and training or self-training facilities in coaching and mentoring are provided.

Promotion grooming

Some companies will do what passes for coaching or mentoring only when someone is being groomed for succession or promotion. While obviously beneficial, coaching only under those circumstances sends a signal to all other employees that the only people in the company worth spending time developing are those receiving promotions. It also sends a signal saying the only time your performance is of interest is just before, during and shortly after your promotions. Not a recipe for a company full of consistently high performers. Far better that coaching should be the norm, with extra briefing being provided

Promotion grooming

during a promotion transition. Live in the real world we must. So if that is the way a company chooses to operate how should it be done? What is involved in the promotion grooming?

1 An assessment of the current skills and knowledge of the promoted person.
2 An assessment of the skills and knowledge required for successful performance in the post.
3 A comparison between the skills they have now and the skills required for the post.
4 Followed by appropriate measures to close the gap.

The promoted person may conduct the analysis with the help of those who know what is required in the new post. The role of the coach or mentor in this situation can vary from that of transition trainer to moral supporter, depending on what the performer wants, what the company decrees and what the coach is capable of.

Role model

Which of us has never tried to emulate a successful other? Much of early childhood learning is based on imitating role models. Can the company provide suitable role models from within? From outside? Role models in the workplace will come from those who have achieved at a high level the performance or kind of performance the performer wants to or is expected to achieve. The performer can be given access to the role model in several different ways: regularly; as and when required; as and when possible; or for a one-off interactive session with a senior company figure or a business celebrity.

Naturally there are problems. Role models often become 'semi-cult figures' whose every movement is analysed for some deep and significant meaning. They quickly become surrounded by myth, fable and fallacious (mis)assumptions. They are attributed with talents and abilities which they do not possess. There is a fine line between role modelling and hero worship. When that line is crossed, the benefits of mentoring are largely lost: rational emulation of the role model's skill and abilities is overshadowed.

Arranging for a commercial celebrity to visit your company is a good way of demonstrating to those in authority the beneficial effects of mentoring; don't be surprised if those most enthusiastic about meeting the person were those most resistant to the idea of coaching.

Group role model

Groups can have role models in the same way individuals can. Their role models can be individuals or other groups. The most effective group role models are those chosen by the group. To be effective the group must have easy access either to the individual or team concerned or to information about them. Group role modelling is most effective as part of a peer group development system. The concept of mentoring can be subtly introduced to a group or team by drawing their attention to a notable success by an individual or team and asking what can be learned from it. Once the group has actively engaged in the discussion and has come to some useful conclusions, you can suggest that there might be some merit in group role modelling and ask 'How can we use this technique on a regular basis?' Once accepted in principle, your implementation programme can move on to whatever you think is an appropriate next stage.

Sponsor system

Sponsoring is a popular way of mentoring. The mentor acts to protect and represent the interests of the developing performer. The mentor (in theory) helps the performer in whatever they wish assistance with. They promote and present the performer to others. In this system, the mentor is less of an information provider and more of an agent. The mentor aims to ease the performer's interactions with important others. But there can only be a limited number of sufficiently high-level managers in each organization to provide high-quality mentoring. The performers who are allocated a less senior or less influential mentor than their peers will regard that as a statement by the company on their comparative worth. The best way to avoid such a problem is to ensure that all mentors servicing a particular level of performer are all of equal status. To ensure there are sufficient to go round may mean mentors are no more than say two levels above the performer. The greatest advantage of this system is its simplicity and the relatively low level of coaching skill required by the mentors.

Strategic skills analysis

We know that strategic skills analysis is done by self-managed developers and other super-performers. They analyse, in various individual ways, the skills required in order to achieve the objectives set. They decide how best to acquire the skills concerned and set about doing so. The role of the coach or mentor with this system is to assist the strategic skills analysis and help the performer in other ways as they require and request.

Strategic skills analysis can be conducted without the availability of coaches. The personnel and/or training functions can co-ordinate the issue and return of self-completed strategic skills analysis forms. Everyone (not necessarily all at once) in the company is requested to analyse the skills, knowledge, contacts, resources necessary to carry out their organizational objectives. The second part of the process is for performers to provide a plan for achieving their objectives, and a plan for acquiring the required skill.

Using this system to introduce coaching enables those in personnel and training who may previously have felt threatened to see first-hand the benefits of giving performers responsibility for their own development. The information

Strategic skills analysis

provided can then be used as the basis for individual coaching with the performers. Absolutely the worst thing that could be done for the cause of coaching, mentoring and staff improvement generally is to seek the information, collect the forms, and then leave them gathering dust in the performer's personnel or training file.

Self-development

This system is the closest practicable to pure coaching. The role of the organization is to provide what the performer needs to manage their own learning and development. We know that the highest performances come from those who take total responsibility for their learning and other achievements. The company which encourages and resources such performance enhancement methods can expect great returns.

What kind of resourcing? Time, access to people and suitable learning resources. If the necessary time is made available, little money will be required. The self-managed developer will use the time to access people, libraries, university staff or whatever else they know will benefit them at minimal cost to the company. Access to people in the organization should be taken as read, but in some companies it may be necessary to brief staff to encourage them to help, and to create the expectation that they can be called on to act as impromptu teachers.

Money in anything other than small amounts will be required only if access to time and people is denied for whatever reason. Even the money in self-developmental coaching can become the responsibility of the performer. He or she can be given control over their own training budget for the year; how they choose to spend it can be up to them. There should be an incentive system whereby the high performer can earn more training credits; the meritocratic organization will no doubt be glad to offer more training to those who have proven that their return justifies the investment. There should also be a system whereby the high performer who achieves without spending the training budget can transfer that money either to the next year's budget or to shares in the company or to their own budget for any project they wish to undertake on behalf of the company. The threat of 'grabbing back' unspent budgets causes irresponsible spending of the kind seen once a year in many public service organizations. There should be no such threat; responsible people tuck away small amounts of money for contingencies and opportunities.

What kind of controls should be in place to ensure that the unscrupulous do not use the company as a free university? Access to a self-controlled training budget and training time should be earned, and the right to continued access should be maintained by evidence of constructive and appropriate learning activity. The judgement of 'appropriateness' must be made very carefully; many intrapreneurs have to deliberately break company rules in order to benefit the company. If the company stops the performer from performing, don't be surprised to see an intrapreneur turning into a successful entrepreneur and doing so in such a big way that they blow their previous employer out of the water. Thwart the highly motivated self-developer at your peril.

Autobiographical and biographical

Which of us has read an autobiography by some ultra-high achiever and not been uplifted and motivated to emulate them? Which of us can claim not to be moved by the many high-quality, motivational success-oriented texts available, particularly when they can cite real-life examples? Who amongst us does not find the mini success stories in the press fascinating and educational? The answer to all these questions is those who don't think they can learn anything useful from the success of others, or those who attribute success to luck, serendipity, chance, fate... In short, those who have decided that success is not first created in the mind.

Autobiographical coaching or mentoring is probably a misnomer. It is really a self-managed development activity. A company wishing to encourage this kind of coaching will provide suitable texts. Some do so by providing a company library or learning centre. My experience is they are under-used and probably a waste of money.

A much more productive way to harness autobiographical learning is to have managers act as librarians. Why? Because part of their responsibility is staff development, and they can use the lending of books as an opportunity to carry out the developmental responsibilities. They can ask the performer what they are hoping to learn from each text, what was actually learned on return, what they would like to implement from what they have learned. The manager can invite requests for assistance, developmental support or coaching from the performer wishing to implement what they have learned. They can ask the performer what from the new knowledge they would like to develop further, either in terms of training or training follow-up, and so on.

Autobiographical coaching can often suffer from a credibility obstacle. Credibility of the hero or heroine can often be dented by the very strengths that enabled their achievements. For instance, most of us learn from our mistakes while deliberately trying to forget the mistakes we learned from. It is therefore likely that many autobiographies offer an incomplete picture: the heroic figure may forget to include some very important, informative and decisive mistakes. Or worse still, they may paint a picture exaggerated by the passing of time, or still worse, exaggerated for the purposes of self-publicity. Numerous examples could be provided, but I am a UK citizen; libel laws loom large and lawyers liking lots of lolly linger longingly.

Manager as coach or mentor

The most common form of coaching and mentoring system in the world today, and usually on an unknowing basis, is where managers act as coach or mentor. Most companies have no formal coaching or mentoring system, but managers are expected to ensure that their staff are sufficiently competent. The only way to do this is to train, motivate, facilitate – to coach – but without the formal structure to do so for optimum effectiveness.

The most serious drawback with this system is the human propensity for hypocrisy. It may be acceptable in our significant others, but not, most definitely not, in our superiors. If our bosses want to lose our respect as rapidly as is humanly possible they need only pay a brief visit to the school of 'don't do as I do, do as I say'. A manager failing to practise what they preach in a coaching session cannot expect their coaching input to be taken seriously or, for that matter, their managerial competence.

We have also mentioned earlier the conflict of interests, the consequences of breaching trust and the best ways to prevent the commission of such a cardinal sin. The greatest benefit of the manager providing the coaching or mentoring input is that he or she has an interest in the performer doing well. They also have an interest in the whole team working well and in developing their coaching skills to the highest possible levels. The better the team are as coaches to each other, the better their department or division will perform, the more likely they are to be promoted, or to be awarded that big bonus and so on.

Despite all the associated problems, the manager is the ideal coach; they have the strongest interest in the performer's performance. As we know, he or she who has the greatest intensity and consistency of purpose is always most effective in the long term. The manager coach fits that role perfectly.

Informal coaching

Informal coaching can be highly effective, but it needs to be prepared properly. That may sound contradictory. It is not. Informal coaching can only occur effectively if the provider is equipped with the appropriate coaching skills and has prepared themselves to coach at a moment's notice. The receiver can be coached without awareness that coaching is taking place. Performers usually respond best to coaching, whether formal or informal, if they know the purpose of the interaction is for both parties to work together to improve their performance.

Companies planning to set up *ad hoc* or informal arrangements should re-evaluate. Unfortunately, commercial experience tells us that informal arrangements very rapidly degenerate into non-existent ones. So even if the coaching is to be informal, or perhaps better called spontaneous, it should still be conducted in a formal and organized way. After agreeing that a coaching session is appropriate, both parties should go to a designated coaching room or area. If changing location is not appropriate, a communication of the purpose of the subsequent interaction should be clearly made.

EXERCISE

Divide the above systems into two categories: long-term and short-term coaching and mentoring.

All of the above were devised to fit into some company's particular circumstances. If your company circumstances lend themselves to the total adoption of one of the above, that's good news: it will save you some work. Since that is unlikely, you will do yourself and your company a lot of good by learning what you can from each of these approaches and devising your own. Only the people in your company can possibly know what is best for you, and only you can know what will and what will not work. Only you will know what is likely to be acceptable, only you will know what the best starting point will be. Experts can tell you what factors you should be considering, but you should make the final decision because you have to live with it and take the consequences if it doesn't work. Confucius might have said, 'Accept cautiously advice from person who is immunized from the consequences of that advice'.

Introducing and implementing systems

As an integral part of the description of the various coaching and mentoring systems, suggestions for implementation were made. Implementation suggestions were also offered in the various barriers sections. What I offer as suggestions is less important than you being able to consider all the factors necessary to decide how YOU are going to implement a system.

If you are the CEO life is relatively easy in terms of implementation. Well, at least you don't have to try persuading the CEO! If you are still on your way to that position you have to do the same as the CEO AND persuade him or her that your proposal is worth implementing. What are the factors you will have to consider when deciding how to introduce and implement a coaching and/or mentoring system? They consist of:

- Researching the options.
- Deciding on a system.
- Fielding the idea.
- Seeking consensus.
- Providing information:

  - The benefits.
  - The logistics.
  - The worries.
  - The reassurances.

- Starting at the top.
- Starting at the bottom.
- Setting an example.
- Briefing pyramids.
- Expectation clarifying.
- Training or self-managed development.
- Information provision.

Researching the options, deciding on a system

As was said at the end of the last chapter, only those inside an organization can know what system will work best in that structure. Discovering what is likely to work will require a considerable knowledge of the organization as it really is, not as it is supposed to be on the organizational chart, and not as it is supposed to be in any operating or procedure manuals. The reality in every organization is that the adoption of any system has less to do with the good it can provide the organization and more to do with what it will achieve for the people running the organization.

Your implementation proposal should therefore consider the needs of those making the final decision. You can test their reactions to some of the options by asking questions like 'If we were to introduce some organized method of improving staff performance and output, what characteristics do you think it would have in order to work in our company? What criteria would it have to fulfil to be acceptable?'

If you obtain sufficiently clear characteristics and acceptance criteria, when your proposal can be shown to satisfy them, resistance is likely to be minimal.

EXERCISE

How will you research and decide on which option to propose? How will you figure out what is likely to work in the company?

Seeking consensus

When seeking consensus, one eye should be kept on what will work most effectively, the other on what most people will accept, and the third eye, if you have one handy, on what will serve the interests of those in authority. However, the adoption of a system that is good for the organization is not beyond hope. It is an unwise underling who actively resists the wishes or apparent wishes of their bosses. Equally it is an unwise general who overrules the wishes of their troops. Now, far be it from me to suggest the use of underhand tactics but if someone were to propose such a reprehensible thing they might say: If the troops think the general wants the system that is best for the organization, which is system X, and the general thinks the troops want system X, regardless of what each originally wanted, they are all more likely to want system X. Right? Your likelihood of success is high.

A note of warning: how can you be sure that you know what is best for the organization? How can you be sure that what you think is best is not actually what is best for you? Despite the known conflict of interest experienced by leaders between their needs and the organization's needs, how can you be sure that the system they would favour is not better for the organization than the one you favour? Their interests are, after all, tied up with the interests of the company. How can you be sure that what people most desire for themselves is not better for the organization? How can you be sure that what people are committed to will not work better than something imposed or effectively imposed because they think the boss likes it?

It is rapidly looking as though using underhand methods to create an apparent consensus may not be so clever. My advice is if you have to use underhand methods, it should only be to introduce a system that will ultimately be accepted, and not to use dirty tricks to impose one system over another. The system that will work best and have the greatest longevity is the one supported by the largest number with the greatest influence; let democracy take its course. The most successful societies in the world are democracies for very good reasons. Devise a systematic way in which you can test and seek consensus for the proposed coaching system.

Researching and deciding on a system – revisited

In the truly enlightened organizations of the world, the people who would be affected by the system will be those who make the decision. Who is affected? Everyone who could be a provider or receiver of coaching or mentoring services. Which means that the system chosen may vary from division to division, between departments and even between department sections. In fact, it makes sense to have different coaching systems operating throughout the company. It sends the right signals to the staff; it says we value you as unique individuals with the wisdom to choose what is best for you and the company. Naturally a self-chosen system will produce a much higher degree of commitment than one imposed from above. The directive or, rather, suggestion from the top could then be to adopt a means of coaching and mentoring your staff that your staff decide – if your staff decide. How can you persuade the top team that letting the staff decide which system to adopt is likely to be the most effective option?

Providing information

In order for staff to decide which system to adopt they need to have the relevant information. The information should be provided impartially in the same way that skilled medical practitioners will tell the patient about the options for treatment. The benefits, the risks, the logistics and all the relevant statistics will be provided for each of the treatment options. The physician will naturally make recommendations and give good reasons for them, but in an ideal situation the patient makes an informed choice and decides which option to select. But in this instance the people receiving information are not ill, they are your commercial athletes. In what ways will you provide staff with impartial information on coaching and mentoring systems?

Providing information

If a decision has to be made to impose a coaching and mentoring system, a different approach is required. Selling, education and reassurance are the order of the day. The approach you take to selling the proposed system will depend on your personal style, the nature of your audience and the other factors mentioned in the section covering persuasion and influence styles (page 126). The educational component will be an integral part of your message. You will have to provide details of how, where, when, who, why, how much and how often. The way you provide the education is up to you. There is an enormous number of options: briefing teams, memos, notice-board signs, personalized letters and so on. Reassurance is best provided by demonstrating that far from being a threat – the main worry about any new system – the coaching programme is a significant benefit to employee and company alike.

Reassurance can also be provided by allowing worried staff to witness a coaching session on video. If you do make such a video, show it as it happens:

don't use any fancy shots, fades, wipes, or graphics. Simply set the camera up in the corner and let it run throughout the session. Why? Anxious employees expect you to try to persuade them. If you show it as it is, problems and all, you will be much more credible. Remember the finding conveyed earlier that the revelation of information that weakens an attempt at persuasion by the persuader paradoxically makes the message more persuasive? Show it as it is, warts and all. Besides which, it is very cheap for someone to bring in their home movie camera and make copies of the resultant tape for distribution to those who wish to see it. Plan your sales campaign for your system.

Starting at the top

Since employees mimic their bosses it is best to implement any new system from the top down. Each level in the organization will want to copy the apparently effective new behaviours in the levels above. If the highest levels are coaching their subordinates, every other level will want to coach their potential successors. Unfortunately some will want merely to be seen to be coaching or mentoring. They can be rumbled by the assessment and evaluation procedures (see later) which will reveal the inferior performance of those they are coaching, compared to those of similar ability being coached in a genuine way.

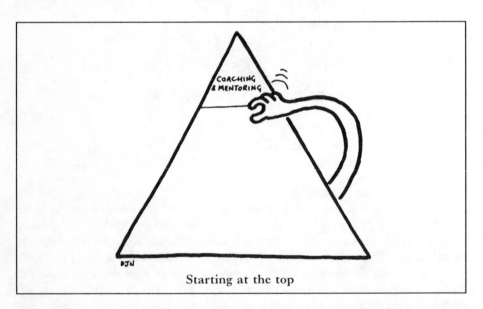

Starting at the top

If you are at the top, one of the most influential things you can do to start the coaching ball rolling is to publicize a new and revised coaching and staff training plan. The plan should be drawn from, and be entirely consistent with, the strategic plan, the marketing plan, the production plan, the 'every other' plan. How can you publicize the coaching and mentoring efforts of the top team?

Starting at the bottom

In some circumstances – namely those in which you are liable to encounter resistance from the top for all the wrong reasons – it is wise to start at the bottom. In one system I set up a few years ago, the track record of top management was such that resistance was inevitable. The strategy adopted was to implement the new system, start it working and achieving its objectives, create widespread support that would be difficult to ignore or overrule, and then present the new system to top management as a *fait accompli*. The predictable reaction of the senior staff concerned was, 'Jolly good idea. We support it entirely. Why didn't you ask for our help earlier?' How can you implement a new system at the lower levels in such a way that it dovetails into the existing responsibilities of those implementing it?

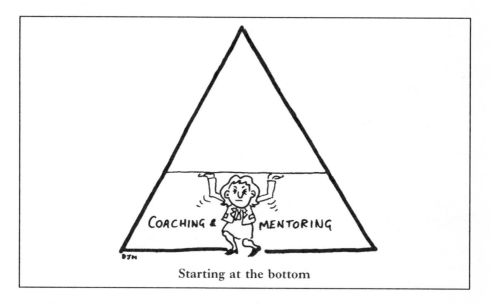

Starting at the bottom

Setting an example

We are all influenced by the successful performance of others in the field in which we wish to excel. The best advert for coaching and mentoring is doing it and obtaining superior results from your staff. The second best advert is that you obtain coaching or mentoring for yourself and are consequently more successful in your own performances. To be credible, you must practise what you preach. Would a book on coaching that didn't practise the principles of coaching be credible? Would an educational text that didn't practise the known principles of maximizing learning be credible? Alas, there are many of both! Write to me to tell me how I can be even more credible in the follow-up to this book. But first, ask those you seek to influence on the matter of coaching how they will be most persuaded to choose a system.

Briefing pyramids

The mimicking effect described in 'Starting at the top' can be formally harnessed by having each level coach the next level down in the techniques of coaching or mentoring. Briefing pyramids are optimally effective if the message about coaching is conveyed using coaching methods, if the person giving the briefing 'walks their talk', as some Americans say. Using what you now know about coaching how will you brief others using the principles of coaching?

Expectation clarifying

The main reason management fashions come and go, but good management principles remain timeless is that fashions create unrealistic and unclear expectations in the hype that surrounds them. If I have been guilty of this misdemeanour please write to me using the following complaint form:

☐

To implement a coaching or mentoring system which is going to be accepted, effective and long-standing, expectations must be realistic and clear. By all means do your best to sell the idea, but make no exaggerated claims, no unsustainable assertions and no unfulfillable promises. How will you ensure that in your various sales pitches you don't create any unrealistic expectations and set the whole system up for failure?

Training or facilitating the self-development of the coaches and mentors

What are the key decisions you have to make about training coaches and mentors? The first is whether or not to train mentors. The second is if you require more of your mentors than role modelling or information provision, to what extent will coaching skills training be required? The third decision is how the training will be provided. The fourth decision is how to support new coaches through their development and then how to continue supporting established coaches as they experience the ups and downs of the role.

Information provision for coaches and mentors

Virtually every profession and every discipline within that profession has a means of exchanging ideas and providing the latest information to all interested parties. Many companies have company newsletters or regular gatherings of various kinds. Providing information to your coaches and mentors is critical to the outcome and continual improvement of their efforts. How will you provide information for your coaches? How will you help them to exchange ideas, methods, techniques and so on?

Barriers to implementation

Some people may block the implementation of a new coaching or mentoring system on the grounds that it is seen as a way of selecting high fliers – that would be divisive. Others will block because they see it as a mechanism through which old boy networks could get a foothold and flourish, and damn it as anti-meritocratic. Still others will block systems for fear they will be seen by staff as the route to promotion. They will worry that the system so linked will rapidly degenerate into one in which participation must be seen and outcome not heard. In other words, the whole system will turn into a 'face time' exercise for all concerned. Senior managers will have to have their faces seen coaching or mentoring to obtain board positions, and junior levels will be expected to be on the receiving end to obtain promotion. All of these fears are realistic. The only way to overcome them is to put checks and balances in place. What balances and checks could you put in place to prevent the above? Clue: outcome assessment.

EXERCISE

What other barriers to implementation are you likely to encounter? How will you overcome them?

Selecting, training and supporting coaches and mentors

Selecting

Selection or self-selection? In many ways those who self-select are much more motivated than those 'volunteered'. Motivation is one part of the equation; skill and coaching competence is the other part. The ideal coaching provider is he or she who wants to do it and who has the bulk of the necessary skills already in place. Only a small amount, if any, of additional training will be required.

How should coaches or mentors be selected or self-selected? If provision contingent provision is in place, selection is automatic; anyone wishing to receive it must provide it. If not, some means of deciding who should coach must be implemented. Ideally everyone who will ever have to manage staff should also be a skilled coach. Practically, only those who currently have responsibility for others are in a position to practise the skills, at least within the company. Others may have social or community responsibilities that give them the opportunity to develop coaching skills.

EXERCISE

With the relevant factors before you, how should you select coaches and mentors in your organization? If you think self-selection is not appropriate, who and how will you select?

Is training needed?

Is it necessary to train mentors? Mentoring can be carried out quite satis-factorily with the skills that most senior managers will have acquired over their years of development. It is extremely unlikely that anyone could reach a high level in an organization without having had to set an example for their staff, thereby acting as a *de facto* mentor. The decision is not necessarily training versus no training; there is a constructive mid-ground. Provide senior staff with some guidelines on what is to be expected in their particular mentor-ing situation. The guidelines provided will clearly depend on the objectives of the mentoring exercise. That statement should lead you to guess the next exercise.

EXERCISE

What are the objectives of mentoring in your organization? What should the guidelines be?

Objective of training

To the extent to which you require more of your mentors than the basic provision of a role model and of information for performers, coaching skills will be needed. For both straight coaches and coaching mentors, training will be required to the degree that they do not already practise coaching methods; you may want to assess their coaching skills. They can be assessed best by making a video or audio recording of a standard performer presenting the same require-ments to each of the coaches to be assessed. The recording can then be analysed and the performance compared against the appropriate criteria. What are the appropriate criteria? Effectiveness of rapport formation, demonstration of listen-ing skills, appropriate questions to enhance focus and ownership as required... in fact all the skills we have been discussing throughout the book. Cue another exercise: Compile a list of the criteria against which coaches should be assessed on video or audio tape.

It may, however, cost more to assess all, and then train some, than it would to provide training for all straight away. Such an approach may create resent-ment amongst those who are already skilled, unless they are asked to offer considerable assistance to their less coaching-literate peers. If you do take this training approach who should organize and prepare the training material?

Training

How should the training be provided? By formal training or self-managed development? The ideal situation is to provide the trainee coach with coaching in coaching by a skilled coach (that is, if you can follow what that means!). There are two possible approaches. The first, as in the provision contingent provision model introduced earlier, is where training in coaching is the first coaching goal. The second is to teach coaching by showing what it can do for them in practice – in other words, to help the performer increase their personal level of achievement using the coaching methods, so they have a full appreciation of just how powerful the techniques can be. Those same methods will later be summarized, re-demonstrated and practised by the performer in anticipation of their helping others with the techniques.

There are other ways of providing training in coaching: team coaching in coaching skills; self-coaching in coaching skills; and text/exercise book based self-coaching (probably what you are doing now).

EXERCISE

What do you think is the best way of teaching yourself coaching or mentoring skills, other than by using simply wonderful texts like this? (Sick bags will be provided later.)

Supporting

How can you support the new coaches through their development? Later, how do you continue supporting established coaches as they experience the ups and downs of the role? There are numerous options: abdication – let someone else worry about it; delegation – check that someone else is worrying about it; provide a coach's coach or a mentor's mentor; set up coach and mentor support groups; encourage the establishment of co-counselling arrangements between coaches; provide a 'scream zone' with punchbags, straitjackets and padded cells. Which system will you choose?

Who to coach/mentor

Now that you have mastered the concepts of coaching and mentoring, decisions have to be made about the objectives of your company's coaching programme and subsequently who will benefit from the introduced programme, that is if you do choose to, or have to, impose a system. Should the system you introduce be selective or universal? Should it apply to a selected few or to all? If selective, who should benefit? The high fliers? The under-performers? The middle-level performers? Should the system be voluntary or compulsory or subtly coercive? Should participation be rewarded or seen as a reward in its own right? If rewarded, should the level of reward be such that everyone wishes to be involved? Or at a level that only the most motivated will want to participate? If not rewarded, should participation be required as a condition for access to something that is seen as a reward?

We now consider these issues under the following headings:

- High fliers, under-performers, middle performers or new entries?
- Voluntary, compulsory or subtly coercive?
- Rewards and incentives.

High fliers, under-performers, middle performers or new entries?

Many companies operate a fast-track mentoring or coaching programme, that is, a system designed, implemented and only available for high fliers, usually the cream of the graduate or postgraduate intake. If you were one of these high fliers, there is no doubt you would feel privileged and valued, and your motivation is likely to be high in those circumstances. But what if you were one of the other ambitious and competent staff who was not receiving such specialist development? What if you'd put in several years of good quality service and those with no proven loyalty to the company were receiving training and coaching that you and the company would benefit from as well as, if not better than, the so-called high fliers? What would be your reaction? No need to speculate: we know you would move to a company where you were valued, where you could be one of the high fliers.

Selective coaching or mentoring has problems in companies where there are many high performers achieving at a similar level and only a few are chosen for special development. It does not seem to be a problem in organizations where there is either a large and obvious capability gap between 'staff' and 'the workers', or in organizations where there is a high element of choice as to into which category one places one's self. For instance, in the armed forces worldwide where officers are trained much more intensively than ratings, there is widespread acceptance of the differential treatment because of the usually wide capability gap. In other organizations where the training investment by individuals is high before they are admitted on to any fast-track scheme and where others have chosen not to invest that time and effort, there is acceptance of differential treatment. Similarly, in professions like medicine, law and accountancy where the training investment by performers is high and over a prolonged period, there is little resentment at further fast-tracking from those staff who have chosen not to undertake training but there would be in those who trained to the same level.

What of the under-performers? Should coaching be directed exclusively at under-performers? Given the law of diminishing returns, is there not a greater level of payback from addressing the 'remedial needs' of under-performers? Probably. So is that where you should invest your coaching effort? Probably not! Why? Because it sends the wrong signals to employees about both under-performance and coaching. It says 'Coaching is for remedial cases', and 'The only time special treatment will be afforded employees is when they under-perform'. If you do want to obtain the high returns possible from addressing the inadequacies of those not living up to expectations, it is best done as part of an overall coaching programme.

What of the mid-level performer? They make up the vast majority of your staff. It is simply not possible to take them all to the levels of the high performers using coaching or any other method, but you can improve their performance *en masse*. Although the returns from individual mid-level performers will be lower than those obtained from under-performers, the numbers involved are much greater. The collective return is therefore much greater.

EXERCISE

Armed with a knowledge of the issues, who should be the focus of your organization's coaching and mentoring efforts?

Voluntary, compulsory or subtly coercive?

One way to avoid the problems mentioned above is to give anyone who wishes it access to coaching and mentoring provision. Make the system voluntary. Some who will benefit little and take much time will use the provision to the detriment of others. Others who would benefit enormously will not take up the offer because they will feel either that they don't need it or that others need it more. Should it be made compulsory? Doing so will ensure all who need it and could benefit from it will receive coaching or mentoring. Force also ensures enormous amounts of waste. Many self-developers don't need it, some others will no doubt engage in passive resistance, still others will find ingenious ways of avoiding it. Subtle coercion may be equally ineffective. Making promotion contingent upon coaching and mentoring activity is likely to engender compliance not commitment, face time not timely effort. In short, compulsion, coercion and punishment don't work as motivators (see Motivation section, page 16). If you want something to happen, you should provide freedom of choice, rewards and incentives. All forms of genuine co-operation are by consent. Under what circumstances can you imagine coaching or mentoring should be imposed?

Rewards and incentives

We know that what is rewarded will happen. If coaching participation is to be rewarded, should the level of reward be such that everyone wishes to be involved? If it is not to be directly rewarded, should participation be required as a condition for access to something that is seen as a reward? In other words should it be indirectly rewarded? What rewards can be offered? Should there be control over their own training budgets for those who volunteer, with no veto option by any higher authority? Should you run competitions for 'most improved performer'? 'Best coach'? 'Most sought-after mentor'? How should you offer recognition and praise to those involved in coaching and mentoring?

Concluding comments and summary

The coaching or mentoring system adopted by an organization will directly reflect the needs and culture of that organization. Only those who know the company well can know what will work best, what will be acceptable, and what will engender the commitment necessary to make the system work. Ideally the people who are coached or mentored will choose the system that they want, and ideally each division, department, section and (being extremely idealistic) individual will have free choice of system. Whichever system is chosen it will almost certainly have to be tailored to suit the needs of the organization.

14

MONITORING AND EVALUATION

Throughout the book we have hinted at some of the issues which follow but have not considered them in any depth. Others we examined in depth, but have sidestepped some important assumptions or consequences to avoid confusion. Naughty, naughty! So now let's look at:

- Placebo and expectation effects.
- Non-directive: real or ideal?
- Dead person's shoes, and over-development.
- System monitoring and evaluation.

Placebo and expectation effects

The commitment put into making coaching work is more predictive of success than the specific system or methods used. From that point of view it can be said that coaching and mentoring are the commercial equivalents of the placebo effect. In medicine, a placebo will work in 70 per cent of cases even if the patient knows that what is being taken is a placebo! The active ingredient of the placebo effect is the mind. The tablet taken is simply the vehicle the mind uses to trigger the effect. That is true in the workplace too. Coaching and mentoring are simply the vehicles through which the active ingredients are delivered. The active ingredients are ownership, focus and a strong sense of expectation of performance. That which is expected has more chance of occurring because expectation is a self-fulfilling prophecy. Coaching and mentoring set up a strong expectation of achievement and are credible vehicles with which to trigger the mind of the performer into believing they can perform. The simple act of introducing a coaching and mentoring system may improve performance before the first coaching sessions take place!

Non-directive: real or ideal?

Throughout the book I have advocated non-directive coaching. To what extent is 'non-directive' achievable? It is not. That's right, this is not a misprint; it is not achievable. Before I explain why, let me first say why it is useful to strive towards non-directiveness as an ideal: doing so contains several benefits. The more you direct yourself, the more ownership and control you have over your performance. The more others expect you to direct yourself, the more likely you are to do so. In most companies, most players expect to either direct or to be directed – advocating non-directiveness will move the accepted norm more toward self-directedness and more toward ownership of performance by the performer.

Non-directiveness is a dream for several reasons. First, we know from numerous experiments on scientists (the people presumed to be most detached, objective and non-directive) that their personal expectations of the outcome of an experiment will affect the outcome, even if they take measures to prevent that influence taking place. Medical scientists now conduct experiments on a 'double blind' basis, that is, neither the experimenter nor the subject knows whether what is being given is real or a placebo. They don't trust themselves not to influence the outcome of their experiments. If people who pride themselves on being and train others to be objective and non-directive don't trust themselves to be so, what hope is there for the rest of us to be non-directive?

It doesn't only affect scientists. Teachers who are told (as part of an experiment) that certain pupils are bright or dull then behave towards those pupils in subtle, virtually undetectable ways which fulfil the description of the pupils' ability, whether or not these pupils are in fact as described!

No teacher would deliberately behave in such a way as to detrimentally influence a pupil's exam results, but the evidence tells us that they unwittingly have that influence. The evidence tells us we all behave in ways that fulfil our expectations of others.

Assuming the achievability of non-directiveness is not only impossible, it is hypocritical: non-directive coaching is based on the expectation (direction) that the other party will be self-directed. So-called 'non-directive' methods actively direct the other to be self-directing. That is directive in any way you care to express it.

Do you still think non-directiveness is possible in coaching? You do? Well, here is some more evidence. We know that all of us alter our language content, style and structure to more closely match that of the person with whom we are conversing. The degree of alteration varies from person to person from the barely detectable to the quite pronounced. You might have noticed yourself or others talking in the other party's accent during or after a conversation with them. Accent alteration is just the tip of the iceberg; grammatical structure, range of vocabulary used and so on are all altered. Why? Because we want to get on with our fellow human beings, so we allow them to influence us in little ways to demonstrate our level of co-operation. In other words we allow others to direct us for the purposes of good two-way communication.

The story doesn't end there. We know that what is thought influences what is said and vice versa. So by altering our communication we allow the language used to affect not only the way we think, but what we think.

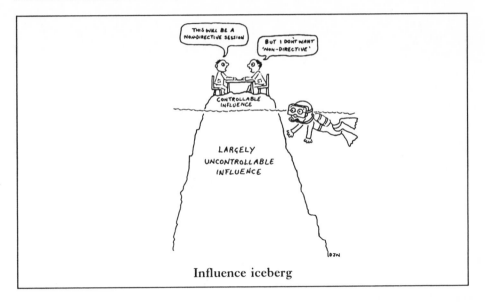

Influence iceberg

Do you still think any human interaction can be non-directive? You do? Well, let's start considering the remaining communication channels (so far unconsidered) which transmit 80 per cent of any message you send and how they can direct another person, shall we? No, I think we've made the point by examining the first 20 per cent. Non-directive coaching, counselling... anything, is a fallacy, but not a harmful one. Striving for non-directiveness as an ideal takes performers closer to ownership of their performance, and coaches further away from depriving others of their self-responsibility.

EXERCISE

Seek out a 'non-directive' coach, psychiatrist or counsellor and ask them to prove that non-directive coaching or counselling is possible. Enjoy the show as they use directive methods to convince you of the achievability of non-directiveness!

Dead person's shoes, and over-development

'Dead person's shoes' presents another problem. What can be done for those staff who are ready for a promotion, but no vacancy exists? The problem occurs more frequently in 'flat' organizations, those with few management layers between the CEO and the entry grade employee. What can be done? Surprisingly, more than could normally be done in a top-heavy organization. The options include greater autonomy, more control over things like the projects undertaken, the independent use of funds for the company's benefit, responsibility for evolving and updating systems – for instance, the implementation

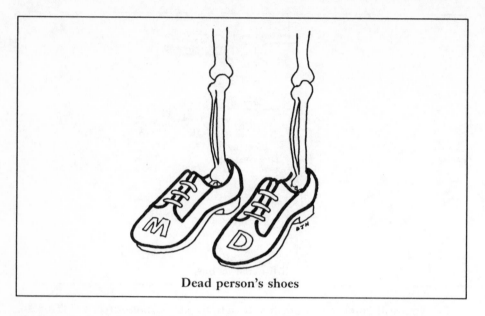

Dead person's shoes

of planned obsolescence (where each system is given a set life span at the end of which it is totally revised or replaced), the acquisition of the skills required in other departments, improving interdepartmental communications, new product development, new division set-ups and so on. In what other ways can your company provide development for those whose potential is beyond their current position? How can you convince those making the decisions that it is in their best interests to do so?

System monitoring and evaluation

The need for evaluation

This is bottom-line time. If the coaching and mentoring system you set up is not systematically evaluated, monitored and shown to be effective, it will be dropped by design or default. No CEO, board of directors or shareholders who are doing their job properly will tolerate the implementation or continuation of a system that is not being monitored or cannot show its effectiveness. It will be no use saying to your inquisitors: 'It is of double benefit to the organization: coaching and mentoring helps both the performer and the provider to develop. The coaches improve their people management and motivation skills; the performer improves their productivity; the organization benefits from both.' Unless you can demonstrate the benefit in hard statistical terms, you'll sound like just another bleeding heart, or empty-promise salesperson.

The same difficulties that plague educational performance measures plague the assessment of coaching and mentoring. With one important difference –

business is not (in this regard) burdened by political ideology, political conflicts between local and national government, education managers and providers and so on. There are difficulties, but their existence is no excuse for not being as accurate and rigorous in measurement as possible. Quite the contrary: the existence of difficulties is even more reason to insist on measurement. Critics can claim 'If it is difficult to measure the benefit of coaching, it is because it has no intrinsic efficacy'. Assessment of coaching and mentoring is required to assure one and all that promised results are being achieved, and if not, the information to discover why not is readily available.

Modern senior managers are so rigorous that there are fewer and fewer who will introduce a system without simultaneously introducing the means of assessment. Systems which went unassessed for decades are now expected to prove they are delivering what is claimed. What then should be the system for evaluating the effectiveness of coaching or mentoring? What kind of measures can be used?

- Existing measures.
- Hard or quantitative measures.
- Soft or qualitative measures.
- Control group measures.
- Process measures.
- Outcome measures.

Existing measures

The easiest and most cost-effective way to assess the efficacy of coaching and mentoring is to use information which is already being gathered. Ideally whichever measures are to be used should not have the possibility of any changes being attributable to other factors: any changes taking place in performance levels should only be attributable to coaching or mentoring. Assuming no other changes, the three most accurate existing measures will be absenteeism, staff turnover rates and production output (sales, widgets made and so on). What other existing measures could you depend on and to what extent?

Hard or quantitative measures, soft or qualitative measures

Hard measures include staff attendance, manager's attendance and other output measures. Soft measures include satisfaction measures, questionnaires, morale, confidence, initiative levels, self-responsibility, knowledge of principles of achievement, other input/process and qualitative measures. Control comparisons are taken by measuring those not being coached or mentored on the same dimensions as those being coached. The purpose of using control comparisons is to determine (amongst other things) whether or not the effects witnessed are due to coaching or some other effect.

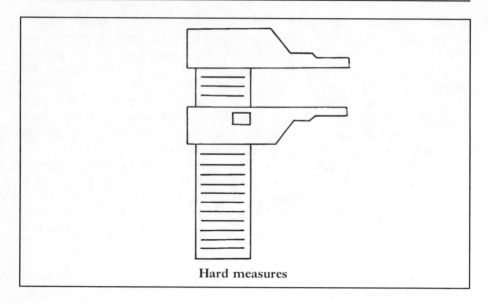

Hard measures

Outcome and process measures

Both the coaching process and its outcome should be assessed. As a guide output/outcome is more likely to be assessable with hard measures and process or input with soft measures. There is considerable cross-over, for instance the number of coaching meetings taking place (input) is a hard measure whereas the morale level (outcome) is a soft measure.

The precise method you use to make measurements on whichever dimensions you deem appropriate will be your choice. If you are not familiar with quantitative and qualitative assessment methods you should seek out either a suitable text or someone in your company who has knowledge of statistical methods.

EXERCISE

Organize the following list into hard, soft, process, outcome and self-assessment measures. Where an entry covers more than one category

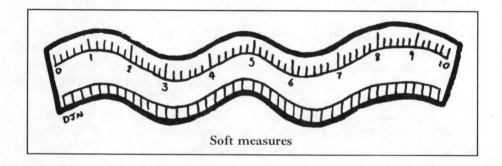

Soft measures

repeat it as necessary. What other measures could you use to assess the effectiveness of coaching or mentoring systems?

- Before and after output measures.
- Individual and group performance measures.
- Cross-group performance comparisons.
- Control group comparison measures.
- Cross-industry performance comparisons.
- Cost-savings measures.
- Profit levels.
- Administration levels and costs.
- Productivity measures.
- Service performance measures.
- Staff retention levels.
- Absenteeism levels.
- Sickness levels.
- Number of staff employment applications.
- Quality of applications.
- Induction rate, time to productivity.
- Numbers and ratios of those obtaining qualifications.
- Numbers engaged in extra company training.
- Ratio of objectives set to objectives achieved.
- Ratio of objectives achieved on time to objectives achieved late.
- Number of assignments undertaken by group not prompted by higher or lower teams.
- Number of problems anticipated and pre-resolved to number not anticipated.
- Crisis management performance.
- Time elapsed from point of crisis to point of detection.
- Time elapsed from point of detection to point of action.
- Time elapsed from point of first action to successful resolution.
- The percentage of objectives completed totally, satisfactorily, barely.
- Number of meetings.
- Time taken to reach decisions.
- Number of decisions per meeting.
- Number of issues covered per meeting.
- Information exchanged.
- Length of meetings.
- Number of ideas generated during meeting.
- Percentage of time wasted, not concerned with process or outcome planning.
- Number of irrelevant or side-issue discussions.
- Percentage of attendances.
- Punctuality of attenders.
- Number of meetings per outcome achievement.
- Number of action points/objectives set per meeting.
- Percentage of action points from previous meetings completed.
- Percentage input per coach and performer per meeting.
- Agenda set at conclusion of previous meeting.
- Number of conflicts.

- Number of conflicts resolved by mutual consent.
- Number of conflicts 'resolved' by agreeing to disagree.

EXERCISE

Which of the above measures will you use to assess the coaching or mentoring system that you have devised and implemented (or will) in your company? Which measures not mentioned will you adopt for your tailor-made system in the unique culture of your organization?

Concluding comments and chapter summary

Coaching and mentoring, as an integral part of a company culture, will result in a change of recruitment policy. The emphasis will be on recruiting self-responsible performers. A coaching-oriented company can expect to become a meritocracy very rapidly after the introduction of the coaching or mentoring system. The mere introduction of the system may improve performance company-wide. A properly implemented coaching or mentoring system will create a performance-positive meritocracy.

Monitoring and assessing the effectiveness of coaching or mentoring is extremely important. If it is assessed it can be improved. If it is assessed, it can be defended. If it is assessed, it is more likely to be introduced. The exact means used to assess your coaching system will depend on the system you have devised and introduced. It will depend on how the system works in practice, not on how it is supposed to in theory.

Book summary and conclusions

Successful coaching comprises six main components:

1 First-hand experience and understanding of achievement in the workplace at a high level.
2 A conceptual understanding of the processes involved in achievement and in coaching others to achieve.
3 Performer-empowering attitudes and assumptions.
4 Strong rapport creation and maintenance skills.
5 Excellent listening skills.
6 Sophisticated questioning skills.

Coaches and mentors can be of most help by asking performers questions which increase the performers' ownership of their goal/task/skill and the performers' awareness of the factors involved in achieving their goal. Performer awareness can be enhanced by observation, analysis or synthesis being conducted separately. The coaching role can be briefly defined as that of helping the performer go through the learning cycle.

Self-motivation is essential for successful performance. Both coach and mentor should help performers develop their motivation by facilitating an awareness of the factors which effect motivation and encouraging the performer to take ownership of those factors.

Successful coaches don't need to be experts in the discipline being coached as long as they are both high achievers in another area of business and skilled coaches. Mentors, by comparison, do require technical expertise in the subject or performance area. As a coach develops in competence using the core skills, opportunities for the development of the more advanced skills will emerge. Because of the unique one-to-one nature of the coaching relationship, the performer can help the coach develop and indeed has an interest in helping the coach improve their skills. The unique relationship allows other benefits not normally available: the performer can have any training they require presented and designed in the way they will most benefit.

At any, and several, of the stages in the coaching process the performer may wish to assess their current position, their desired position, or the means of getting there. The coach has a range of assessment and analysis tools to achieve that desire. Successful coaching enables the performer to take charge of their own development. Some will not welcome the use of analysis tools; others will strip them down to the bare essence. The coach should be sensitive to, and actively encourage, such assertive ownership of their development by the performer.

Obstacles, barriers and problems of all sorts will face the developing performer. Stress, personal paradigm barriers, and even barriers created by the coaching process itself can all be overcome by the performer and coach working together using a few simple principles. As with all other performance, the key factors in overcoming barriers are ownership and awareness – identifying the barriers and accepting responsibility for overcoming them in some way.

The coaching or mentoring system introduced and implemented must be one that fits the organization. Ideally it should be a system wanted by the people who stand to benefit from it and will carry it out. Commitment to the system is essential for it to work. Being ideal in the extreme, the system should be flexible enough for each individual in the company to choose the way they are coached or mentored.

Creating a coaching culture will bring enormous benefits to a company. It will have a positive effect on every aspect of company functioning. It will create an atmosphere in which performance is valued and expected. It will create a meritocracy. Coaching and mentoring can be the vehicles with which performers give themselves permission to perform. Coaching can turn training into self-development. It can turn the idea of empowerment into reality. It can change resented authoritarianism into revitalizing self-responsibility, coercion into co-operation, stifling dependency into staff dynamism. Coaching is about working well for your staff to enable them to work well for you. How hard are you prepared to work at coaching?

EXERCISE

Go through the book and translate each of the concepts and terms you wish to use into your own terminology. Making your memory work within your own language structure is much more effective than accepting my language.

EXERCISE

With the knowledge you now have, which sections and exercises would be worth revisiting to take your knowledge and ability even further?

EXERCISE

And now the most important exercise of all: devise your own coaching or mentoring skills development plan. Set your goals in terms of the knowledge, attitudes, behaviours and skill levels you wish to reach in the short, medium and long term. Use the information I have provided, not as your finishing point, but as your start. You have all my best ideas, but I don't have yours, so with practice you are bound to become a better coach. Give me five more reasons why you can become a better coach!

Part V

Skill checklists

This section aims to provide coaches and mentors with a one page checklist of the key factors involved in helping performers with the most frequently coached business and organizational skills. The skills will be covered in 4 areas:

- Personal skills (chapter 15)
- Management skills (chapter 16)
- Functional skills (chapter 17)
- Holistic skills (chapter 18)

The format throughout will be:

1 Performer adopts ownership of...
2 Performer to take responsibility for...
3 Areas of focus or analysis...
4 Some factors for the performer to consider...

15

PERSONAL SKILLS

Introduction

The personal skills dealt with in this chapter are:

- Time management.
- Stress management.
- Emotional management and happiness maintenance.
- Assertiveness.
- Negotiation.

TIME MANAGEMENT

Performer adopts ownership of their:

- Beliefs about time management.
- Knowledge of time management methods.
- Attitude towards time management.
- Time management behaviour.
- Continuing development of time management skills.

Performer to take responsibility for:

- Establishing their time management objectives.
- Identifying the factors which are involved in time management.
- Analysing and planning time management behaviour.
- The methods and strategies used to achieve effective time management.
- Preparing and managing time as a company resource.
- Monitoring, evaluating and improving time management processes and outcomes.

Areas of focus or analysis

- All things done which:

  - increase the effectiveness of time management.
  - decrease the effectiveness of time management.

- All things not done which:

  - increase the effectiveness of time management.
  - decrease the effectiveness of time management.

Some factors for the performer to consider

- Causes of time waste: correspondence, callers, meetings, travel, working methods, personal preferences.
- Pareto analysis of time use, keeping a time-use log.
- Set up systems to minimize time waste and disruptions.
- Correspondence: managing it faster, more effectively.
- Telephone: managing incoming and outgoing calls, ending conversations firmly.
- Travel: make better use of travel, multi-purpose travel, travelling when quickest with the least delays.
- Delegation: maximum use of staff to save time.
- Personal preferences: utilize personal preferences to maximize use of time.
- Energy levels: use energy level peaks and troughs to maximize time use.
- Peak, prime-time usage.
- Prioritizing.
- Urgent, important, to ignore, to do during slack periods.

STRESS MANAGEMENT

Performer adopts ownership of their:

- Beliefs about stress management.
- Knowledge of methods involved in stress management.
- Attitude towards stress management.
- Stress management behaviour.
- Continuing development of stress management skills.

Performer to take responsibility for:

- Establishing their stress management objectives.
- Identifying the factors which are involved in stress and its management.
- Analysing and planning stress management behaviour.
- The methods and strategies used to manage stress.
- Preparing and managing self to protect against stress.
- Monitoring, evaluating and improving the processes and outcomes of stress management.

Areas of focus or analysis

- All things done which:

    - increase the effectiveness of stress management.
    - decrease the effectiveness of stress management.

- All things not done which:

    - increase the effectiveness of stress management.
    - decrease the effectiveness of stress management.

Some factors for the performer to consider

- Causes of stress, both internal and external.
- Methods of analysing stress levels and causes.
- Honesty about overload level.
- Tolerance of self and others as a stress prevention factor.
- Problem anticipation and crisis contingency planning as stress prevention methods.
- Saying no to extra burdens and other people's crises.
- Relaxation: planned, spontaneous and regular.
- Quiet periods.
- Use of routine to minimize stress and unpredictability.
- Use of laughter, fun and distractions.
- Sleep, hobbies, exercise, socializing.
- Support for and from others.

EMOTIONAL MANAGEMENT AND HAPPINESS MAINTENANCE

Performer adopts ownership of their:

- Beliefs about happiness and emotional management.
- Knowledge of methods involved in maintaining happiness and successful emotional management.
- Attitude towards emotional management and happiness maintenance.
- Emotional management and happiness maintenance behaviour.
- Continuing development of emotional management and happiness maintenance skills.

Performer to take responsibility for:

- Establishing their emotional and happiness objectives.
- Observing and identifying the factors which are involved in emotional and happiness management.
- Analysing and planning emotional management and happiness maintenance behaviour.
- The methods and strategies used to achieve emotional mastery and happiness.
- Preparing and managing their emotional mastery and happiness.
- Monitoring, evaluating and improving the processes and outcomes of their emotional/happiness management.

Areas of focus or analysis

- All things done which:

  - increase the effectiveness of emotional mastery and happiness.
  - decrease the effectiveness of emotional mastery and happiness.

- All things not done which:

  - increase the effectiveness of emotional mastery and happiness.
  - decrease the effectiveness of emotional mastery and happiness.

Some factors for the performer to consider

- How to choose happiness at a moment's notice.
- How to learn about successful emotional management.
- Emotional management of setbacks and failures.
- How to avoid exposure to negative events and people.
- Removal of human and non-human causes of misery.
- Successful management of life's irresolvables.
- How to focus on the positive.
- Positive, empowered attitude maintenance.
- Methods of obtaining and maintaining an empowered positive attitude.
- How to renew a positive attitude and how to resist creeping negativity.
- How to spot emerging disempowering beliefs.
- How to make others happy.
- Seek empowering interpretations of life's events, both positive and negative events.
- Reinterpret negative experiences from the past in a positive, empowering way.
- Maintenance of physical and mental health.
- Self-pampering, self-valuing, self-support.
- Be true to yourself.
- Head games, unrealistic view of self, the future, personal control.
- Mutual support arrangements.

ASSERTIVENESS

Performer adopts ownership of their:

- Beliefs about being assertive.
- Knowledge of methods involved in assertion.
- Attitude towards being assertive.
- Assertive behaviours.
- Continuing development of assertion skills.

Performer to take responsibility for:

- Establishing their assertion objectives.
- Identifying the factors which are involved in asserting one's self.
- Analysing and planning assertive behaviours.
- The methods and strategies used to achieve assertiveness.
- Preparing and managing assertiveness.
- Monitoring, evaluating and improving the processes and outcomes of assertive behaviour.

Areas of focus or analysis

- All things done which:

    - increase the effectiveness of assertive behaviours.
    - decrease the effectiveness of assertive behaviours.

- All things not done which:

    - increase the effectiveness of assertive behaviours.
    - decrease the effectiveness of assertive behaviours.

Some factors for the performer to consider

- Identifying and recognizing passive, aggressive and assertive behaviour in self and others.
- Understanding the motives and consequences of each type of behaviour.
- The negative consequences of passive or aggressive behaviour.
- Observing assertive others.
- The advantages of being assertive in terms of performance, communication and relationships.
- Practising assertion in terms of body language, voice, eye contact and so on.
- Rehearsing, practising and making habitual the appropriate inner dialogues.
- The rights acquired and defended by being assertive, such as the right to self-expression, make and deny requests, criticize and accept or reject criticism, to make mistakes, to have physical space and so on.
- Ways in which one can assert one's self.
- Types of assertion.
- Responding assertively to non-assertive behaviour in others.
- Making clear, direct and specific requests or statements to others.

NEGOTIATION

Performer adopts ownership of their:

- Beliefs about negotiation.
- Knowledge of negotiation methods.
- Attitude towards negotiation.
- Negotiation behaviour.
- Continuing development of negotiation skills.

Performer to take responsibility for:

- Establishing their negotiation objectives.
- Identifying the factors which are involved in negotiation.
- Analysing and planning negotiation behaviour.
- The methods and strategies used to achieve negotiation objectives.
- Preparing and managing negotiations.
- Monitoring, evaluating and improving processes and outcomes of negotiations.

Areas of focus or analysis

- All things done which:

  - increase the effectiveness of negotiation skills.
  - decrease the effectiveness of negotiation skills.

- All things not done which:

  - increase the effectiveness of negotiation skills.
  - decrease the effectiveness of negotiation skills.

Some factors for the performer to consider

- Stages of negotiation: preparing, discussing, positioning, bargaining, agreeing, committing.
- Research, background information, establishing negotiation needs of other party.
- Self-control, patience, staying calm, being persistent, being flexible, bluff, acting, being human.
- Negotiation tactics and approaches: aggressive, co-operative, conciliatory and so on.
- Rapport, listening, asking constructive questions, common ground, other party's language style.
- Know the other party's weaknesses, expect them to know yours (but don't assume they do).
- Deciding on your best outcome scenario, the worst acceptable outcome.
- What is open to concession, what will be conceded in exchange for what.
- Authority, deadlines, time, money, discounts.
- Summaries, confirming memos, contracts, quotations, conflicts of interest.
- Objections, strategies, tactics, pressure and games of the other party.
- Walking away, not agreeing if harmful to do so.
- Winning too great a victory, bad will, contract sabotage, resentment and hidden clawbacks.

16

MANAGEMENT SKILLS

Introduction

The management skills in this chapter are:

- Motivating.
- Leading.
- Delegation.
- Decision making and problem solving.
- Project management.

MOTIVATING

Performer adopts ownership of their:

- Beliefs about motivating others.
- Knowledge of motivation methods.
- Attitude towards motivating others.
- Other motivating behaviour.
- Continuing development of staff motivation skills.

Performer to take responsibility for:

- Establishing their staff motivation objectives.
- Identifying the factors which are involved in motivation of staff.
- Analysing and planning staff motivation.
- The methods and strategies used to achieve staff motivation.
- Preparing and implementing motivation efforts.
- Monitoring, evaluating and improving the processes and outcomes of motivational attempts.

Areas of focus or analysis

- All things done which:

  - increase the effectiveness of motivation efforts.
  - decrease the effectiveness of motivation efforts.

- All things not done which:

  - increase the effectiveness of motivation efforts.
  - decrease the effectiveness of motivation efforts.

Some factors for the performer to consider

- Assessing staff motivation levels.
- Tuning into and responding to motivation of staff.
- Provide an optimally motivating environment.
- Behaving in ways which maximize motivation.
- Helping staff maximize their self-motivation.
- Protecting and maintaining motivational levels in self and others.
- Interfacing between organization and staff to protect their motivation.
- Work environment, salary, security, bonuses, perks, fairness and equality in treatment.
- Recognition, acceptance, relationships.
- Challenge, interest, development, self-control.

LEADING

Performer adopts ownership of their:

- Beliefs about leadership.
- Knowledge of leadership methods.
- Attitude towards leadership.
- Leadership behaviour.
- Continuing development of leadership skills.

Performer to take responsibility for:

- Establishing their leadership objectives.
- Identifying the factors which are involved in leadership.
- Analysing and planning leadership behaviour.
- The methods and strategies used to achieve effective leadership.
- Preparing for leadership.
- Monitoring, evaluating and improving the processes and outcomes of leadership efforts.

Areas of focus or analysis:

- All things done which:
  - increase the effectiveness of leadership.
  - decrease the effectiveness of leadership.
- All things not done which:
  - increase the effectiveness of leadership.
  - decrease the effectiveness of leadership.

Some factors for the performer to consider

- Attending to individual needs, supporting individuals, encouraging individuals to support group.
- Inclusion, affection and influence needs, trust and respect.
- Encourage group to support individuals, encourage group cohesion.
- Encourage self-leadership of team by team, encourage sharing of leadership responsibilities.
- Group participation, norms and norm formation stages, group self-regeneration.
- Decision-making style, delegation, motivation, conflict-resolution methods.
- Vision, purpose, mission, task objectives, shared responsibility.
- Encouraging enthusiasm and commitment.
- Performing: preparing, energizing, activity, rest and recovery.

DELEGATION

Performer adopts ownership of their:

- Beliefs about delegation.
- Knowledge of delegation methods.
- Attitude towards delegation.
- Delegation behaviours.
- Continuing development of delegation skills.

Performer to take responsibility for:

- Establishing their delegation objectives.
- Identifying the factors which are involved in delegation.
- Analysing and planning delegation.
- The methods and strategies used to delegate effectively.
- Preparing and managing delegation.
- Monitoring, evaluating and improving the processes and outcomes of delegation.

Areas of focus or analysis

- All things done which:

  - increase the effectiveness of delegating.
  - decrease the effectiveness of delegating.

- All things not done which:

  - increase the effectiveness of delegating.
  - decrease the effectiveness of delegating.

Some factors for the performer to consider

- Delegation versus abdication.
- When to delegate: staff development needs, speed of completion, cost-effective completion, time saving and so on.
- Delegation in relation to overall objectives.
- Whom to delegate what; whom not to delegate to.
- How to delegate: written or verbal.
- Ensuring successful understanding.
- Setting or agreeing the objective generally, leaving the specifics to the delegate.
- Delegate authority not just responsibility.
- Agree to provide or arrange input if required.
- Agree measures for the outcome, set feedback and monitoring sessions.
- Agree the targets and time-scales are achievable.
- Reviewing targets if the situation changes.
- Monitoring: preventing an error versus allowing self-development.
- Recognizing successful completion, building on non-completion of objective.

DECISION MAKING AND PROBLEM SOLVING

Performer adopts ownership of their:

- Beliefs about decision making and problem solving.
- Knowledge of decision making and problem solving methods.
- Attitude towards decision making and problem solving.
- Decision making and problem solving behaviour.
- Continuing development of decision making and problem solving skills.

Performer to take responsibility for:

- Establishing their decision making and problem solving objectives.
- Identifying the factors which are involved in decision making and problem solving.
- Analysing and planning decision making and problem solving.
- The methods and strategies used in decision making and problem solving.
- Preparing and managing decision making and problem solving.
- Monitoring, evaluating and improving processes and outcomes of decision making and problem solving.

Areas of focus or analysis

- All things done which:
    - increase the effectiveness of decision making and problem solving.
    - decrease the effectiveness of decision making and problem solving.
- All things not done which:
    - increase the effectiveness of decision making and problem solving.
    - decrease the effectiveness of decision making and problem solving.

Some factors for the performer to consider

- Anticipating and becoming aware of problems or the need for decisions.
- Specifically identifying and analysing causal/involved factors.
- Dimensions of the problem: importance, urgency, who, where, how big, how often and so on.
- Ownership of problem: consequences for whom of non-solution?
- Methods of problem solving and decision making.
- Power, authority and remit.
- Group decision making.
- Defining the criteria for an acceptable solution.
- Whose needs must be considered?
- Methods of generating solutions, enhancing solutions, evaluating solutions.
- Previous solutions to the same problem.
- Devising an action plan, implementing and monitoring solutions and decisions.
- Delegating decision making and problem solving, using it as a developmental exercise.
- Resources available for solving and implementing solution/decision.

PROJECT MANAGEMENT

Performer adopts ownership of their:

- Beliefs about project management.
- Knowledge of project management methods.
- Attitude towards project management.
- Project management behaviour.
- Continuing development of project management skills.

Performer to take responsibility for:

- Establishing their project management objectives.
- Identifying the factors which are involved in project management.
- Analysing and planning project management.
- The methods and strategies used to manage projects.
- Preparing and implementing project management.
- Monitoring, evaluating and improving processes and outcomes of project management.

Areas of focus or analysis

- All things done which:

  - increase the effectiveness of project management.
  - decrease the effectiveness of project management.

- All things not done which:

  - increase the effectiveness of project management.
  - decrease the effectiveness of project management.

Some factors for the performer to consider

- Project proposal, the project life cycle, the project sub-objectives, planning and scheduling, managing the team.
- Feasibility studies, precise definition of objectives, planning tools: bar charts, critical path analysis.
- Task analysis: description, time, staff and other resources to complete.
- Task analysis: dependent on which other tasks, feeding into which other tasks?
- Planning for slack and delays: sequential tasks, floating tasks.
- Project finance: income/benefits, costs/expenditure, budgets, finance and financial controls, cash flow.
- Project profitability: time to payback period, longevity of payback, optimum project completion time.
- Risk/reward pay-off assessment, minimizing: time, duration and costs of project.
- Maximize: stability of progress, use and availability of resources.
- Substituting thought, effort and creativity for lack of other resources.
- Client and project team management.
- Quality controls, progress monitoring, delegation, staff development.

17

FUNCTIONAL SKILLS

Introduction

In this chapter, checklists will be provided for the following functional skills:

- Sales skills.
- Sales management.
- Marketing management.
- Financial management.
- Production management.

SALES SKILLS

Performer adopts ownership of their:

- Beliefs about selling skills.
- Knowledge of selling methods.
- Attitude towards sales skills.
- Selling behaviour.
- Continuing development of sales skills.

Performer to take responsibility for:

- Establishing their selling objectives.
- Identifying the factors which are involved in selling.
- Analysing and planning sales behaviour.
- The methods and strategies used to achieve sales.
- Preparing and managing sales.
- Monitoring, evaluating and improving the processes and outcomes of selling efforts.

Areas of focus or analysis

- All things done which:

  - increase the effectiveness of sales skills.
  - decrease the effectiveness of sales skills.

- All things not done which:

  - increase the effectiveness of sales skills.
  - decrease the effectiveness of sales skills.

Some factors for the performer to consider

- Prospecting methods.
- Pre-approach background work.
- Methods of qualifying prospects, from suspects to prospects.
- Means of making appointments.
- First impressions, rapport creation, unconscious communication.
- Analysing the customer's needs, the methods of presentation.
- Answering objections, providing information in response to concerns.
- The art of persuasive questioning, gradual progression of agreement.
- Gaining and solidifying commitment.
- Methods of after-sales support, long-term relationship management.
- Handling complaints to enhance goodwill.
- Proposals, quotations, tenders, delays.
- Maintaining a positive attitude, handling rejection in an empowering way.
- Handling failure in an empowering way.
- Self-motivation methods and maintenance.
- Time management in sales.
- Self-development of sales skills.
- Developing and maintaining the desire to win business.

SALES MANAGEMENT

Performer adopts ownership of their:

- Beliefs about sales management.
- Knowledge of sales management methods.
- Attitude towards sales management.
- Sales management behaviour.
- Continuing development of sales management skills.

Performer to take responsibility for:

- Establishing their sales management objectives.
- Identifying the factors which are involved in sales management.
- Analysing and planning sales management.
- The methods and strategies used to manage sales.
- Preparing and implementing sales management.
- Monitoring, evaluating and improving the processes and outcomes of sales management efforts.

Areas of focus or analysis

- All things done which:

  - increase the effectiveness of sales management.
  - decrease the effectiveness of sales management.

- All things not done which:

  - increase the effectiveness of sales management.
  - decrease the effectiveness of sales management.

Some factors for the performer to consider

- Sales objectives, forecasts, planning, pricing.
- Product, industry and customer needs knowledge.
- Cost of sales in terms of time, materials, salaries, support costs and so on.
- Service requirements of existing customers, finding new customers.
- Matching output targets to staff input targets.
- Training objectives and methods for product knowledge, presentation skills, rapport creation, objection handling, induction training, handling rejection, self-motivation techniques.
- Support and mutual support for sales team.
- Managing and supporting motivational levels.
- Recruiting sales staff, pay and incentives, appraisal and feedback.
- Monitoring and control systems, managing the sales office.

MARKETING MANAGEMENT

Performer adopts ownership of their:

- Beliefs about marketing management.
- Knowledge of marketing management methods.
- Attitude towards marketing management.
- Marketing management behaviour.
- Continuing development of marketing management skills.

Performer to take responsibility for:

- Establishing their marketing management objectives.
- Identifying the factors which are involved in marketing management.
- Analysing and planning marketing management.
- The methods and strategies used to manage marketing.
- Preparing and implementing marketing management.
- Monitoring, evaluating and improving the processes and outcomes of marketing management efforts.

Areas of focus or analysis

- All things done which:
  - increase the effectiveness of marketing management.
  - decrease the effectiveness of marketing management.
- All things not done which:
  - increase the effectiveness of marketing management.
  - decrease the effectiveness of marketing management.

Some factors for the performer to consider

- Strategic direction of marketing efforts.
- Legal and financial aspects: pricing policy.
- Market analysis, market research, marketing research, buyer behaviour and decision methods.
- Product differentiation, brand identity, brand maintenance.
- Planning the marketing mix, marketing processes, methods, sales channels, sales communications and so on.
- Planning for the short, medium and long term.
- Organizing marketing resources, implementing the marketing plan.
- Measuring, evaluating and improving the marketing methods and strategies.
- Managing resources: people, time, money, outsiders.

FINANCIAL MANAGEMENT (FOR NON-FINANCE MANAGERS)

Performer adopts ownership of their:

- Beliefs about financial management.
- Knowledge of financial management methods.
- Attitude towards financial management.
- Financial management behaviour.
- Continuing development of financial management skills.

Performer to take responsibility for:

- Establishing their financial management objectives.
- Identifying the factors which are involved in financial management.
- Analysing and planning financial management.
- The methods and strategies used to manage finances.
- Preparing and implementation of financial management plans.
- Monitoring, evaluating and improving the processes and outcomes of financial management.

Areas of focus or analysis

- All things done which:

  - increase the effectiveness of financial management.
  - decrease the effectiveness of financial management.

- All things not done which:

  - increase the effectiveness of financial management.
  - decrease the effectiveness of financial management.

Some factors for the performer to consider

- Planning, preparing, managing and monitoring: a budget; cash/funds flow; profit and loss statements; the assets and liabilities of an organization; the raising of finance; the financial elements of a business plan.
- The accounting cycle: financial event occurs; event is measured; event recorded; events summarized and classified; events reported in financial statements.
- Financial statements' content and structure (forecast and actual): profit and loss statements, cash/funds flow statements, balance sheets.
- Other financial documents: invoices, purchase orders, credit notes.
- Planning issues for accounting: statutory requirements, management information requirements and so on.
- Working capital, fixed assets, current assets, creditors, debtors.
- Pricing/volume/cost relationships.
- Pricing, costing, fixed costs, variable costs, break-even points.
- Sales, purchase, stock, nominal and other ledgers and records.
- Tax allowances, purchase and value taxes.
- Components of a business plan.
- Raising finance: the sources, the relative costs, risks and responsibilities.
- Using ratios to assess performance.

PRODUCTION MANAGEMENT

Performer adopts ownership of their:

- Beliefs about production management.
- Knowledge of production management methods.
- Attitude towards production management.
- Production management behaviour.
- Continuing development of production management skills.

Performer to take responsibility for:

- Establishing their production management objectives.
- Identifying the factors which are involved in production management.
- Analysing and planning production management.
- The methods and strategies used to manage production.
- Preparing and implementing production management.
- Monitoring, evaluating and improving processes and outcomes of production management.

Areas of focus or analysis

- All things done which:

  - increase the effectiveness of production management.
  - decrease the effectiveness of production management.

- All things not done which:

  - increase the effectiveness of production management.
  - decrease the effectiveness of production management.

Some factors for the performer to consider

- Specifying and designing the product:

  - Research and development, initiating market research.
  - Product design and market feedback, manufacturing feasibility, final design.

- Designing the manufacturing process:

  - Location of site, layout, sequence of manufacture, manufacturing methods, equipment type, capacities, staff.
  - Stock control, materials handling, stock storage and distribution planning.
  - Order and delivery management, stock held, delivery times, delivery reliability.
  - Manufacturing/service provision sequence, work in progress.
  - Flexible working, system failure and staff shortage planning.

- Controlling and monitoring production:

  - Managing materials, labour and other resources.
  - Inspection and other quality control measures.
  - Record keeping, monitoring, evaluation, computerization.

18

HOLISTIC PERFORMANCE SKILLS

Making different skills work together

Performer adopts ownership of their:

- Beliefs about their overall performance skills.
- Knowledge of skill–combining methods.
- Attitude towards integrating skills.
- Holistic performance behaviour.
- Continuing development of achievement skills.

Performer to take responsibility for:

- Establishing their holistic performance objectives.
- Identifying the factors which are involved in achievement.
- Analysing and planning achievement.
- The methods and strategies used to manage achievement and performance.
- Preparing and implementing holistic performance.
- Monitoring, evaluating and improving processes and outcomes of holistic achievement efforts.

Areas of focus or analysis

- All things done which:
  - increase the effectiveness of overall performance.
  - decrease the effectiveness of overall performance.
- All things not done which:
  - increase the effectiveness of overall performance.
  - increase the effectiveness of overall performance.

Some factors for the performer to consider

- Interaction between separate skills.
- Integrating separate skills.

- Applying each skill to improve other skills.
- Observing the factors which affect the constructive interaction of skills.
- Skill dualling: combining skills to achieve more than one objective.
- Multi-tasking of skills: using several skills simultaneously for different purposes.
- Skill-isolation awareness: which skills must be practised on their own.
- Skill-combining assessment: which skills can be practised with others.
- Situational and contextual factors: when which skills can be used to greatest effect.

EXERCISE

Using the format style of all the preceding checklists, compile a coaching/mentoring checklist for whichever skills you feel I have missed or left out because they have already been covered in sufficient depth in the text, for example training, public speaking, appraisal, praise, criticism, feedback, influence...

APPENDIX: DOCUMENTATION AND ADMINISTRATION

Because there are so many different coaching systems with an infinite variety of implementation options there can be no 'standard' coaching and mentoring documentation. Each company should devise its own forms for its own systems. Here is a sample of the many types of possibly useful documents:

- Achievement plan (see page 294 for example).
- Belief/paradigm change plan as appears in the paradigm change section.
- The coaching/mentoring log, progress sheet. Log of coach's activities/ discussions with performer.
- The skills acquisition portfolio: a log of the skills a performer is acquiring.
- The coach/mentor feedback form: to enable the coach/mentor's own development.
- The performance review document: consists of a listing of the job-relevant assessment criteria.
- The performance review guidelines: issued to both performer and assessor.
- The career plan: specifies the performer's career goals in terms of short-, medium- and long-term objectives and the necessary programme of skills acquisition to fulfil those objectives.
- The 'what to expect from coaching' introduction sheet: a guide for those about to be coached.
- Benefits of coaching/mentoring to performer: an alternative or an addition to the above.
- Ingredients of successful coaching/mentoring guide: a guide and checklist for coaches/mentors using the company's unique system.
- Procedure for complaint or exemption or coach change request: for those who wish to complain about a coach, mentor or performer, or those who wish to avoid being coached, or those who wish to cease coaching a difficult performer.
- Checklists of various kinds as *aides-mémoire* for coaches/mentors or performers.
- System flowcharts: as per the question formation and others.
- Additional coaching resources in the company: to give performer and coaches information about the location of relevant resources such as video or audio tapes, books, self-teach training courses and so on.
- Addresses and contact names: location and telephone numbers of human coaching and mentoring resources.

Name of performer:

Achievement goal defined:

Date now: Planned date of achievement:

Sub-goal 1:

Specific tasks to achieve sub-goal

Task i

Task ii

Task iii

...

Sub-goal 2:

Specific tasks to achieve sub-goal

Task i

Task ii

Task iii

...

Sub-goal 3:

Assessment of achievement

Criteria/dimension	Here/now starting point	There/then sub-goal	To be achieved by when	Assessment method
1				
2				
3				
4				
...				

Performer's signature   Coach's signature:

Achievement plan

Some documents will be presented in tabular formats for a sequence of different entries over a prolonged period. Others you will design as one-off documents. Still others will be used to provide information to new performers or novice coaches. And finally some may be used to remind both coach and performers of key issues.

REFERENCES AND BIBLIOGRAPHY

Adair, J. (1983) *Effective Leadership*. Gower, Aldershot, and Pan, London.

Alexander, R.S. (1989) *Rhinoceros Success*. Success Publications, Bridgnorth.

Atkinson, M. (1984) *Our Master's Voices*. Methuen, London.

Atkinson, R.L., Atkinson, R.C. and Hilgard, E.R. (1983) *Introduction To Psychology*. Harcourt, Brace, Jovanovich, London.

Back, K. and K. (1982) *Assertiveness at Work*. McGraw-Hill, Maidenhead.

Barranger, J. (1988) *Knowing When To Quit*. Thorsons, Nothamptonshire.

Beer, M. (1990) *The Joy of Winning*. Mercury, London.

Bennis, W. and Nanus, B. (1985) *Leaders*. Harper & Row, London.

Berne, E. (1964) *Games People Play*. Penguin, London.

Bettinghaus, E.P. (1980) *Persuasive Communication*, 3rd Ed., Holt, Rinehart & Winston, London.

Bindra, D. and Stewart, J. (1966) *Motivation*. Penguin, London.

Blanchard, K. and Johnson, S. (1983) *The One Minute Manager*. Collins/Fontana, Glasgow.

Bond, T. (1986) *Games For Social and Life Skills*. Hutchinson, London.

Brown, J.A.C. (1963) *Techniques Of Persuasion*. Pelican, London.

Calvert, R., Durkin, B., Grandi, E., Martin, K. (1990) *First Find Your Hilltop*. Hutchinson Business Books, London.

Chapman, E.N. (1991) *How To Develop A Positive Attitude*. Kogan Page, London.

Collins, E.G.C. and Devanna, M.A. (1990) *The Portable MBA*. John Wiley & Sons, New York.

Conner, D. (1989) *The Art of Winning*. Thorsons, Northamptonshire.

Cooper, C. and Hingley, P. (1985) *The Change Makers*. Harper & Row, London.

Deaux, K. and Wrightsman, L.S. (1984) *Social Psychology In The 80s*. Brooks Cole, California.

De Bono, E. (1985) *Tactics: The Art and Science Of Success*. Collins, London.

Deverell, C.S. (1985) *Business Administration and Management*. 5th Ed., Van Nostrand Reinhold, Wokingham.

Drucker, P. (1955) *The Practice of Management*. William Heinemann, London.

Drummond, H. (1991) *Power*. Kogan Page, London.

Firestone, R. (1976) *The Success Trip*. Playboy Press, Chicago.

Fletcher, W. (1983) *Meetings, Meetings*. Michael Joseph, London.

Freemantle, D. (1985) *Superboss*. Gower, Aldershot.

Gallwey, W.T. (1986) *The Inner Game of Golf*. Pan, London.
Gallwey, W.T. (1988) *The Inner Game of Tennis*. Bantam Books, London.
Garfield, C. (1986) *Peak Performers*. Hutchinson Business Books, London.
Gibb, C.A. (ed.) (1969) *Leadership*. Penguin, London.
Glass, L. (1991) *Confident Conversation*. Piatkus, London.
Goldsmith, W. and Clutterbuck, D. (1986) *The Winning Streak Check Book*. Penguin, London.
Gould, S.J. (1981) *The Mismeasure of Man*. Pelican, London.
Hamilton, R. (1993) *Mentoring*. The Industrial Society, London.
Hamlin, S. (1989) *How To Talk So People Listen*. Thorsons, Northamptonshire.
Hampshire, S. and Jaap, T. (1981) *How To Realise Your Potential*. Institute of Personnel Management. London.
Handy, C. (1990) *The Age of Unreason*. Arrow Books, London.
Handy, C. (1991) *Waiting For The Mountain To Move*. Arrow Books, London.
Hanson, P.G. (1989) *Stress For Success*. Pan, London.
Harri-Augstein, S. and Thomas, L. (1991) *Learning Conversations*. Routledge, London.
Helmester, S. (1992) *Life Choices*. Thorsons, Northamptonshire.
Honey, P. (1980) *Solving PeopleProblems*. McGraw-Hill, Maidenhead.
Hopkins, T. (1983) *How to Master The Art of Selling*. Grafton Books, London.
Hopkins, T. (1985) *The Official Guide To Success*. Grafton Books, London.
Huse, E.F. and Bowditch, J.L. (1977) *Behaviour In Organisations*. Addison-Wesley, London.
Johnson-Laird, P.N. (ed.) (1977) *Thinking, Readings In Cognitive Science*. Cambridge University Press, Cambridge.
Kenney, J. and Reid, M.A. (1990) *Training Interventions*. 2nd Ed., Institute of Personnel Management, London.
Koren, L. and Goodman, P. (1991) *The Haggler's Handbook*. Century, London.
LeBoeuf, M. (1985) *The Greatest Management Principle In The World*. Berkley Books, New York.
McCormack, M. (1984) *What They Don't Teach You At Harvard Business School*. Collins, London.
McLaulighlin, B. (1971) *Learning and Social Behaviour*. The Free Press, London.
Miller, S. (1975) *Experimental Design and Statistics*. Methuen, London.
Morehouse, L. and Gross, L. (1980) *Maximum Performance*. Granada Publishing, London.
Moss, G. (1991) *The Trainer's Desk Reference*. Kogan Page, London.
Mulligan, J. (1988) *The Personal Management Handbook*. Sphere Books, London.
Palladino, C.D. (1989) *Developing Self Esteem*. Kogan Page, London.
Parsloe, E. (1992) *Coaching, Mentoring and Assessing*. Kogan Page, London.
Peale, N.V. (1985) *Positive Thoughts For The Day*. Cedar, London.
Pease, A. (1981) *Body Language*. Sheldon Press, London.
Poissant, C.A. (1989) *How To Think Like A Millionaire*. Thorsons, Northamptonshire.

Robbins, A. (1992) *Awaken The Giant Within*. Simon and Schuster, London.

Roger, J. and McWilliams, P. (1993) *Wealth 101*. Thorsons, Northamptonshire.

Roloff, M.E. and Miller, G.R. (1980) *Persuasion: New Directions In Theory and Research*. Sage, London.

Rose, C. (1985) *Accelerated Learning*. Accelerated Learning Systems, Aylesbury.

Rowntree, D. (1989) *The Manager's Book of Checklists*. Gower, Aldershot.

Rusk, T. and N. (1988) *Mind Traps*. Thorsons, Northamptonshire.

Semler, Ricardo (1993) *Maverick*. Hutchinson, London.

Shea, M. (1988) *Influence*. Century, London.

Smith, P.B. (1980) *Group Processes And Personal Change*. Harper & Row, London.

Stammers, R. and Patrick, J. (1975) *The Psychology of Training*. Methuen, London.

Stewart, D.M. (ed.) (1992) *Handbook of Management Skills* 2nd Ed., Gower, Aldershot.

Stone, C.W. (1990) *The Success System That Never Fails*. Thorsons, Northamptonshire.

Tack, A. (1979) *1001 Ways To Increase Your Sales*. Cedar Books, Surrey.

Tack, A. (1983) *How To Succeed As A Sales Manager*. World's Work, Surrey.

Thomas, L. and Harri-Augstein, S. (1985) *Self Organised Learning*. Routledge, London.

Thouless, R.H. (1953) *Straight and Crooked Thinking*. Pan, London.

Tillet, A.D., Kempner, T. and Willis, G. (1970) *Management Thinkers*. Pelican, London.

Trump, D.J. (1987) *The Art of The Deal*. Century, London.

Walker, S. (1975) *Learning & Reinforcement*. Methuen, London.

Whitmore, J. (1992) *Coaching for Performance*. Nicholas Brealey Publishing, London.

Zimmer, M. (1987) *Effective Presentations*. Sphere Books, London.

Zuker, E. (1991) *The Seven Secrets of Influence*. McGraw-Hill, Maidenhead.

INDEX

Change and the Bottom Line

A Gower Novel

Alan Warner

- How do you plan organizational change?
- How good are you at managing change?
- How do you monitor progress?
- How can you identify resistance – and deal with it?
- What concepts and techniques are available to help?

These are some of the questions addressed in Alan Warner's latest business novel. He takes the characters already established in his two earlier books – *The Bottom Line* and *Beyond the Bottom Line* – and sets them in a new context. Phil Moorley has become CEO of a family firm in the North of England, where his main task is to change its culture so that it can meet the challenges ahead. Once again he enlists the aid of Christine Goodhart, now a training consultant.

We follow Phil's attempts to create allies and pacify enemies, and we share with him the pains and the triumphs involved. We learn about some of the methods that can be used to bring about change and we see how they work – or fail – when put to the test.

Change and the Bottom Line is another highly effective case study, given life by the fictional treatment. An added feature is the detailed commentary provided by the author, drawing on his personal experience of working closely with change specialists. The result is an entertaining introduction to one of the key areas of management responsibility.

1995   200 pages   0 566 07560 1

Gower

Empowering People at Work

Nancy Foy

This is a book written, says the author, "for the benefit of practical managers coping with real people in real organizations". Part I shows how the elements of empowerment work together: performance focus, teams, leadership and face-to-face communication. Part II explains how to manage the process of empowerment, even in a climate of "downsizing" and "delayering". It includes chapters on networking, listening, running effective team meetings, giving feedback, training and using employee surveys. Part III contains case studies of IBM and British Telecom and examines the way they have developed employee communication to help achieve corporate objectives.

The final section comprises a review of communication channels that can be used to enhance the empowerment process, an extensive set of survey questions to be selected on a "pick and mix" basis and an annotated guide to further reading.

Empowerment is probably the most important concept in the world of management today, and Nancy Foy's new book will go a long way towards helping managers to "make it happen".

Contents

1994   288 pages   0 566 07436 2

Gower

Facilitating

Mike Robson with Ciarán Beary

How to manage change, and how to ensure continuous improvement: these are perhaps the two most important challenges confronting businesses today. And increasingly facilitating is being seen as the best way to deal with both.

Facilitators – and managers operating in a facilitative style – work on helping individuals, groups and organizations to enhance their performance. This book shows how that can be done. The first part deals with the nature of facilitation and why those involved need to understand the basis of human behaviour. The second covers the management of change at different levels. The third provides practical guidelines on the relevant skills. The fourth looks at the kinds of situation where facilitators can be effective and includes case studies from a wide variety of settings. The final part deals with facilitative styles of management.

For any manager or trainer determined to release the unfulfilled potential of their organization and the people in it, this book is the ideal starting point.

Contents

1995   224 pages   0 566 07449 4

Gower

How Managers Can Develop Managers

Alan Mumford

Managers are constantly being told that they are responsible for developing other managers. This challenging book explains why and how this should be done.

Moving beyond the familiar territory of appraisal, coaching and courses, Professor Mumford examines ways of using day-to-day contact to develop managers. The emphasis is on learning from experience - from the job itself, from problems and opportunities, from bosses, mentors and colleagues.

Among the topics covered are:
- recognizing learning opportunities
- understanding the learning process
- what being helped involves
- the skills required to develop others
- the idea of reciprocity ("I help you, you help me")

Throughout the text there are exercises designed to connect the reader's own experience to the author's ideas. The result is a powerful and innovative work from one of Europe's foremost writers on management development.

1993   240 pages   0 566 07403 6

Gower

It's Not Luck

Eliyahu M Goldratt

Alex Rogo has had a great year, he was promoted to executive vice-president of UniCo with the responsibility for three recently acquired companies. His team of former and new associates is in place and the future looks secure and exciting. But then there is a shift of policy at the board level. Cash is needed and Alex's companies are to be put on the block. Alex faces a cruel dilemma. If he successfully completes the turnaround of his companies, they can be sold for the maximum return, but if he fails, the companies will be closed down. Either way, Alex and his team will be out of a job. It looks like a lose-lose situation. And as if he doesn't have enough to deal with, his two children have become teenagers!

As Alex grapples with problems at work and at home, we begin to understand the full scope of Eli Goldratt's powerful techniques, first presented in *The Goal*, the million copy best-seller that has already transformed management thinking throughout the Western world. *It's Not Luck* reveals more of the Thinking Processes, and moves beyond *The Goal* by showing how to apply them on a comprehensive scale.

This book will challenge you to change the way you think and prove to you that it's not luck that makes startling improvements achievable in your life.

1994   288 pages   0 566 07637 3

Gower